Confessions of a Wall Street Insider

How to Profit From the Growing 2009 Monetary Crisis

Disenchanted with the sales oriented environment of Wall Street firms, J.S. Kim left the corporate world to launch his own companies, SmartKnowledgeU™, an investment research & education firm, and Blue Ocean Investing™, an investment consulting firm. Before leaving the corporate world, J.S.'s diverse work experiences included managing money for some of the richest people in the world at Fortune 500 companies and developing healthcare programs for some of the poorest Americans at a community healthcare corporation.

His life-long passion for martial arts led to a black belt in aiki-jutsu with special weapons skills earned under the tutelage of a U.S. Navy SEAL as well as additional training in Mansekan Aikido, Seidokan Aikido, Chin-na, and Northern Shaolim Gung Fu, both in the U.S. and in Japan. J.S.'s other passion, traveling, has led to a life abroad in Thailand, Japan and perhaps Argentina in the near future.

Though J.S. earned a degree in Neurobiology from the University of Pennsylvania and two master degrees (a Master in Public Policy and a Master in Business Administration) from top U.S. graduate programs at the University of Texas at Austin, he found his creative passions infinitely more helpful to his development of the first new investment strategies in over half-a-century that do not rely on fundamental or technical analysis as a primary screening method to select stocks.

J.S. maintains an investment blog, www.theUndergroundInvestor.com, where he informs investors of how to interpret the news behind the news. He is also a regular contributing author to Seeking Alpha, a website that compiles the best investment stories from around the world daily. Currently, J.S. splits his time between Asia and the United States.

J.S. Kim

Confessions of a Wall Street Insider
How to Profit From the Growing 2009 Monetary Crisis

To my late mother, who gave me the opportunities and freedom that I have today. To my father, for providing me the help to transform this book from a possibility into a reality.

Contents

INTRODUCTION

In writing this book, I hope to introduce you to wealth building concepts that have never before been discussed in any other book. In this book, I will discuss in detail a topic that I have named wealth literacy, a topic markedly different than any material previously covered by the numerous books written about financial literacy. Quite simply, wealth literacy bridges a critical gap left unfulfilled by financial literacy. The topics that constitute financial literacy today may grant you a broad-based knowledge of fiscal responsibility but they still firmly leave you outside the boundaries of wealth building. The topics within wealth literacy provide the skill set and knowledge necessary to transform fiscal responsibility into actual wealth.

Secondly, I will spend a great deal of time discussing the psychological mindset that often prevents people from building wealth. Without establishing a proper investment mindset, it is nearly impossible to build wealth, yet the topic of investment psychology is rarely discussed at all. By revealing the subtle, institutionalized nature of an investor's psyche at all levels, from primary and secondary education as well as investment education and forums provided by your friendly commercial investment firms,

I will teach you how to break the limiting beliefs instilled in you about building wealth through stocks.

Thirdly, I will explain why the flattening of the investment world has made the utilization of a blue ocean of revolutionary investment strategies not only possible but necessary for anyone that wishes to achieve significant success in stock investing. The rise of Asia's importance in global stock markets, the significant merger and acquisition activity in the investment industry, the explosive growth of massive derivative markets, and the increasing importance of newly developing technology that has created "dark pools" necessitate a completely different approach to investing than in past years.

Fourthly, in this, the third edition of this book, I have added an additional chapter that discusses the very dangerous dollar crisis that will threaten every stock market in the world in 2009 with poor performance and massive volatility, with the most serious threat posed to U.S. and European stock markets. Whether this threat materializes into a full-blown crisis strongly depends upon the actions of the world's top Central Banks, but currently, this threat is real, imminent, and growing. In fact, the actions of the world's leading Central Banks to begin 2009 seem to indicate their desire to cement this crisis.

And finally, to inject an old topic with a fresh perspective, as financial markets and investing are topics that people generally read when they can't fall asleep, as an avid martial artist that has trained in mixed martial arts for over a decade now under the tutelage of an ex-Navy SEAL in Philadelphia, an Aikido master in Kumamoto, Japan and a Northern Shaolim Gung Fu master in Los Angeles, I will further reveal how tenets of martial arts often yield intelligent guidelines for building wealth. My decision to leave corporate America was spurred by a series of epiphanies that gave rise to my current companies, Blue Ocean Investing™, LLC and SmartKnowledgeU™, LLC, and a subsequent desire to share what I had learned about the investment industry with you, the retail investor. Whether your portfolio is $100,000 or $50 million, I truly believe that every investor will significantly benefit from the material that I present in this book.

This book was born from a singular moment several years ago. After having worked for 15-years in finance, including extended periods with two U.S. Fortune 500 companies and a Wall Street firm, I woke up one day with the disturbing realization that I didn't know anything more about building wealth than when I had started my career as a Private Banker and a Private Wealth Manager. I thought to myself, "How could I have earned a degree from the University of Pennsylvania, an Ivy League school perennially ranked with Yale and Harvard as one of the best universities in the world, earned two master degrees (a Master in Public Policy and a Master in Business Administration) from top U.S. graduate programs at the University of Texas at Austin, worked for 15 years in finance and still not know anything about the key secrets of building wealth in the stock markets?"

When I couldn't answer this question, I realized that almost everything I had learned in my life through forums of traditional education and through corporate America about building wealth was wrong. I at once knew that the average investor also would have zero clue about how to invest properly even though he or she was certain to believe that he or she knew much more about investing than he or she truly did. After all, if I had spent my entire career in the finance and investment world while receiving training at the world's top corporations and did not know, how could the average investor that watches Bloomberg and MSNBC for their investment news have any clue? I realized that I had not been able to build great wealth because almost all the information I had learned in school and in the global commercial investment industry amounted to a huge mass of misinformation. It was at this point, I decided to embark on a journey to discover the keys to successful investing. I realized that those that were privy to this information would never offer it freely. I realized that if I wanted to learn how to profit not only in bull markets, but also more importantly, in times of crises, I would have to independently seek this information.

Bruce Lee, one of the greatest martial artists of all time, once said, "Don't get set into one form. Adapt it and build your own, and let it grow. Be like water." In his martial arts instruction, Bruce used to frequently refer to the power of water. Water was gentle enough to flow around an obstruction seamlessly, he would say, yet strong enough to grind a rock into sand over time. When I realized that my seven years of higher education and my additional seven years in corporate America at top investment firms did not enable me to build wealth, I realized I had committed the cardinal sin of being "set into one form" - the theories and investment strategies promoted by the commercial investment industry.

Convinced that I could unlock the secrets to building wealth that were not provided within the realms of corporate America and formal institutions of education, I started to dig deeper into my diverse foundation of knowledge to develop a new investment paradigm rooted in applicability and performance. Consequently, I drew upon my knowledge of psychology, my knowledge retained from speeches and lectures I attended given by former U.S. Presidents, U.S. Secretaries of Defense, and Governors, the knowledge I gained from reading seminal books about economics and world politics, and my knowledge of information technology. Using this broad base of unconventional knowledge, I formed a new investment paradigm that consistently predicted significant stock price appreciation. At the same time, I decided to abandon all of the investment strategies that I had learned from commercial investment firms and Wall Street as I realized that they were rooted only in the achievement of asset gathering and the generation of sales.

My development of my own investment paradigm led me to the conclusion that all freely offered and easily accessible information is free for a reason – free information, especially institutional information, is hardly worth knowing, for ulterior motives almost always lurk behind this information. Conversely, the knowledge I present to you here is knowledge that is not freely offered nor widely known. I hope that after reading this book, that you too will abandon every harmful belief about investing that has ever been taught to you by the establishment so that you may truly free your mind as well and immediately begin your journey in unlocking the secrets to building wealth in the stock markets.

1

WHY WEALTH LITERACY, NOT FINANCIAL LITERACY SHOULD BE YOUR FOCUS

Today, we are on the cusp of a global economic crisis. I can near guarantee you that despite the parade of investment pundits on TV that declare the bottom will come in 2009, the crisis is just beginning as of January, 2009. In fact, I foresee stages of full-blown panic and worldwide civil unrest as probabilities greater than not. Depending upon when you are reading this book, we may already be in the midst of panic. These statements are not meant to frighten you but are meant to merely convey the severity and gravity of this crisis as the major media has failed miserably in their journalistic responsibilities for two consecutive years now to inform you of the truth regarding this crisis. The possibility of a collapse in the US Treasury Bond market and the US dollar market is real, and if you don't understand this, there is no way that you will take the necessary steps to protect yourself as this monetary crisis deepens in 2009. If you can't realize that the roots of all economic problems in the Ukraine, Iceland, Mexico, South Korea, Singapore,

Hong Kong, China, Spain, Germany, the UK, and the US can be found in the fraudulent US dollar, there is no doubt in my mind that you will risk your family's livelihood in the next several years. And even if we do experience a boost in major global stock markets at some point in 2009, the boost is likely to be temporary and still be detrimental to your overall wealth (I'll explain what I mean by this in the last chapter of this book).

However, before I delve into this topic, I will first cover numerous topics essential to understanding this crisis. Knowledge alone is not power. As this crisis has been unfolding, I have told many of my friends what they needed to do not only to protect their assets but also to make a fortune. Out of curiosity, several months later, I often ask them if they took my advice. About 90% of the time, they have not. By remaining passive, many have lost considerable amounts of money when they had a clear opportunity to make considerable amounts of money. If you wonder why anyone would refuse to listen to guidance that would make him or her rich, and instead, choose to engage in behavior that makes him or her poor, the answer is simple.

Most of us have been brainwashed by the commercial investment industry, the mainstream investment media, and the talking heads on TV to believe numerous concepts about investing that simply are not true. When it comes to personal relationships, how many times have you known someone that has stayed in an unhealthy relationship far too long because of misguided beliefs about their partner? The same also occurs in investment relationships. Many of us stay in investment relationships that are toxic due to our misguided faith and belief in firms, financial consultants, and the information we read in financial publications.

The most difficult aspect about making lots of money, by far, is the psychological aspect. Most of us are much more comfortable doing the same thing as the Joneses, even to the detriment of our portfolio returns. If we stand apart from the rest of the crowd, not only do we fear looking foolish, but we also constantly question whether or not we are doing the right thing. We convince ourselves that if 99% of the people we know are adhering to strategy A, then strategy A must be the correct approach, even of 99% of these people lose money 99% of the time. I have no doubt that many of you will read the concepts in this book, shake your head, and tell yourself that what you are reading is just not true. After all the elite bankers of this world have conditioned you through decades of education in which they have pushed their agendas at the world's top business schools and through corporate training programs worldwide where they reinforce their agendas and belief system about investing so that you internalize the misinformation they want you to believe. It is thus critical that you understand the psychology behind your investment beliefs. If you take the time to really do so, then you may just be able to finally shed yourself of harmful investment beliefs and completely rewire your brain to learn the truths about investing.

For example, psychological studies have illustrated that the forces of conformity are so strong that even intelligent people, when subjected to a room full of people stating that 3+4=8, will eventually reply after an initial period of resistance, that 3+4 also equals 8. The commercial investment industry knows that the powers of conformity are overwhelming and have used this knowledge to misinform, deceive, and sometimes flat out lie to you. Thus, I have named my book, <u>Confessions of a Wall Street Insider, How to Profit from the Growing 2009 Monetary Crisis</u>. If I am to truly inform each and every one of you how to make a fortune from this crisis, then it is 100% necessary for me to discuss not only the factors that have led us to this clear and imminent global crisis, but also to discuss the necessary paradigm shift that must occur in your thinking for you to take advantage of the knowledge that I am presenting to you. Thus, to truly make a fortune from this coming crisis, I urge you to please read not just the last couple of chapters of this book, but this book in its entirety.

Breaking the Mindset of the Unsuccessful Investor

Although financial literacy is still a hot topic today, financial literacy achieves virtually nothing in granting us the necessary skill set to build wealth. Many of the reasons many of us believe that financial literacy is so important is that our formal educational system and commercial investment industry reinforce these erroneous beliefs. These beliefs trickle up to the highest levels and then trickle back down to us, the retail investor. The first step in disproving the significance of financial literacy is to break the mindset that leads to the belief in its importance. To do so, we must understand the origins of financial literacy, starting with its roots in our educational system and its role within the investment industry. A solid understanding of the roots of institutional education will enable us to realize that the pursuit of most traditional education places us in monetary debt, instills within us a harmful psychological mindset, and never imparts the necessary knowledge or skill set required to build wealth.

Why Traditional Education is Nearly Irrelevant to Building Wealth

Most of us, no matter where in the world we are educated, go through our educational lives learning precisely how to become robots. An authority figure tells us that A+B =D and if we disagree and argue that A+B = C, then our reward is a less than satisfactory grade. As students, we are institutionalized to spit back exactly what our teachers tell us to think. For our obedience, our reward is a good job with a top company. It's a perfect process to produce the perfect cog in the machine, the pod people represented in the film "The Matrix".

To attend higher education at a top ranked global institution, many times it was necessary for us to accrue between USD$80,000 and USD$200,000 of debt. With education inflation, our children will accrue even more debt than we did. In essence, for those of us that chose to attend a top school, in essence, we made a decision to trade an "elite" education for a lifetime of debt. Even for those of us that are wealthy enough not to accrue enormous debt if we choose to send our children to top schools, that legacy won't necessarily be passed on to our children. Before students graduate, they will need to start establishing "debt" if they wish to successfully apply for a car loan or a home mortgage in the future. I have substituted the word "debt" for the word "credit" because I believe debt to be a much more accurate word than credit.

For example, to establish good "credit", we must necessarily first accumulate lots of debt. Hardly makes sense that we can't establish good credit unless we accumulate loads of debt, does it? Unless we can demonstrate that we can pay off huge sums of debt responsibly, then we will have "bad credit" instead of "good credit". Without "good credit", even if we eventually accumulate $1 million of cash in the bank, we still will have no credit. And with no credit, we won't be able to get a car loan or a home mortgage. Not even with $1 million in the bank. Not unless the $1 million of cash is offered as collateral for a secured loan. And we as Americans wonder why we are known as a debtor nation? Our system not only encourages it, but it flat out requires it.

To be quite frank, credit cards should be renamed "debt cards" and institutions of higher learning should be renamed "institutions of higher debt" so that every young bright, doe-eyed 18-year-old has no misconceptions about the significant role traditional education will play in their future life. It is no coincidence that the moneyed elites founded almost all of the top universities in every country in the world. In the United States, the moneyed elites founded Temple University, Vanderbilt, Johns Hopkins, Cornell, Duke, the University of Pennsylvania, Columbia University, Harvard, and Stanford just to name a few. In the seminal book Education and the Rise of the Corporate State, Joel Spring wrote: "the development of a factory-like system in the nineteenth-century classroom was not accidental". Russell Conwell, a member of the wealthy elite, validated Spring's assertion with statements he made when he founded one of America's oldest educational institutions, Temple University:

"The men who get rich may be the most honest men you find in the community…Ninety-eight out of one hundred of the rich men in America are honest. That is why they are rich. That is why they are trusted with our money…It is because they are honest men….the number of poor who are to be sympathized with is very small. To sympathize with a man whom God has punished for his sins….is to do wrong."

That is one of the most ridiculous statements I have ever read in my life (especially in light of all the financial shenanigans that have been perpetrated by some of the richest men in American this decade), but it is important to note because it validates many of the reasons the American educational system was founded: (1) to sustain an unspoken caste system of rich and poor; (2) to promote the ideas and goals of the wealthy, and (3) to provide a steady stream of "factory workers" to serve the wealthy – a modern version of the Medieval Lord-Serf caste system if you will. In the late 1800's and early 1900's, masses of students were trained to conform in their thinking, and any dissent to the teachings of these universities was discouraged and punished with poor grades. Even though this was a hundred years ago, not much has changed with the modern educational system. For the most part, in classrooms all over the world, conformity is still King. Though brief, this examination of the origins of educational institutions is important to our discussion of financial literacy. It should aptly demonstrate why financial literacy, a knowledge set that provides no empowerment, is freely given, while wealth literacy remains so secretive.

Don't be Lured by the Pot of Fool's Gold that Waits at the End of College Graduation

Regarding the perceived importance of traditional education, yes, I know the rebuttal. But note that I use the word "perceived" because its perceived importance is far different than its real importance. Good exam scores are important, because they help you get into good schools, and good schools help you get good jobs, right? But then what? I scored in the very top 1% of all test takers in the United States on my SATs. That accomplishment gained me entry to one of the best universities in the world. Graduating from this university helped me gain employment at Fortune 500 companies and Wall Street firms. Still, none of this made me rich, and it won't make you or your children rich either. And even if you are one of the rare persons that migrates to the very top of the food chain, you may eventually be rich, but will you be free (meaning can you come and go as you please, and generally have the freedom you desire)? Probably not. During the entire time I was getting "smart", I was never learning how to become wealthy.

No one taught me how to leverage U.S. $50,000 in savings into U.S. $500,000. Learning how to do this would have been far more important than getting an "A" in an advanced calculus or an "A" in an economics course. Simply put, going to a great school and getting a good job is of fairly low utility unless you are going to become a doctor, lawyer, engineer or architect. Otherwise, nothing you learn at a top school anywhere in the world will ever help you become wealthy.

To demonstrate how focused most of us are on getting the wrong type of education, today, as parents, we spend more than $2 billion a year on courses designed to ensure that our children can earn the highest scores possible on a variety of college prep and graduate school examinations.[1] Courses that only teach our children how to get good grades are depleting assets and accomplish nothing beyond draining our wallets. Instead, our children would be much better served if we re-directed the money we spent on college-prep courses into courses centered on wealth-building concepts.

It's been almost a decade since I earned my MBA and my Master in Public Policy, and from the stories I've heard from my former classmates, the smartest & brightest minds in my class are nowhere near the wealthiest of my classmates now. The "dumb" knowledge you learn in exam prep courses and in traditional institutions of learning will not make you wealthy. Consider these recent statistics. In 1965, CEOs in America earned about 24 times as much as their employees. In 2006, CEOs in America earned 262 times as much as their employees,[2] and they didn't earn this money because they were 262 times smarter than their average employee. In fact, most large firms have many employees much smarter, much more creative, and much more visionary than the CEOs that make 262 times more money than them. What these regular employees didn't have is the key network. They weren't part of the old boy's network that pushes these men on a fast track into "CEOhood".

One only needs to examine performance to know that those employees in the U.S. that earn the most money are far from the brightest minds at their respective companies. In 2005 and 2006, CEOs from the 11 largest U.S. firms took (as opposed to earned) $865,000,000 in salary at the same time their "leadership" caused a decline of $64,000,000,000 in stock market capitalization of their respective firms.[3] While some CEOs of huge global corporations have undoubtedly worked very hard to attain their position, they still would not have made it to the top without the best networks in the world. If anything, it is only the network of people to whom elite educational institutions expose their students, and not the educational curriculum of these institutions, that have any worth in predicting future wealth. However, our children can still build elite networks without attending an elite university, and without accruing that elite debt (but more about this in a later chapter).

How Traditional Education Kills the Most Important Skill in Building Wealth – Critical Thinking

To provide an illustration of how the ulterior motives of yesteryear's educational focus is still applied in modern day classrooms, I distinctly remember a university course in which I strongly dissented with the professor's opinion. The professor's argument just didn't hold any weight in my mind. Though I crafted entirely well constructed arguments to support my dissenting view on the next exam, the professor "rewarded" my critical thinking with a C+. On the following examination, having learned my lesson, I provided the exact answers that I knew my professor wanted to hear, even though I still disagreed with them. For my utter lack of critical examination of any of the key issues, I was rewarded with an "A". This lesson in conformity occurred within the revered and hallowed halls of an Ivy League institution. Such manufactured conformity routinely spills over into the corporate world once these institutions graduate their students.

If Copernicus had accepted the Catholic church's teachings that the earth was the center of the universe, mankind would have continued believing that the sun circled the earth for a hundred more years. If the Wright brothers had accepted the universal belief that flying was for birds only and quit due to the ridicule heaped upon them for their "unachievable" pursuits, man still might not be able to fly today. To illustrate how blindly we accept what we are told, recently I read an article where astronomers agreed that Pluto was not a planet. Consequently, they stripped Pluto of its accepted planetary status since 1930.

Yet when I was a child, if I had not mentioned that Pluto was a planet on a science exam, my answer would have been marked wrong, even if I had given the exact same arguments that astronomers provided today. I am sure my teacher would have told me, "Look, it's in our science book. Pluto is a planet," and another lesson in conformity would have taken place. If a hundred years ago, somebody started teaching the world that the moon was made out of cheese, everybody today would believe the moon appears as a yellow orb in the sky because it is made out of cheese. It is only when the tenets that comprise universally accepted beliefs are questioned that groundbreaking progress will be achieved. The same is true in building wealth.

It is this manufactured consent and manufactured conformity to universal beliefs about the value of traditional education that destroys much of our ability to build wealth. Any death of our critical thinking skills places financial institutions, instead of us, firmly in control of our financial destinies. During our educational lives, we learn that taking courses in economics, statistics, and marketing will improve our financial literacy and thus help us build wealth. In reality, the value of such courses is minimal or non-existent. Furthermore, as students, most of us completely miss the mark regarding the true lessons taught through formal educational forums. When I attended business school, many of our projects were structured as team projects in which every member of the team received the same grade.

Our professors told us that they adopted the teamwork structure to simulate real life scenarios in which teamwork is often integral to a project's success or failure. Many students bitterly complained about this structure due to its encouragement of a free rider mentality. Almost every group project had a free rider, someone that performed little or no work yet received the same grade as everyone else. Though not necessarily fair, the real world is hardly fair either, and if there was one lesson to gleam from this example, it was that those students who learned how to manipulate the system the best were often the ones that won. Not the smartest, not the brightest, and not the hardest working. Currently, our educational systems are designed to keep you ignorant about the most important aspects of wealth building. Again, you can only win if you learn to manipulate our current systems for your own benefit.

Stop Passing Erroneous Myths on to Your Children

Let me conclude this segment about traditional education with a conversation I had with a good friend of mine, a trust officer at a very large financial services institution. Recently, when I asked her how her teenage son was doing, she expressed concern that her son didn't seem to be taking an interest at all in preparing for the SATs and for college. Of course, my response was that attending an elite college was hardly correlated to building wealth, so I wouldn't worry about her son's lack of academic interest for now. My friend countered by offering her belief that a strong college education was still important in the eyes of future employers, and as proof, she quoted the insane salaries that recent Harvard Business School graduates were commanding in today's job market. Although I hate to use my good friend's mindset as an example, it is exactly this mindset that you must shed. Although traditional institutions of education will never teach our children or us how to build wealth, most of us still believe that the only way to build wealth is through the pursuit of an elite education and an elite job. When we pass this faulty deduction on to our children, we prevent our children from ever learning how to build wealth. I guarantee you that I can take an18-year-old teenager and teach him or her knowledge that will make him or her far wealthier than any child that spends four years in college.

Even if we make the decision to send our children to school, if our children eventually earn $300,000 to $400,000 a year, this still hardly guarantees that they will be able to parlay that salary into significant wealth. For the same reason that we as parents today are so ill equipped to build wealth, so are our children. Thus, even though a recent Schwab brokerage study revealed that a very high percentage of teenagers want that their parents to teach them about money, the great majority of us can only pass on financial literacy skills, a vastly inferior subset of knowledge to wealth literacy skills. Again, the reason why information about wealth literacy is not freely shared should be self-evident. The financial and investment services industry is a multi-trillion dollar industry worldwide. If wealth-building courses were part of every student's regular curriculum and every student became proficient in the art of investing by the time they graduated college, every young adult would be able to spot, from miles away, the wizard that manipulates the retail investor from behind the proverbial curtain. Consequently, the number of clients that the commercial investment industry would be capable of securing would severely deteriorate.

The handful of wealth literacy courses that should constitute the backbone of every young adult's education is astonishingly and conspicuously absent from traditional education and therefore must be sought independently of the mainstream education avenue.

Help Your Children Bridge the Gap Between Reality and Fantasy

According to a 2007 Charles Schwab study, today's American teenagers have huge delusions about the type of wealth that they will build as young adults. Of the 1,000 teenagers that participated in the survey, boys on average expected to earn $173,000 a year while girls expected to earn $114,200 annually.[4] The reality, however, of course, will be much different. Only 5% of all wage-earning adults in the U.S. earn six figure salaries, and of this 5%, only those that focus on gaining wealth literacy, not financial literacy, will successfully build wealth.

The aforementioned Schwab survey further reported that nearly two-thirds of American teenagers between 13 and18 years-of-age believed that they were knowledgeable about money management, including budgeting, saving and investing. Despite this typical teenage braggadocio, barely a third of them admitted to knowing how to budget money (41 percent), how to pay bills (34 percent), and how credit card interest and fees work (26 percent).[5] However, this is where this survey was lacking and where a crucial gap in understanding must be bridged. The type of knowledge the Schwab survey focused on is perhaps necessary to assume a baseline of fiscal responsibility but hardly the type of knowledge that will ever help young adults achieve wealth.

Many of us mistakenly assume that our children have zero interest in learning how to build wealth, but the Schwab studies reveal otherwise. According to the Schwab survey, "nearly 9 in 10 [teenagers] say they want to learn how to make their money grow (89 percent). Two-thirds (65 percent) believe learning about money management is 'interesting,' and 60 percent say that learning about money management is one of their top priorities."[6] Still, only one thing will help bridge the gap between a young adult's desired wealth status and his or her actual future wealth status – a course on wealth literacy that covers topics such a precious metals, currency markets, networking, interpreting the financial media and other subjects that have a direct correlation to building wealth (but more on this later).

The Inadequacies of Financial Literacy Courses

Just as many of us wrongly focus on traditional education as the key to attaining financial freedom, many of us also focus on building financial literacy because we believe that this knowledge will help us build wealth. While it is true that many of us are woefully ignorant of our own finances and we contribute too small a percentage of our salaries to our retirement plans, spend too large a percentage of our salaries every month, and know too little about assets such as stocks, options, and real estate, many of us erroneously believe that taking actionable steps towards financially literacy will actually help us build wealth. Most concepts of financial literacy are so basic, so fundamental, so logical, and so general that achieving financial literacy does little more than make your knowledge base average. And average knowledge will not build wealth. In other words, if you are currently not wealthy, gaining financial literacy will only succeed in transforming you from a fiscally irresponsible person into a fiscally responsible person, but accomplish almost absolutely nothing in regards to real wealth transformation.

Just because many young adults are financially illiterate does not mean that they should strive to become financially literate. Many books parade the need for our young adults to become financially literate merely because they are not. This, as a reason that something should be pursued, is a horrible reason. Many kids don't know how to manufacture MDMA (the designer drug ecstasy) in a chemical lab but that doesn't mean that they should learn how to do this either. Financial literacy knowledge may very well create noticeable changes in our wealth if applied over a period of time that spans decades but certainly will not provide significant changes within a shorter timeframe. Because the concepts of wealth literacy can create noticeable differences in our wealth within a matter of several years, this is precisely why the pursuit of financial literacy is not adequate.

If one were a power forward in the NBA, the comparable value of a financial literacy course would be to learn that you need a good array of post-up moves, a sweet outside shot to make opponents respect your range, a quick first step that allows you to create shots off the dribble, and a solid defensive game. However, after gaining this knowledge, there would be no further explanation but a wish of "good luck" and a pat on the back. Perhaps after ten years, one could become a premier NBA forward simply be practicing all of the above skill sets and by learning how to accomplish everything after much trial and error. Ultimately, this is exactly what financial literacy knowledge is lacking - specific knowledge that will produce significant results within a short timeframe.

Why Financial Literacy Knowledge is Freely Given and Wealth Literacy Knowledge is Kept Secret

There is a very simple reason why financial literacy programs stop well short of giving us the knowledge we need to achieve financial independence. Most financial literacy programs are sponsored by investment and financial companies that greatly benefit from a more financially literate but still wealth-illiterate customer base. University and graduate school courses such as accounting and corporate valuation classes again fall conspicuously short of providing the kind of knowledge to build wealth in the real world. Financial literacy courses grant us just the minimum amount of knowledge to know that we should be doing more with our money to make it work for us yet they don't grant us the specific knowledge we need to do it ourselves.

Iconic businessman Henry Ford once stated, "It is well enough that people of the nation do not understand our banking and monetary system, for if they did, I believe there would be revolution before tomorrow morning." This statement still holds true today. Ninety-nine percent of people, even the very people employed by banks, still have no true understanding of how banks (including the World Bank, the International Monetary Fund, and the world's central banks) control economies. And control and manipulate economies they do. In reference to the U.S. Federal Reserve's attempt to assist Great Britain's loss of gold reserves in the late 1920's, a famous man made this comment: "The Fed succeeded; it stopped the gold loss, but it nearly destroyed the economies of the world, in the process." Most people would be shocked to learn that that comment was made in 1966 by future U.S. Federal Reserve Chairman Alan Greenspan. It is knowledge of this nature, knowledge that I categorize as wealth literacy, and not financial literacy, that is essential to building wealth.

The scheme of financial literacy is in fact, brilliant from a marketing perspective. It is similar to any retailer's strategy of getting children hooked on its product from a young age to provide a built-in customer base for many future years. The education and investment industries have very cleverly created a state of learned helplessness (a concept coined by University of Pennsylvania professor Martin Seligman) in retail investors that creates a belief that we have no choice but to continue feeding their bottom line. However, this belief is nothing more than a perception that has zero basis in reality. Our learned helplessness is merely a product of a critical gap in our level of knowledge. By bridging the gap between financial and wealth literacy, we can easily break our chain of dependency and our erroneous beliefs that "slow and steady" is the best way to build wealth.

We can all start TODAY in building our foundation of wealth literacy knowledge. All we need is a healthy perspective regarding problem solving and an even healthier dose of curiosity. Ask yourself the following question:

How many trailblazers do I know in the business world? - the type of person that makes me stand up and take note for truly pioneering a different way of doing something?

Those of us that are able to cultivate a vision that most people are incapable of seeing are the ones that will ultimately build great wealth. Following traditional paths and traditional lines of thinking and climbing the corporate ladder may still lead to substantial wealth, but only for less than 1% of the entire population.

In the future, when I hire employees for either of my companies, I will always hire C+ students that never went to college but that had started their own successful businesses or had pioneered a new way of doing something rather than A+ students with PhDs that had never accomplished a single non-traditional pursuit in their entire lives. Why? Because traditional book smarts can never provide the "right" type of intelligence when it comes to building wealth. In today's global world, if you cannot adapt your business strategies to account for cultural differences, you will fail. If you surround yourself with "yes" men and don't consider as many alternatives as possible in your decisions, you will fail. And in investing, if you don't challenge the most widely accepted mantras and realize that they are pure sell-side mantras, you will fail.

If investment firms truly provided the type of education that we need to independently build wealth, then it would render their own services obsolete and unnecessary. No firm would ever willfully engage in such self-defeating behavior. This would be analogous to a tobacco firm voluntarily sponsoring classes about the deleterious effects of smoking for their most prized customers. As if it isn't already damaging enough that traditional institutions of education and investing provide poor advice when it comes to building wealth, investment professionals reinforce this poor advice by continually forcing their beliefs upon their employees which are then inevitably passed on to their clients.

To illustrate this point, let me recount a story regarding an interview I once had with a nationally recognized and prominent investment U.S. firm located in California. At the time of my interview, this firm had successfully gathered more than $20 billion of assets under management. During the course of my interview, I gave my interviewer answers that he did not want to hear. For example, the interviewer believed that asking me to state the exact level at which the Dow Jones Industrial Average (DJIA) had closed that day tested my knowledge of the stock market.

Ask me that question today, and some days I still wouldn't even be able to give you a ballpark figure. Back then, when confronted with that question, I answered, "I don't know and I don't care because frankly, it's irrelevant." I then politely responded with, "Can you please tell me where the London Stock Exchange is trading at today? Can you tell me where the SET at Thailand closed yesterday? Can you tell me where the Nikkei 225 closed at today? And, Can you tell me where the TSX in Canada is currently trading at?"

I asked him those questions to make my point that big investment firms such as his were dinosaurs not only for thinking that only U.S. markets had relevance in our global economy but also for believing that knowing a bunch of statistics had any relevance to building wealth in stock markets. Of course, the interviewer answered that he didn't know because those markets were irrelevant. His firm claimed to be revolutionary and creative. yet its top employees were bogged down in useless statistics that would never help a single soul discover a phenomenal stock opportunity. His interview questions conjured up memories of other useless things I had learned during my career, such as how to uncover companies that had just laid off tons of workers so I could call on their human resource departments to discover if anyone was advising their employees about rolling over their 401(k) plans.

Unsurprisingly, my answers did not please my interviewer, so he continued to pepper me with even more remarkably unfocused questions. "Do you think the market is a bull or bear market?" he asked next. "In what country and in what industry?" I replied. "Real estate, technology, pharmaceutical, precious metals, or oil and gas?" He didn't answer, stunned that I would even need to ask that question. Finally he spoke. "In general, a bull or bear market? And in the U.S. of course," he replied, conveniently ignoring my clarification request for industries.

"Well it doesn't really matter to me, because I look for stock opportunities globally. I believe it's too narrow-minded just to focus on the U.S. market's potential," I answered. Needless to say, the questions never got any better, and I did not receive a second interview. However, I was absolutely amazed that this guy was a senior level person at a firm that managed more than $20 billion of assets. The truth is that most investment firms would not have hired me with those answers. The greater point of this story is that if I really wanted the job, I knew exactly what answers the interviewer was looking for. Just as I had learned in college, I could have very well given the answers the big shot interviewer wanted to hear.

This experience undoubtedly confirmed in my mind that commercial investment firms do NOT want to hire independent thinkers because independent thinkers are dangerous to the very ability of these firms to survive and to continue pushing pure sell-side investment strategies on to their clients. Instead, commercial investment firms want robots, good little soldiers that will unquestionably always tow the company line,

especially when it helps them sell terrible investment strategies to their unsuspecting clients. However, as we have seen in 2008, such a status and agenda of maintaining the "status quo" can be irreversibly harmful to your personal welfare if you fall victim to such tactics. Just because a wealth manager drives a 7-series BMW, wears a $5,000 suit, and works for a large international firm has zero correlation to his ethical and moral constitution.

On a larger scale, these firms are the exact same ones that are working furiously to spread their concepts about financial literacy and investing to millions of people all around the world. If top management at these firms fail to recognize that the concepts they use to manage billions of dollars of assets are poor concepts, would you really want to trust any of the concepts that they teach you about investing?

The amount of non-conventional thinkers in the investment world today that regularly gain exposure in the financial press can probably be counted on one hand. Before I started to have real success with my own portfolio, in the range of 20% to 40% annual returns, I had to "unlearn" virtually everything that I had learned in school and at nationally recognized investment houses. I had to reset my mind to tabula rasa per se. Only when I formulated my own ideas, my own strategies, and utilized creativity did I begin to have great success with investing in stocks. In some ways, it's quite ironic that I had to leave the commercial investment industry and Wall Street to truly learn how to invest properly. In other ways, it's perfectly logical.

THE 14 RULES OF INVESTING I LEARNED FROM A NAVY SEAL

Throughout my life, I have always been very goal oriented. Sometimes so much so that sometimes I've needed to step back, take a breath, and remember that enjoyment of the journey is as important, if not more important, than reaching the destination. After I graduated from college, martial arts became a way of life for me. I initially trained under an ex-Navy SEAL for several years in the arts of Kyokushinkai Karate and Aiki-jutsu with special weapons training. Eventually, I added Aikido and Northern Shaolim Gung Fu to my toolkit as well.

Below are 14 lessons I learned while training in martial arts under the instruction of a Navy SEAL for four years. These lessons continue to help me immensely in my work and I offer them here in hopes that they will also greatly enhance the performance of your portfolio as well. Stick to these rules as an investor and I guarantee you that your portfolio returns will significantly improve. Without further ado, here they are.

1. Master the basics and you will be a good operator.

Paper trade first if you have never invested in stock markets before. You cannot be a great investor without mastering the basics first. Paper trading entails setting up an account with "fake" money and monitoring your success and failure for a minimum period of six months to one year. Better to make mistakes with play money rather than with your real, hard-earned dough.

2. Never make the same mistake twice.

Though you should experiment a little bit when you paper trade, you should strive to never make the same mistake twice. You want paper trading to be of utility, not to be a useless exercise. In real life, when we make a mistake, most of us will study our mistake and learn from the experience. When dealing with money, it is essential to not make the same mistake twice. By the way, this rule also applies when you begin investing with real money.

3. Strive for perfection. You'll never get there; perfection doesn't exist for SEALs but we can always do better.

This is one of the most important traits you can develop. Many financial consultants take pride in making money, not in earning great returns. It is quite possible for a financial consultant or fund manager to earn huge salaries while simultaneously losing great sums of money for clients. Just ask Brian Hunter at Amaranth hedge fund. In 2006, he lost over $6,000,000,000 of clients' money in a matter of weeks. What was his personal pain? Besides getting fired, that's about it. And he still had the estimated $75-100 million that he earned from the prior year to ease that pain.[4]

Striving for perfection means that you ultimately must step up to the plate and take responsibility for the creation of your own wealth instead of handing that responsibility off to someone else. Refer to Appendix 1, 101 Reasons Why You Need to Manage Your Own Money, for further detail.

4. A SEAL's job is not eight to five. You cannot be number one in the world and not put in extra hours.

I've worked at large investment firms during very bad markets and observed that the majority of financial consultants never changed their hours or worked any later than normal. Many financial consultants claim that they believe in working smarter, not harder. That's just a euphemism for the fact that they don't want to work hard. To be the best, you always have to work harder than everyone else. There are no shortcuts to this in any endeavor, whether in investing or in martial arts. To receive my black belt in martial arts, training during regular sessions wasn't enough. I always sparred on weekends or worked on submissions with my training partners outside of regular class hours. Investing is the same. If you're lazy, you're not going to achieve phenomenal returns in your investment portfolio.

The Navy SEAL trident pin is represented by an American eagle with his head bowed. The eagle's head is bowed to represent that the SEAL is humble and knows that perfection is unattainable. However, it is this attitude that leads to a level of expertise as close to perfection as possible. This attitude in investing also is the correct one as well.

In eight years of working at the private wealth management offices of Fortune 500 companies, not once did I ever hear a story of a financial consultant or private wealth manager that performed research for clients on his or her own time. Not once in two thousand, nine hundred and twenty days. But I heard at least a hundred stories of advisors that met with clients over weekends in an effort to close sales. When it comes to earning phenomenal investment returns, this work is going to have to come from you.

5. Become a Subject-Matter Expert (SME) in your field.

SEALs divide knowledge responsibilities among their teams. Their expertise in certain areas is nothing short of astounding. SEAL communications experts have more knowledge than electrical technicians, able to build radios out of almost anything. Others become combat medic experts, their knowledge in infectious disease and combat inflicted wound repair more specific and extensive than Harvard-educated doctors.

Just like Navy SEALs, when it comes to investing, every one of us should also gain industry specific knowledge. Whether you choose the alternative energy industry, the pharmaceutical industry, precious metals, oil and gas, it doesn't matter. Just become an expert. And form an investment group. You'll be able to leverage the knowledge of other specialized experts if you do, for you'll have very valuable insight to offer in return. This is a win-win situation for everyone.

6. Train as you would fight.

In this case, since we are not SEALs (well, I suppose that there is a chance that some of you out there may actually be SEALs), there is no fighting to be done here. The only fight we have as investors is against the U.S. Federal Reserve, the weakening U.S. dollar, and global inflation.

This rule only really applies to beginners and those just learning to invest in stocks. When you start investing with real money, your paper trading results will serve as a good proxy for how you will perform when you start using real money. So experiment at first, but don't experiment for any longer than three months. Within this time, develop your buying and selling strategies and industry specific leanings. After three months, start paper trading as if you were using real money.

7. Think ahead and stay organized.

In combat situations, SEALs will win most times if they stay just one step ahead of the enemy. But they aren't satisfied with being just one step ahead. They want to be three, four, or five steps ahead of the enemy. In investing you'll never win unless you are also at least one step ahead of the "thundering sheep herd (my euphemism for the mindless public masses), but preferably three, four and five steps ahead.

When global markets sharply corrected in May, 2006, many people were caught completely off guard. And when it inevitably happens in the future, the same people will be caught off guard once again. You can't win in the stock market just by thinking about today or tomorrow and reacting to what is happening now. The only way to win is to think ahead and to dig deep below the surface to root out the real facts so that you may understand what is likely to happen in the future. It has been stated that chess masters think seven steps ahead when forging a strategy. You should strive to do the same when it comes to investing.

8. When you have a good idea that benefits your team, share it with others.

Although this sounds like a rule from kindergarten class, it is actually a principle tenet of SEAL teams. And it should be a principle tenet of your investment group. If one person has a great idea, it will benefit the entire team, but you must have a team first. See Rule #5 for the reasons I highly recommend that you form or join an investment group if you are not a member of one.

9. If you don't know or didn't understand, ask. It is your responsibility to find out. Research. Demonstrate an unquenchable desire to know everything about your job.

This principle of being a member of the Navy SEAL teams is particularly applicable to investing. You should never buy a stock without understanding everything you can about what makes it a good stock to buy and what might possibly make it a dangerous stock to buy. Just because Warren Buffet or George Soros bought a particular stock does not constitute a reason why you should buy it. Even if you subscribe to my Global Stock Picker newsletter at my SmartKnowledgeU™ website, you should still never buy a stock just because I state that I love the stock's potential.

You should always fully research the positives and negatives of a stock and formulate an independent opinion before making a decision to buy. If there are things that you uncover about a company that seem important but you don't understand how it may affect the company, it is your responsibility to ensure that you understand this information before making a decision to buy. Don't just ignore or disregard information that you believe might be important to the future performance of the stock price because you don't understand it. Research it until you do.

10. If something is broken or not right, take the initiative to fix it or make it right. Don't wait for someone else to take action.

I used to hear people say in terrible bear markets that they would cease checking their portfolio because it was too depressing to look at. And I used to hear **LOTS OF PEOPLE** say this. This is the absolute worst thing we as investors could do. We know it's broken, yet we continue to ignore all the signs that scream for us to fix it. If our portfolios are performing poorly, we must take proactive steps to fix it. Better yet, we should fix our portfolios before they are even broken (you have one such opportunity to do this right now if you are reading this in early 2008). Ask yourself,

Am I over-weighted in industries that no longer possess the strong points that convinced me to invest in them in the first place?

Is my portfolio over-diversified into mediocrity and thus in need of major re-structuring and re-allocation?

If so, don't just ignore the problem. Fix it.

11. Listen and take notes during all Patrol Leader orders. Prior to going into the field, know the minimum.

Since we are the "Patrol Leader" of our portfolios, we must always take notes when we purchase stocks so that we do not forget the reasons why we purchased them. Though this sounds simple, this is an invaluable exercise so make sure that you do it. For example, we may decide to sell a certain stock, but after researching the stock, discover that the stock price will probably receive a nice bump in price after the release of their earnings report next month. If we don't note this discovery somewhere in a place that we check frequently, then one day we may notice that we still hold the stock in our portfolio and prematurely sell out of our position.

12. ALWAYS rehearse/dirt dive everything.

SEALs call rehearsing an operation "dirt diving" it. Paper trading is our "dirt dive" of trading with real money. If you're currently in the markets and haven't "dirt dived" your situation yet, get out. For SEALs, failing to dirt dive a tactical operation may get them killed. For us, failing to dirt dive our financial situation may not kill us, but it most certainly will lead to financial disasters.

13. The easy way out may not be the safe way out.

During SEAL operations, the easiest way to infiltrate or exfiltrate enemy targets is often not the safest route. Similarly, the easiest way to invest (handing our money over to a firm to manage) is almost NEVER the safe way as well. All too often, the financial consultants we choose compound our mistakes by also assuming the easiest route in investing our money. Owning individual stocks is always the better, though much more difficult route in investing. Mutual funds are the easy way out.

In May 2006, some of the best performing emerging market mutual funds in Russia and Turkey corrected very steeply, shedding some 40% to 60% in just a few weeks. We will see this situation happen with the mutual funds of other emerging markets at a future point in time as well. Own the best stocks within these emerging markets and you're a lot less likely to take as deep a hit.

14. Do K.I.M. exercises as much as possible.

Being a SEAL requires much more mental resolve than the majority of civilians realize. What separates those that make it through Hell Week and BUD/S (Basic Underwater Demolition SEAL training) and those that do not is often not physical ability but pure will. Those that are the best swimmers and best runners sometimes are among the very first DORs (drops on request) while those that are not as physically gifted sometimes endure until the end. You just cannot measure will until severe physical duress is imposed. That's where separation becomes apparent.

As part of their training to sharpen their mental acuity and observation skills, SEALS constantly engage in KIM (Keep In Mind) exercises. If SEALs are on a subway train, they may try to remember facial features and the clothes of everyone on their subway car. And they may do the same thing while eating in a public restaurant. So should you. Take note if the door opens inward or outward. Does it open to the left or to the right? Is it made out of steel, wood, or glass? Where are the exits located and how many exit points are there? How many wait staff? Doing KIM exercises repeatedly automatically sharpens and trains the mind to be more observant and aware.

I'll end this chapter with a short story of an encounter with my SEAL instructor. I remember one time spotting my instructor on the streets of Philadelphia. I ran up behind him and when I caught up with him, he casually looked over and broke into an easy smile.

SEAL: I heard you coming.

Me: What do you mean?

SEAL: I knew from the sound of your footsteps that you were a man because the footsteps were too heavy to belong to a woman or a child. And from the beat of your steps I could tell that you were a "friendly" and not a "hostile". Your footsteps weren't at a pace of a mugger or robber.

I looked at him like he was crazy. I thought to myself "Who in the world thinks like this?"

But as I learned later, he was merely doing a classic KIM exercise - the sign of a truly observant SEAL.

So how can KIM exercises help your investment performance? Believe it or not, KIM exercises will increase the amount of stock opportunities you uncover. Although you probably haven't realized it, if you travel a lot, you've already been exposed to lots of public companies in their infancy stage of growth that have exploded upward in share price. For example, if you've traveled in a country with a booming economy and have played a round of golf on a five-star golf course that had been recently developed, did you take time to discover who developed the course? Or if you've ever been in a city with booming construction, have you ever looked at the names plastered on the heavy machinery that is in plain site? And what names were plastered on the cement trucks? Or have you ever vacationed in Macau and while gambling in their casinos, learned that all Casino chips possessed RFID chips for identification? Who manufactured those RFID chips?

While still living in the U.S. in 2004, I had purchased my first Chinese stock, Tom Online (TOMO), and it promptly went from $13 a share to $27 a share in about 18 months, at which point I sold out. I knew that Tom Online was owned by the same owner as Hutch mobile phones and a conglomerate called Hutchison Whampoa, Li Ka Sheng. Living in Asia, a couple of years ago, I noticed that many billboards in Thailand advertised Hutch mobile phones. So I researched Hutchison Whampoa, and discovered that they were like the Berkshire Hathaway of Asia. I discovered that Hutchison Whampoa owned ports, real estate, telecommunication, properties and hotels, and retail and energy divisions that had business dealings in 54 different countries, with many of their business dealings concentrated on the fastest growing countries in Asia. And who held a huge stake in Hutchison Whampoa? Cheung Kong, another Li Ka Sheng company.

So there you are. The 14 lessons from Navy SEAL training that will provide you with the mindset you need to take advantage of the other lessons in this book.

3

THE FATALLY FLAWED PSYCHE OF THE UNSUCCESSFUL INVESTOR

Often many harmful notions are imbedded within the average person's psyche. A healthy psyche has always been paramount not only to the health of a martial artist but also to the financial health of the retail investor. Mind, body and spirit must become one. When training in martial arts, a strong body with a weak mind will create all kinds of psychological problems while a strong mind paired with a weak body will create numerous physical ailments. One of my martial arts teachers always stressed the importance of sparring and training as if you're life depended upon it. He stated, "If you learn a martial arts technique that could save your life, but you have no confidence that it will work in a real-life situation, then it is worthless." I absolutely agreed with him. Knowing effective martial arts techniques without confidence in their efficacy is not worth knowing at all.

For most novice investors, even those with significant amounts of money, the psychological relationships they have had with commercial investment firms have been very damaging. Commercial investment firms manipulate an investor's fear or greed to employ ineffective, asset-gathering investment strategies to manage their money. In pursuing the bottom-line goal of maximizing corporate profits, a financial consultant must spend the majority of his or her time gathering assets. This leaves little time for deciding how those gathered assets should be invested. Therefore, investment strategies that require very little time must be utilized to manage clients' money. Thus, the mantra of diversification was born.

Kime

The concept of "kime", or "tightening the mind" is a concept that martial artists are familiar with. The overwhelming majority of investors, if they also employed "kime", would be able to accomplish returns five to ten times better than usual. I sincerely believe that. Five times better than what we have accomplished in the past is not out of the question. Unfortunately, it is a lack of desire or laziness that prevents most of us from properly learning how to build wealth. Instead, we opt for the mistake of turning our money over to any number of commercial investment houses that have accomplished nothing more than the production of mediocre returns for decades. Master the "kime" of investing and your returns will explode.

Miso No Koro

In martial arts, a lot of practitioners never become "zen" and despite a chronological adult age, continue to behave like petulant, attention-needy, misbehaved children. It is said that everyone that had ever met Mas Oyama, the Korean founder of Kyokushinkai karate, was at once in awe of the sense of tranquility that seemed to hang over him. Oyama once stated, "Karate is not a game. It is not a sport. It is not even a system of self-defense. Karate is half-physical exercise and half-spiritual. The karateist who has given the necessary years of exercise and meditation is a tranquil person. He is unafraid. He can be calm in a burning building."

My very first martial arts instructor, an ex-Navy SEAL, once told me that had I continued to train with him (I only left his instruction because I moved to a different part of the country), he would have taught me to lose all sense of fear. He said that it was possible to have someone walk up to you, put a gun to your head, and have your heart rate never change. I only wish that I had been able to train with him long enough to reach that state. This state of Zen or calmness in the midst of a highly stressful situation is known as miso no koro, or "a mind like still water". In investing, miso no koro is necessary as well. A mind like still water is necessary to have the clarity to spot and avoid all the sales traps and sales strategies of commercial investment firms that ultimately damage our ability to build wealth.

Unfortunately, psychology is one of the most overlooked components when it comes to building wealth. Throughout my investment career, I have discovered that "poor investors", investors that will never considerably grow their wealth in the stock market due to a primary mindset of failure, generally fall into three distinct categories:

(1) Poor Investor #1: Poor Investor #1 manages his or her own money, reads every investment book ever published about "how to build seven figure portfolios", and sticks firmly to mainstream investment strategies. However, because he lacks creative vision, he only achieves mediocre returns that never exceed 15% a year.

(2) Poor Investor #2: Poor Investor #2 wants to learn new investment strategies because he or she is smart enough to realize that almost all investment strategies advocated by investment firms are selling strategies. However, Poor Investor #2 never learns to prioritize correctly, and thus never sets aside any time to learn new investing concepts. Thus, Poor Investor #2 wallows in the same mediocre returns as Poor Investor #1.

(3) Poor Investor #3: Poor Investor #3 believes the large firms' spoon-fed sales strategies that annual returns of 20% or greater are not possible without the assumption of great risk. Poor Investor #3's sub-par returns result from a psychological mindset that does not question the deceptive claims of authority figures. Consequently, Poor Investor #3 entrusts management of his $1,000,000+ investment portfolio to a commercial investment firm and consequently averages mediocre 8% to 10% annual returns.

The common denominator with all three poor investors is the adoption of negative psychological beliefs. However, psychology has strong transformational powers when it comes to building wealth and can easily turn a "poor" investor into a "rich" investor. For precisely this reason, I will devote substantial sections of this book on debunking the widespread investment myths that create the adoption of poor mindsets that severely hurt our ability to build wealth. Ultimately, the commercial investment industry is not solely responsible for the poor psychological mindset of investors. The recency effect, or the tendency to remember only the latest details of the most recent action, also greatly contributes to the "poor" investor mindset.

Understanding the Recency Effect

Stocks oddly enough seem to be the one commodity that the overwhelming majority of people only buy when it is selling at extremely high premiums. If you show a group of people a nice pair of dress shoes that cost $275, and find 1000 people that would pay that price for those shoes, if you then offered that same pair of shoes to them for $500, 999 of those 1000 people would probably no longer buy them as its price would seem bloated compared to its value. However this is not the case when it comes to stocks. People, and this includes analysts as well, only seem to jump on board the bandwagon when the price of a stock goes up.

Let's take BHP Billiton, the world's largest, diversified mining company, to illustrate how the recency effect works. In 2006, when BHP Billiton was trading below $40 a share, and it stayed below $40 a share for weeks, I told several friends that were looking for something to buy that BHP under $40 a share was a good buy. For two months, they could have bought BHP between $37 and $40 a share, yet I doubt that any of them did. Why? I know the mindset of most investors. Most investors want to see large increases in price before buying into a stock instead of buying it when it is beaten down in price. From a psychological standpoint, when they see a stock leap up 15% to 20% in price, they think they can hop on board and continue riding the wave higher.

Sometimes this works, but the majority of times it does not. Back then, I noticed that analysts finally upgraded BHP after it increased in share price by 19% from $37 a share to $44 a share. And this is why analysts contribute to the poor decision making of investors. Investors should have bought BHP when it was an ignored stock and trading at $37 a share. Instead, they foolishly wait for analysts to tell them when to buy and end up paying a needless and unnecessary 19% premium on the price.

When evaluating more volatile stocks than BHP, the average investor will probably pay upwards of a 25% to 50% premium on the same stock than a forward-looking investor. When we consider the fact that average investors are paying anywhere from 10% to 15% higher prices on blue chips and 25% to 50% higher prices for mid and small cap stocks, obviously there will be a huge and marked difference in the absolute returns of the portfolio of an average investor versus that of a forward looking investor.

The Best Investment Style? Low-Risk, High-Reward Investing, Hands Down

Although today, many investment newsletters tout value, value, value, this is not what I promote or what I believe. I don't believe in growth investing and I don't believe in value investing. I only believe in low-risk, high-reward investing, because I believe this style trumps all others. When I worked for a large Wall Street firm before venturing into my own entrepreneurial pursuits, I remember periods when investment firms that focused on a value style performed horribly for years at a time. Value companies can underperform for three distinct reasons: (1) A company can appear to be a great value, but it may be undervalued because it deserves to be, and ultimately will only head lower (think housing stocks that were touted as great value in 2007 by many commercial investment firms, yet continued to drop 30% to 50% more after firms had rated them a value buy), (2) A company can truly be a great value, but may currently dwell in a business sector that is out of favor, and thus will continue to underperform; and (3) A company may be a great value but if there are no compelling stories specific to that company or attached to their industry, its stock price can still languish for a long time.

Today, rather than trying to guess whether "growth" or "value" stocks are in vogue, a forward looking investor can always select stocks that outperform by focusing on the intimate relationship that exists among financial institutions (and the economy), governments and corporations to uncover low-risk, high-reward stocks.

If you think that, up to this point, I have spent too little time discussing P/E to growth ratios, working capital ratios, debt structure, etc., it's not just because I believe that number crunching is incredibly boring, which it is, by the way. And it's not because I absolutely ignore these numbers, because I don't. *It's because I believe that number crunching alone is a prehistoric method of picking stock winners.* How many of you think that Heads of States and U.S. Senators that have significantly outperformed every money manager in the world for decades are actually sitting at home with a calculator, happily number crunching away?

Heads of States, Presidents, Parliament members, and Senators have understood for decades that government-banking-corporate relationships are much better predictive indicators of whether a stock's share price will significantly appreciate as opposed to a reliance on fundamental evaluation. While it is true, that in the past, the average person could not, and did not have access to this type of information, the flattening of the information world through technology has dramatically changed this game, with many of these dramatic changes occurring just within the past five years. Don't get me wrong, **number crunching has its place, but only as a supplemental piece to the puzzle and never as a primary driver of decisions**. Just being a value stock picker is a very incomplete system to finding huge winners. While I don't expect 60% to 80% gains in less than a year from BHP as I do from many other stocks I hold, purchasing stocks like BHP that have great stories when they are out of favor makes sense as a long-term core holding to build a portfolio around. While I don't own too many stocks that most investors have ever heard of, having a few with strong upside potential as long term core holdings is never a bad idea.

The Story of Miyamoto Musashi

One of my favorite stories about one of the most famous and accomplished samurai ever, Miyamoto Musashi, aptly illustrates the proper psyche that must be established by a successful investor. Thus, it's a fine way to conclude this chapter.

Miyamoto Musashi's reputation as a fearsome samurai in Japan was legendary. He was said to be equally adept in using the sword with either hand, or even using two swords at the same time. Legend was that Mushashi never lost a sword fight in his entire life. A young samurai, well aware of Musashi's reputation, decided to seek an apprenticeship under Musashi as he desired to become a master swordsman as well. After much persistence, the young samurai was able to convince Musashi to be his sensei.

At first, Musashi instructed the young samurai to engage in nothing more but chopping wood and fetching buckets of water from a far away spring. The young samurai viewed this as paying his dues in the master-student relationship so he didn't complain. The days of chopping wood and fetching water soon turned into weeks, and soon, the weeks turned into months. Still, the young apprentice did not complain. He continued to chop wood and fetch water but eventually the months turned into a year, the year into two years, and the second year into yet another. After doing nothing but chopping wood and fetching water for years, the young apprentice began to question if Musashi was just using him as a servant or if he was ever going to start his apprenticeship as a samurai.

Fine, Musashi replied, you have been incredibly patient so I will finally begin teaching you as you wish.

Musashi next instructed the young samurai to go to his dojo and carefully walk around the edge of the tatami mat without missing a single inch. Again, the apprentice faithfully listened. He walked from morning to evening every day. Once again the days grew into weeks, the weeks grew into months, and the months grew into a year. Still the apprentice did not question Musashi. Finally, after an entire year of this arduous walking, the young apprentice begged of Musashi, Please, I want to learn the true way of the samurai.

Musashi listened to the pleas of his obedient apprentice, and replied, Yes, yes. You have been very patient. Today I will begin teaching you.

Musashi then proceeded to lead the apprentice to a deep ravine. There, a tree trunk spanned its fatal depths. Musashi looked at his apprentice and said, Walk across.

When the apprentice hesitated, Musashi said, You have walked along a thin line, not missing a single step, everyday from sunup to sundown, for an entire year, yet you can not walk across a log that is much wider along a distance that is a tiny fraction of the distance you walked every day?

Upon hearing this logic, the young apprentice's fear of dying dissipated, and he strode with confidence across the log to the other side. When the apprentice reached the other side, Musashi informed him that his training was complete.

He told the apprentice, I trained your body for three years by having you chop wood and carry buckets of water. I trained your mind not to waver by having you walk along a narrow line for an entire year. Finally, I solidified the harmony among your mind, body, and spirit when you faced death and were not afraid.

So what is the point of the above story? The point is that in martial arts, no progress is possible with those that have a mindset of immediate gratification. The belt system so many are familiar with in the Western world – white, yellow, green, blue, purple, brown, black – is a Western invention to appease the need for immediate gratification, i.e. the thought process of "if the belt color around my waist is not changing, then I am not learning." In Asia, in many schools, there are still only two belt colors – white and black. You are either a student or master, and just because your belt remains white does not mean you are not learning. Musashi's apprentice became a true Samurai with a "warrior spirit" precisely because of his patience to learn the proper way.

In building wealth today, it is extremely rare to see people with the patience it takes to become "samurai investors". People will spend a lifetime learning to play an instrument or learning a sport but yet refuse to invest several hours a week for just a single year to learn the most important endeavor of their lifetime – how to invest properly. People spend $100,000 a year for an exclusive country club membership but are unwilling to pay a fraction of that cost to learn how to make multiples of that figure in investment profits.

Today, it is very rare to see the patience displayed by Musashi's young apprentice in learning a craft. Today, it is likely impossible to find one child anywhere in a developed country that would have the patience to last even two months if he or she had to train similarly to Musashi's apprentice. All would undoubtedly quit. In investing, the equivalent of Musashi's apprenticeship would require just a fraction of the effort - a few hours a week for a year, with ongoing refinement and customization of investment strategies for several more years - yet, people are still unwilling to invest this minimal effort.

Understand that investing a fraction of the effort of Musashi's apprentice in learning how to build wealth will yield results beyond your wildest dreams.

4

KNOW YOUR ENEMY

In the previous chapter, my goal was to help you to begin establishing the type of mindset that each one of us needs to win at investing. In this chapter, I'll take things a step further by revealing the psychology behind all modern theories of investing. By understanding the psychological culture of commercial investment firms, it will be much easier to rid yourself of past erroneous beliefs and transform your belief system into a winning mindset.

In his seminal book on warfare strategies, The Art of War, Sun Tzu preaches that you must know your enemy. Keep your friends close but your enemies even closer – advice that we as investors, rarely heed. As investors we often place far too much responsibility for our future financial freedom in the hands of investment industry professionals without adequately knowing them. Is it fair to call the investment industry "your enemy"? Hopefully, the very first chapter of this book alerted you to the fact that this is indeed a war for your financial life, and it is a war that the investment industry has heavily and unfairly equipped itself to win at your expense. And win it does.

Logic would tell us that an educated investor is an investor that doesn't need the investment industry. Thus, the job of the investment industry is to keep the average investor ignorant about how to make money and keep the investor dependent upon them. Thus, it is neither illogical nor foolish to consequently view the industry as "your enemy". In order to avoid being taking advantage of, learning the tricks of the trade and insider industry secrets is a must. If you've never been on the inside, it might be impossible to know your enemy. That is what this chapter as well as others in this book will grant you – a solid opportunity for you to get to know the enemy on an intimate basis.

For those of us that use the far too utilized scapegoat of "lack of time" as the reason we refuse to manage our own money, this excuse is simply a rationalization for the fact that we are not truly committed to building wealth. Many Taoists say that there is no such thing as "try" but only "do". They say that if you say you are "trying" to change, that your heart is not sincere. If you sincerely wished to change, you would not try, but rather just "do". The famous Nike slogan "Just do it" in fact was co-opted from this very Taoist concept. Let me explain. Real estate, outside of the stock market, is another industry that immediately comes to mind when we think of how people have built fortunes. How many of you have ever met a single real estate tycoon that built his or her fortune simply by giving someone else $1,000,000 and letting him or her handle every aspect of his or her real estate portfolio?

Yet, this is exactly what most of us do every day in regard to our stock portfolios. The cardinal sin of almost every one of us when it comes to investing is that we profess to be serious about building wealth, but when push comes to shove, we still want something for nothing. We believe that investment firms will produce great wealth for us yet still desire to remain largely disengaged from the process. We let investment professionals tell us what is best for us, and how and where our money should be invested without ever independently challenging or even attempting to verify any of this advice. This is the lazy man and woman's approach, consistent with what Taoists would say is "trying" but not "doing."

In this chapter, I will discuss why the cards are stacked against us when we utilize professional money management services.

The Investment Industry and a History of Selling

If you've ever wondered if you would be best off with an independent financial consultant, with a huge investment firm, or managing your own money, to understand the answer to this question, let us first separate investment fiction from investment fact.

The key to sorting through all the "noise" that investment firms and financial consultants throw at us is to be able to deconstruct the myths they propagate. What is ultimately so confusing about working with big investment houses is that they combine fact and fiction into a top-notch marketing campaign to convince us to entrust our hard-earned dollars to them.

For example, let's consider the oft-repeated investment firm strategy of being fully invested in the market almost all the time. Though being in cash can be an intelligent short-term strategy, there is always money to be made somewhere in the world, whether in put options, in non-stock assets, or by investing outside of the country you call home. Thus for the most part, I don't have a huge beef with this strategy. However, I do have a problem with the way Wall Street firms use fear to achieve this. Let's re-visit the commonly quoted sales statistic:

"If you had missed the best 90 performance days in the market from 1963 to 1993 your average annual return would have dramatically fallen from 11.83% to 3.28% a year." (Source: University of Michigan)

Salesmen and women masquerading as Financial Consultants often quote this statistic as proof that you are much better remaining fully invested in markets even during extended bear markets. However, if we analyze the assumptions behind this statistic, it soon becomes enormously easy to disprove. Is it truly realistic to think that anybody's luck would be so bad as to miss the best 90 days over a 30-year time span even if they chose to be in and out of the market at certain times? What are the chances that you, as an investor, would miss all 90 of the best performing days? One in a million? What if, when you were out of the market, instead of missing the best 90 performance days, you missed the worst 90 performance days? Then what would your annual average returns be? 30% instead of 11.83%? See how deeply flawed this argument is. And this is the argument that financial consultants always use to sell you the concept of staying fully invested.

This argument is doubly flawed because most commercial investment firms convince you to stay fully invested in only financial products with which they are familiar. For example, if you live in Hong Kong, your financial consultant will most likely buy almost all Hong Kong/ Chinese stocks. If you live in the U.S., your consultant will certainly purchase a portfolio consisting almost entirely of U.S. stocks. Their "fully invested" strategy is a fee generating strategy versus a return maximization strategy. In fact, this strategy is often combined with the strategy of Modern Portfolio Theory to maximize the amount of assets gathered by each financial consultant. "Modern" portfolio theory was once revolutionary when it was developed way back in the early 1950's, but not anymore.

In simple terms, Modern Portfolio Theory calls for diversification of your stock positions across various sectors and industries to offset the potential of a poorly performing sector. In other words if you own stocks in trucking and shipping companies, Modern Portfolio Theory would dictate that you own oil companies as well because if oil companies lag, then cheaper fuel costs should translate into gains for trucking and shipping companies. The only problem with this theory is that investing is about maximizing our portfolio returns and not merely trying to create a zero sum game.

Mu Shin Ryu

In martial arts, the concept of mu shin ryu, loosely translated, means to "abandon the mind." Every credible school of martial arts will teach some variation of this concept. Even Bruce Lee's famous "Feel. Don't think" quote from Enter the Dragon was an extension of mu shin ryu. In martial arts, one practices techniques until they become second nature so that mind, body and spirit can act in harmony without the process of thought slowing down one's reactions. Instead, thought and reaction become instantaneous. In investing, we need to recognize this concept and how investment firms apply it to our disadvantage.

In many aspects, global investment houses have become demagogues when applying this concept. They have convinced investors over decades to "abandon the mind" and to trust them explicitly, so much so that they can make simple statements through the media and literally move millions of investors to behave exactly how they desire. Even though most of us recognize that the quality of publicly accessible investment information has grown by leaps and bounds over the past decade, most of us will still unfailingly "abandon the mind" and blindly accept the singular method taught by every global investment house – diversification – as the best way to invest.

On a broader scale, every single unscrupulous business that only wants your money will try to convince you to "abandon the mind", including shady investment newsletters, shady investment software programs that make outrageous claims of predicting every market correction and bull run at precise points, multiple "get rich at home" schemes, and so on.

How many "get rich quick" pitches have you ever heard that present unlimited upsides with seemingly no downside? How many meetings have you had with financial consultants that tell you,

"Listen, if you think about it, there is no comparison between the financial products that existed 25 years ago and the ones that exist today. Back then we didn't offer baskets of foreign currency to hedge against a declining dollar; or caps, collars, and swaps; or commission free trading." The difference between financial product selection today and even just 10 years ago is like night and day.

With so much evolution on the financial landscape, how can it be that commercial investment firms' recommended investment strategies of Modern Portfolio Theory and diversification have not evolved at all?

Commercial investment firms cleverly employ the concept of mu shin ryu, or "abandonment of the mind" against us. They constantly send us subliminal messages that state, "We're the experts", "Trust us", and "This is what you need to do with your money". The concept of mu shin ryu can both be dangerous and beneficial to us as an investor. It can be dangerous if we abandon our minds and allow ourselves to be manipulated like robots by commercial investment firms. It can be beneficial, however, if instead, we choose to abandon all the knowledge ever taught to us by commercial investment firms. To have a free mind in this aspect and to question all questionable theories and strategies imposed upon us will undoubtedly make us much better and much wealthier investors.

With the manner in which the internet has rapidly flattened our world, access to information is so good today that every investment firm should invest loads of time to teach their financial consultants how to access the type of corporate information that is much more strongly correlated to stock performance than the information contained within corporate financial statements. The way to stay ahead of the game today is to ensure that investment strategies evolve with technology. However, as I've stated before, the commercial investment industry does not exist to make you rich. They exist to make themselves rich. What other industry employs a fee structure whereby if they fail to deliver, you still have to pay them significant sums of money? I can't think of another one outside of the investment industry. Thus, investment firms will continue to dwell in outdated strategies that help them sell, sell, sell and continue to feed their bottom line rather than provide the re-education their consultants need to improve the performance of their clients' portfolios.

Why Investment Firms' Goals Don't Include the Maximization of Your Portfolio Returns

The origin of almost all universally accepted investment principles is their effectiveness in gathering assets, a completely different objective than the maximization of your portfolio returns. Throughout this book, I will continue to deconstruct many investment myths and expose them as nothing more than sales tools that have specifically been designed to gather assets. To understand why this is so, it is helpful to discuss the mentality of most commercial investment firms.

To illustrate the mentality I speak of, let's take a quick ride through history with Citigroup. I don't want to single out Citigroup, because without exception, almost every large global investment firm has been subjected in past years to multi-million dollars of fines that arose from suspect and unethical behavior. However, since it would be overkill to discuss the infractions of every single large financial institution, let's start off by recounting some of the past infractions of Citigroup.

In June, 2005, the United Kingdom's Financial Services Authority ruled that Citigroup "failed to consider risks or consequences when, in August of 2004, it authorized six traders in London to unload €12.8 billion of securities in 18 seconds," a trade that helped Citigroup earn $18.5 million of profits in one day after they chose to re-purchase some of these securities at lower prices a mere seven minutes later[7]. When the details of this transaction, which ironically had been bestowed with the code name of Dr. Evil, became public, Citigroup's executive management admitted no wrongdoing, and in fact, declared that the transaction was entirely within the confines of securities law. Only after realizing that the transaction had caused a huge credibility gap among European countries that eventually translated into significant amounts of lost business did Citigroup back off its original stance of innocence and finally issue official statements of regret.

Incredulously, a mere one month later, the lessons from this debacle apparently ended up being lost in translation. In September, 2004, Japanese regulators expelled Citigroup's private bank in Japan for engaging in profitable transactions that failed to adequately police possible acts of money laundering. The infractions were so egregious that Japan informed Citigroup's private banking unit that they could not operate anywhere in their country for the next five years, with the earliest possible date of re-instatement sometime in 2009[8]. But this wasn't all. The next year, Citigroup, along with JP Morgan, was forced to spend an additional $4.6 billion to settle lawsuits that accused them of covering up wrong-doing associated with the securities collapses of Enron Corporation and WorldCom, two former powerhouses in the energy and telecommunication industries[9].

Again, Citigroup was hardly a lone wolf in committing industry infractions. In the mid-2000s, other major investment firms also indicted on fraudulent activities included JP Morgan, Morgan Stanley, Goldman Sachs, Credit Suisse First Boston, Lehman Brothers, UBS Warburg and U.S. Bancorp Piper Jaffray. Each of these firms, as a result of these infractions, was required to pay fines between $32,500,000 (Piper Jaffray) and $400,000,000 (Smith Barney)[10]. While these figures may seem huge at first glance, for a major global investment firm, the size of these fines were little more than a minor nuisance (consider that for Goldman Sachs, the average salary package in 2006 for all full-time employees was more than $622,000 and that their 2006 earnings topped $9,340,000,0005)[11].

So where are the honest investment industry professionals?

In all my years working in the Private Client Services divisions of two Fortune 500 companies, I never encountered a financial consultant that I would feel comfortable entrusting with the management of my own money (other than myself of course!). There were always three reasons for my feelings: (1) I couldn't trust the consultant to do the right thing for me before he or she would do the right thing for his or her wallet; (2) I knew that the consultant was too committed to the firm's investment discipline to ever build any real wealth for me; or (3) the consultant possessed both faults (1) and (2).

I'll recount a couple of quick stories that illustrates the pervasive greed that is typical of investment industry professionals. I once overheard one of the top financial consultants at a leading investment firm, a man that had been in the business for at least 20 years, call a client and tell his client that it was time to take profits on a large block of a particular stock. Not a minute after he placed the sell order, he called another client and informed him that it was now a good time to buy the very same stock. Is this the kind of man you would trust with the management of your money?

Another well-circulated story at a leading US investment firm revolved around the methodology that one of the top consultants had utilized to build an impressive book of high-net-worth clients.

According to the story, the manner in which this top financial consultant managed to convince wealthy investors to trust him was to demonstrate his ability to pick stocks that performed phenomenally well. To accomplish this, the financial consultant would find a very thinly traded stock that had a history of volatility. He then would pay for a list of high net worth clients, call ten people on that list and tell them he was a top financial consultant at his firm. Of course, this would not get the attention of these wealthy individuals because they did not know him from Adam. Knowing they would be hesitant to hand their money to him and begin a relationship with him, the consultant would acknowledge their reservations and then proceed to ask them to write down the name of this volatile stock that he had researched. He would then tell these 10 individuals that his stock picking methodology was so good that he was 100% sure that if they invested in this stock, they would make a healthy profit in a short period of time.

Then he would take the next 10 people on the list, repeat this scam, but instead, tell these 10 people that he was 100% sure that they would make lots of money if they purchased put options on this stock. With his ingenious plan in place, the financial consultant would then wait several weeks until the stock moved 25% or more in either direction. If the stock gained, he would call the 10 people that he told he was 100% sure they would make lots of money from buying the stock. If the stock lost 25% or so, he would forget about the 10 wealthy individuals he had told to purchase the stock and instead call the 10 people he had told to short the stock. When he called these individuals, they were amazed that he was right regarding a stock that they had never heard of, and many agreed to give lots of money to him.

I tell you this story because schemes like this are commonplace in the investment industry. They are cleverly designed to make it appear as though these investment "professionals" really know what they are doing, when in fact, they are selling nothing more than emperor's clothes to you. So now that we have discussed some of the proverbial bad apples of the investment industry, where are the honest financial consultants, you may ask? Unfortunately, most end up in financial consultant heaven.

In 2001, Chung Wu, a Houston based financial consultant at UBS Paine Webber, sent an email to his clients warning them of liquidity problems he discovered at Enron and advising them to sell Enron stock. An Enron employee, Aaron Brown, in turn, responded harshly to UBS PaineWebber executives, and sent the Houston branch office manager a note stating: "Please handle this situation. This is extremely disturbing to me." Within three hours, Patrick Mendenhall, a UBS branch manager, fired Chung Wu.[12]

According to a filing with the National Association of Securities Dealers, Mr. Wu wrote: "Enron management was not pleased and due to the employee stock option relationship UBS PaineWebber has with them, the pressure came from my corporate office to dismiss me." UBS claimed they fired Wu over an email protocol infraction even though they immediately retracted Wu's email and sent a new email to their clients informing them that Enron stock was "likely heading higher than lower from here on out."[13] UBS's clients that listened to the corporate retraction of Mr. Wu's email and subsequently held on to Enron stock lost everything they had just a few months later as Mr. Wu's allegations turned out to be correct and Enron declared bankruptcy. (Source: The New York Times, March, 2002).

Although I could fill an entire chapter with stories of deception that I witnessed as an industry insider, it is only important that you understand that commercial investment firms virtually have devised unlimited ways to defraud and deceive us. If a consultant must choose between making the mortgage payment on his $2 million house and doing the right thing for you, hopefully by now, you have a fairly good idea of the decision he or she is likely to make.

What about the analysts?

Unfortunately, the story about analysts is not any better. Given recent history, if there are honest analysts out there that try to protect their clients, it seems that such an analyst won't last long in the investment industry. According to biotechnology analyst Matt Murray of the American investment bank Rodman & Renshaw, he was fired after wanting to lower the rating of client Halozyme Therapeutics despite the objections of his firm[14]. In Hong Kong, Morgan Stanley's chief economist and star analyst Andy Xie was allegedly forced to resign because of an internal memo that he scripted that was later leaked to the public. Xie upset the firm with his criticism of Singaporean officials. In the memo, Xie spoke disparagingly of Singapore and stated, "Actually, Singapore's success came mainly from being the money laundering center for corrupt Indonesian businessmen and government officials. Indonesia has no money. So Singapore isn't doing well. To sustain its economy, Singapore is building casinos to attract corrupt money from China."[15] But Xie wasn't the only one that was let go. According to the Greater China News, Morgan Stanley amazingly also fired two bankers that had merely distributed Xie's memo.

Unfortunately, analysts and financial consultants at major investment firms are under extreme pressure to hold the party line and not to upset corporate relations even if their honesty may save clients hundreds of thousands or even millions of dollars.

The important question you must now ask yourself is,

Can these firms really have my best interests at heart when it comes to my stock portfolio?

Your answer to this question is critical because every investment strategy that drives your investment portfolio is predicated upon your response to this question. If you believe the answer is yes, then you might as well stop reading here and set this book down now. The reason I cited the "Dr. Evil" Citigroup bond trading story above is that if one firm's trading activity can move prices in a bond market, you better believe that the largest investment firms have the ability to move prices in the stock market as well. During the 1990's, the flurry of mergers and acquisitions that consolidated the financial powerhouses into even fewer, more concentrated financial powerhouses was bad news for the average investor.

Firms such as Merrill Lynch, Goldman Sachs, UBS, and Morgan Stanley grew so big in the early 2000's that it was estimated that only a handful of institutions control the majority (meaning greater than 50%) of trading volume in the entire U.S. stock market every single day. Now with the failures of multiple major Wall Street firms in 2008, this problem will become even worse as the concentration will deepen. This means that when the largest firms on Wall Street decide to buy or sell millions of shares of a particular stock, they most likely know that the stock's price will move higher or lower based upon the sheer volume of shares they are moving.

Though most people realize that investment firms have grown exponentially in the amount of assets they manage, it is still amazing to consider that a single financial institution can own blocks of half a billion U.S. dollars or more in a single stock. There is no doubt that large financial institutions move the prices of certain stocks and that they know in advance of either you or I if that price movement is going to be favorable or unfavorable.

Thus, in the end, you must consider everything you have learned here. If the behavior contained in this chapter was not the behavior of a corporation but was the behavior of one of your friends, ask yourself, Would I trust this friend with my hard-earned money? Despite the egregiously poor behavior of many firms, remember that most global investment firms' first choice of a targeted marketing message is one that incorporates the concept of trust. The fact is that millions of people still trust them because they don't understand how they operate. The rest of this chapter will reveal how they do.

The Sell-Side Strategies of the Modern Investment Firm

Modern day commercial investment firms continually tell us that it's impossible to predict what industries will be up in certain years and what industries will be down; thus the necessity of Modern Portfolio Theory. Again, this is a smoke & mirrors ploy designed to confuse the average investor. In today's information technology age, access to information is so good that it is possible to predict with a high degree of accuracy what sectors will trend upward in a given year, and even to predict at times, what sub sector within those sectors will trend upward. So why would firms not utilize technology to maximize returns for you the client? The answer is quite simple.

Though this is possible, doing so still takes time, and to commercial investment firms, time is money. Any time spent maximizing returns for client portfolios detracts from the time financial consultants can dedicate to gathering more assets for the firm. In the end, earning 8% returns for $100 million of assets will earn a firm much more money than earning 25% returns for only $10 million of assets. Thus, investment firms engage in purposeful deception about the feasibility of earning 20% or higher returns every year and lowball client expectations to 6% to 8% a year. By lowballing expectations for decades, firms have been able to minimize the amount of time their financial consultants spend trying to earn portfolio returns while maximizing the amount of time they have to gather assets.

A big story that made the rounds in the financial media in December of 2006 was Jim Cramer's (of CNBC TV and theStreet.com fame) statement that some hedge fund managers spread false rumors about a company to large trading desks and the media to drive a stock price lower. Many people found this admission shocking, but I've known all too well that these types of practices have been utilized against the retail investor for decades. Cramer said this practice is illegal, but easy to do "because the SEC [Securities Exchange Commission, the U.S. regulatory body] doesn't understand it."[16] Furthermore, the extremely wealthy former hedge fund manager boasted, "What's important when you are in hedge fund mode is to not do anything remotely truthful, because the truth is so against your view."[17] Such practices are so commonplace in the financial and investment industry that I don't even understand why stories like this make headlines.

As a former industry insider myself, I've been saying for years that the investment industry is full of investment professionals, everyone from financial consultants to private wealth managers to professional money managers, hard at work weaving the emperor's new clothes. However, only when a big mouth like Cramer speaks of the dishonesty that netted him great wealth does it attract attention. For those of you not familiar with the fable "The Emperor's New Clothes" let me summarize it here.

Long ago in a fabled kingdom, there lived an emperor whose vanity was legendary. Two swindlers, Guido and Luigi Farabutto, knew that they could capitalize on this emperor's character flaw to make a huge profit. They approached the emperor and told him that they would sew him the finest suits of a very expensive special cloth that would be invisible to anyone that was stupid or of low character. The emperor, fearing that he would not be able to see the clothes, sent two of his men to go see the suits.

The men returned, and afraid to tell the emperor they could not see the clothes, told the emperor that the suits were the most beautiful suits they had ever seen. When the emperor went to see the Farabuttos, knowing that his servants had been able to see the clothes, he did not want to admit that he could not see the clothes for fear of being considered stupid and of low character. So he proceeded to allow himself to be dressed in non-existent clothes for a parade through town and proceeded to walk through town in his underwear. When he came upon a young boy that pointed at him and said, "But he has no clothes", only then did the emperor realized that he had been swindled.

It is amazing to me that many of us, even those of us with millions being managed at investment firms, actually believe that our advisor or our firm has our best interests at heart. I understand that everyone of us that has given an investment firm permission to manage our money would like to believe that our advisor or financial consultant is the one man or woman at the firm that actually cares about our financial security. On the contrary, I, by no means, am saying that every single financial consultant only cares about the bottom line. However, as a former industry insider, I have no problem going on record and saying that even if your financial consultant or private wealth manager is your friend, it is still next to impossible for your friend to maximize returns on your investment portfolio.

Why?

Because they are limited to utilizing firm-endorsed investment strategies (diversification, asset allocation, and low volatility) that are pure sales strategies to manage your portfolio. Though the strategies we are all familiar with may sound great to us, that's exactly what the very best of all sales strategies accomplish. They are designed so well that they make us feel comfortable and in charge. The very best emperor's clothes "sell" customers without the customers realizing that they had been highly selected targets.

My estimate of the percent of investment professionals that weave emperor clothes every day is 99%. Of course, not all 99% of these investment professionals are Machiavellian or dishonest. Some, maybe even a lot, may actually believe that the investment strategies taught to them by their firm are the best strategies for you. Such is the nature of the game that is played every day. However, despite what the intent of an investment professional may be, these strategies will undoubtedly leave us financially naked, so much so, that even children with no level of financial sophistication would understand that those of us who allow ourselves to be deceived will end up with no wealth. Always remember that Jim Cramer, someone that built an estimated fortune of $100 million by manipulating wealthy clients, stated, "What's important when you are in hedge fund mode, is to not do anything remotely truthful, because the truth is so against your view."[18]

Many of the topics I write about in this book, I am only at liberty to do so because I no longer work for the commercial investment industry. If I was still there, I probably would have to write under a pseudonym for fear of some type of reprisal or backlash. But the greater, much more significant question to ask is, "How did greed become such a huge monster that when analysts and financial consultants speak a truth that serves to protect the interests of clients, their reward is a pink slip?" For those honest analysts and financial consultants that still work at large investment firms, after reading about the fates of Xie, Wu, and Murray, do you really think that any of them will ever step forward now to warn their clients of impending disasters?

The Manufactured Consent at all Global Investment Firms

As I've stated earlier in this book, investing has revolved around the same universally accepted beliefs for at least the last half-century. Although the same principles have been applied to retail investors' portfolios for many decades, almost every single one of them is heavily flawed and incorrect if the end goal is to maximize portfolio returns. Nobody questions the principles taught by the Merrill Lynches, Bear Sterns, Goldman Sachs, and Smith Barneys of the world even though some are of such questionable merit that a college freshman that has just completed a Logic 101 course could easily deconstruct them. Hardly anyone ever considers that an ulterior motive, such as the maximization of bottom-line corporate profits, could be the driving force behind today's most widely accepted investment principles. As a friend of mine once stated, repeat a rumor enough times and eventually it will be accepted as truth.

The manufactured consent* that is well established and constantly reinforced through a young adult's educational life is in turn greatly leveraged by the investment industry. (* manufactured consent is a term coined by media expert Noam Chomsky in regard to the media's manipulation of public opinion). The investment industry has long used their well-established perception as an authority to maximize their profits at the expense of their clients. Just look at how many large investment firms' marketing campaigns revolve around some variation of the central theme of trust. Slogans such as "Trust us" or "Managing Wealth Successfully for 50 Years" are commonplace. Investment industry employees, no matter how inexperienced and how inept, enjoy a "perceived" expert status despite a large gap between this manufactured perception and reality.

Although I can't prove that a consensus of sales-oriented investment principles has been manufactured among and by the major global investment firms, all logical analysis would lead to this conclusion. If you were to speak to a financial consultant from the largest global investment firms in London, Tokyo, Paris, New York, Sao Paulo, Santiago, Mexico City, Hong Kong, Shanghai, Mumbai, Singapore, or Berlin, they would all sell you basically very similar investment strategies. It seems more than just coincidental that every firm has evolved to produce almost the exact same investment strategies for their clients despite the many cultural differences that exist between various countries and locations throughout the world.

The President of Archer Daniels Midland, when meeting with a Japanese competitor in the mid-1990s, once stated, "We have a saying at this company. Our competitors are our friends, and our customers are our enemies".[19] He stated this to convince their competitors that collusion was necessary in the industry to maximize bottom-line profits (Archer Daniels Midland is one of the top agri-business companies in the United States). Certainly, we, as investors, must consider the possibility that global investment firms have formed a similar alliance to convince the public of the "infallibility" of their investment principles.

5

THE BIG 4 INVESTMENT MYTHS DEBUNKED

The investment industry is full of great myths, with the most prominent ones regarding diversification, the risk inherent in foreign stocks, the alleged 100% efficiency of markets, the impossibility of market timing, and the benefit of mutual funds. So far, I've touched on many of these myths throughout this book. However, in this chapter, I'll more thoroughly deconstruct what I call the BIG four investment myths: (1) Diversification; (2) Foreign Markets Equals Risk; (3) Market Timing; and (4) Mutual Funds.

BIG MYTH #1: Diversification is the Best Investment Strategy

To hammer home how ludicrous the most-widely accepted investment theories are, and how, in reality, they prevent us from building real wealth, let's start with the investment strategy of asset allocation

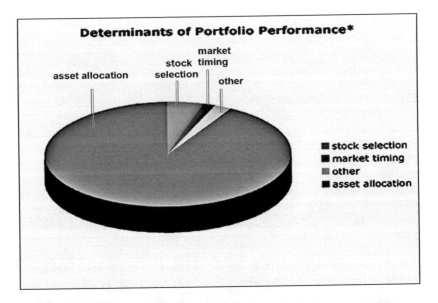

Figure 1. "Determinants of Portfolio Performance II, An Update".
Source: Financial Analysts Journal, May-June 1991

Almost every single person that has ever employed a commercial investment firm has seen the above chart, one that is universally used by the financial consultant as his or her "bible". Financial consultants recite that studies too numerous to count have been performed that prove the above "facts". But by whom? By people they hire? I'm not really sure who has performed these studies and I really don't care. I know they're wrong and that's all you or I need to know. Just like tobacco firms hired doctors to tell us that cigarettes weren't responsible for giving you lung cancer, investment firms will continue telling you certain things that are not true as well. I've stopped believing many of these disseminated investment myths a long time ago and since then, my stock portfolio returns have tripled and quadrupled over the returns I used to earn when I foolishly believed these myths.

Figure 1 claims that only 4.6% of portfolio performance is attributable to stock picking. If this were true, then why demand that your financial advisor spend more than thirty minutes deciding how to allocate the $10,000,000 you just gave him? You wouldn't. But you should, simply because the conclusions of the pie chart in Figure 1 are heavily flawed. Do you really think that if you owned five biotech companies with the best management and the most competent research divisions in the industry as opposed to five companies with the worst, bumbling, shortsighted management teams and research teams with no credentials, that their share performances would be comparable?

Or how about a commodity company that has forward sold contracts at lower than market prices during a commodity bull run? Do you really think this company's stock performance will be the same as a company that has unhedged contracts? Yet financial advisors always claim that these factors are irrelevant as long as you own the right asset classes in your portfolio. What if technology is tanking in the United States but booming in India? The above chart implies that it doesn't even matter what country you are investing in as long as you are in the proper asset classes. For example, commercial investment houses will almost always tell us that individual stock selection is not as important to our portfolio performance as being invested in the right sectors.

For the individual stock investor, no matter if you have $50,000 or $5 million, you can only be confident that your portfolio returns will be maximized when you assume control of its management. From time to time, during the course of my business travels, I will overhear a Financial Consultant, Vice President, or Private Wealth Manager pitching his or her firm's investment strategy to a client or a prospect in hotel lobbies or in restaurants. Listening to these clowns (though that is a harsh term to use, in general, that is my honest assessment of 99% of them) pitch and convince their clients of faulty sell-side investment strategies that line the firm's pockets is analogous to watching naïve city slicker students during my college days become victims to a ubiquitous urban scam. It's painful to watch, it's preventable, and it should never happen.

When I worked for an unnamed Wall Street firm, one of the most successful financial consultants in the office told me that once I had convinced a prospect or client to hand over his or her money to me, not to "waste" time deciding how to invest it. Paraphrasing him, he told me to immediately turn over the money to an outside money manager and move on to the next sale. In essence, he encouraged me to be true to the job title of "broker" and to not expend a single ounce of effort beyond brokering the deal between the client and the investment firm. In fact, during my employment in the investment industry, I was repeatedly informed that the only tactic I could use to possibly distinguish myself from another Wall Street financial consultant was the provision of better service, not the provision of better returns. In essence, because every major firm delivered the same products and roughly the same results at roughly the same fees, the predominant industry belief was that superior service was the only methodology to win more clients.

If investment firms truly strove to deliver performance to the retail investor, then significant variance among returns should be the natural result. Thus, investment returns, not service, would be a distinguishing factor among firms. The reason this variance does not exist is because investment firms have likely colluded to sell the same junk to millions of investors, and in the process, have limited the returns they can produce by sticking to the same sales-oriented investment strategies. Thus, believe it or not, instead of devising new investment strategies to boost portfolio returns, firms waste time thinking of preposterous marketing ideas such as sending clients Thanksgiving cards to stand apart from all the other consultants that send their clients Christmas and Chanukah cards.

Investment portfolio performance is 100% about investing in the RIGHT COMPANIES at the RIGHT TIME in the RIGHT COUNTRIES. Period.

The below pie chart, almost a complete inverse of the previous pie chart I discussed, is a graphic I produced that I believe much more accurately reflects the real "Determinants of Portfolio Performance".

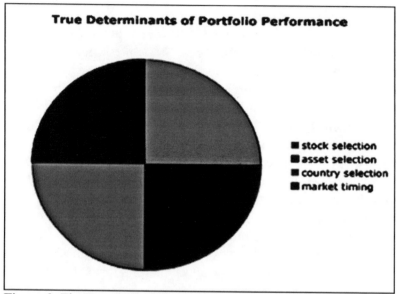

Figure 2. The True Determinants of Portfolio Performance
Source: SmartKnowledgeU™

The utilization of asset allocation theory usually leads to the additional error of diversification, so let's discuss the flaws of diversification. Once again, I'm going to illustrate the erroneous ways of diversification with a martial arts story. In one of the seminal books about martial arts strategy, "The Book of Five Rings" Miyamoto Musashi states that learning any more than five cutting techniques for the sword is unnecessary and that doing so actually detracts from progression in mastering the sword. Musashi stated that there are only a finite number of ways to kill someone with a sword and that he "failed to see the reason for practicing hundreds of little tricks to do it. Better to be the master of a few techniques than the student of many."

It is just not possible to master 10 completely different techniques brilliantly in even a span as long as ten years. In fact, many martial artists of legendary folklore status spent decades mastering just ONE technique that they would then use to defeat opponents of all different styles.

Today, many martial art students still fail to realize the concepts Musashi promoted hundreds of years ago. Perhaps it is Western civilization's obsession with the Gordon Gecko theme of "Greed is good" (from the Oliver Stone movie Wall Street) that leads many of us to believe that more equates to better. As I have trained in martial arts for over 15 years, I recognize that I have been blessed with superior masters that realized that preparation of the spirit was as important as technique and strengthening the body. My senseis and sifus have always instilled in me the philosophy of "better to be a master of few techniques than be an average practitioner of many." Yet, whenever I have trained friends, I have still not trained a single one that takes my advice of "Go practice this technique a hundred times every day for several months now."

Those I have trained always get bored quickly and think that they understand a technique when there is no way they could ever use it effectively in real combat. Perhaps it is the immediate gratification, attention-deficit-disorder, get-rich-quick, high-payoff-with-no-effort society that we live in today that instills this type of mentality in us.

It is this very mentality that also encourages us to quite foolishly adopt a diversification strategy in our portfolios. Diversification is the jack-of-all-trades approach in investing. Because diversification requires us to spread our portfolios so thin across so many industries, we become the master of no asset classes. Even if we own several stocks in an asset class that rise a phenomenal 180% to 300% in one year, if we have employed diversification strategies, our benefit will be greatly constrained due to the diluted performance of those outperforming stocks. However, if we have the foresight to overweight those stocks, our overall returns would significantly benefit. In other words, as an investor, utilizing the diversification approach makes us the master of nothing. Diversification is a distraction that prevents our progression of learning.

Using another martial arts analogy, diversification theory is like the mixed martial artist that knows 30 techniques but none of them with a decent level of mastery. When this martial artist enters a bout with another martial artist that has spent the last ten years, or even five years, mastering just 3 attacks, he will lose 99 times out of 100. If we have a financial consultant that applies the Modern Portfolio Theory of diversification to the management of your portfolio, think about how many asset classes he or she can speak of in terms of mastery. Then think about how many topics like energy, transportation, retail, etc. that he or she can speak of in very general terms. Who do you think will win the battle of portfolio returns between a financial advisor that is the master of very few asset classes and therefore can select stellar individual stocks in each of a few asset classes versus a financial advisor that is a generalist and will pick mediocre stocks in 10 different asset classes year after year?

For the reasons I have explained above, I hate mutual funds. Mutual funds are the equivalent of the Modern Portfolio Theory of diversification to the nth degree. They are a tool by which a managers' lack of expertise leads to terrible returns and great returns are achieved by luck. I know that sometimes financial consultants at large investment firms will tell you that you are best invested in mutual funds at levels less than $50,000 or $100,000. The only reason this may be true is that due to the time constraints placed on all financial consultants and the pressure to gather assets, this is the best possible way for financial consultants to manage your money. However, outside the time constraints of a large commercial investment firm, in the real world, we are far better off identifying individual stocks in a few asset classes in which to invest our money.

From March 2005 to March 2006, I achieved a 40% return in my portfolio with 100% long positions using the proprietary investment strategies that I developed. From May 2006 to May 2007, I was up another 30%. My investment newsletter, the SmartKnowledgeU™ Global Stock Picker, since its launch in mid-June 2006, has returned 19.68% returns in my Model Portfolio in a 7-½ month time span that included the entire month of January, when stock market indexes worldwide shed between 15% to 27% from their December highs. Furthermore, my Currency Portfolio, in a 5-½ month time span that included January of 2008, rose an incredible 37.42%. Thus, if I am able to consistently achieve these returns year after year through a strategy of concentration, this leads me to the following conclusion.

THERE IS NO DOUBT IN MY MIND THAT DIVERSIFI-CATION IS A PURE SALES STRATEGY & ONE OF THE WORST INVESTMENT STRATEGIES OF ALL TIME.

Although I would like to claim that I've been able to attain these returns because I'm extraordinarily smart, there's actually a much simpler explanation. I've simply chosen to be the master of just a few asset classes and a few choice strategies (proprietary strategies that I've developed) versus choosing to be an average student of many. To illustrate how little even investment professionals understand the importance of concentration, the question I'm most frequently asked after relaying the returns I've been able to achieve is the following: "What assets are you speculating in?" Given this question, it is crystal clear that many investment professionals do not understand that it is possible to achieve such returns without speculation and without high risk. Again, their lack of understanding originates from the fact that these professionals have become a victim of their own firms' training.

Realistically, every investor only needs to own three to five different asset classes to be diversified enough to protect your portfolio while being concentrated enough to significantly benefit from the areas we've chosen to master. Owning assets in transportation, technology, pharmaceuticals, retail, consumer, biotech, commodities, manufacturing, and agriculture is just plain silly. We will never build wealth this way. This approach hasn't worked for the last hundred years and it won't work for the next hundred. It's a great asset-gathering tool for investment firms, but as a wealth-building tool, it has no value.

As investors, we have all seen the table presented in Figure 3 on the following page. Figure 3 primarily represents the U.S. stock markets (except for the MSCI EAFE index which represents the aggregate performance of 21 country indexes in Europe, Australia, and Asia). However, similar charts exist for almost all major developed markets and are utilized by investment professionals to demonstrate that diversification among large cap growth, large cap value, mid cap growth, mid cap value, small cap growth and small cap value stocks is necessary (according to them) because of the apparent random nature of asset style performance.

Financial consultants state that this year's loser could be next year's winner, so in order to be "safe", you must invest a little bit in all styles. In order to further solidify this theory in the minds of retail investors as a valid theory, many investment firms hire prominent Wharton and Harvard business school graduates to develop asset-allocation models for their clients (see Figure 4 on page 77) based upon these charts. Surely if a Harvard MBA has developed the asset allocation model that will be used to manage your portfolio, you should be impressed, right? Wrong.

To help you fully understand the content of this particular chapter, please recall what I've previously stated about traditional education and statistics. Having a Harvard or Wharton degree is largely irrelevant to knowing how to build wealth or achieving significant portfolio returns. Again, firms hire employees from prestigious universities because they know that retaining such employees on their staff can convince retail investors to hand their money over to them. The fact is that although these models may appear to be sophisticated, they produce guidance that is nothing more than garbage. How sophisticated can any investment strategy be that virtually guarantees that you will hold underperforming asset classes? Firms will use such models to convince you that they are adding lots of value to the management of your portfolio by periodically overweighting certain asset styles, maybe shifting a greater allocation towards growth, value or emerging markets from quarter to quarter. However, there is one maxim that will never change.

If you feed a model incorrect input, no matter how sophisticated your model may be, wrong input is going to produce wrong output. Let's discuss the two things about Figure 3, the Periodic Table of Investing, that are fundamentally flawed.

2000	2001	2002	2003	2004	2005	2006
Russell 2000 Value 22.83%	Russell 2000 Value 14.02%	LB Agg 10.26%	Russell 2000 Growth 48.54%	Russell 2000 Value 22.25%	MSCI EAFE 13.54%	MSCI EAFE 26.34%
LB Agg 11.63%	LB Agg 8.43%	Russell 2000 Value -11.43%	Russell 2000 47.25%	MSCI EAFE 20.25%	S&P/Citi 500 Value 5.82%	Russell 2000 Value 23.48%
S&P/Citi 500 Value 6.08%	Russell 2000 2.49%	MSCI EAFE -15.94%	Russell 2000 Value 46.03%	Russell 2000 18.33%	S&P 500 Index 4.91%	S&P/Citi 500 Value 20.81%
Russell 2000 -3.02%	Russell 2000 Growth -9.23%	Russell 2000 -20.48%	MSCI EAFE 38.59%	S&P/Citi 500 Value 15.71%	Russell 2000 Value 4.71%	Russell 2000 18.37%
S&P 500 Index -9.11%	S&P/Citi 500 Value -11.71%	S&P/Citi 500 Value -20.85%	S&P/Citi 500 Value 31.79%	Russell 2000 Growth 14.31%	Russell 2000 4.55%	S&P 500 Index 15.79%
MSCI EAFE -14.17%	S&P 500 Index -11.89%	S&P 500 Index -22.10%	S&P 500 Index 28.68%	S&P 500 Index 10.88%	Russell 2000 Growth 4.15%	Russell 2000 Growth 13.35%
S&P/Citi 500Growth -22.08%	S&P/Citi 500 Growth -12.73%	S&P/Citi 500 Growth -23.59%	S&P/Citi 500 Growth 25.66%	S&P/Citi 500 Growth 6.13%	S&P/Citi 500 Growth 4.00%	S&P/Citi 500 Growth 11.01%
Russell 2000 Growth -22.43%	MSCI EAFE -21.44%	Russell 2000 Growth -30.26%	LB Agg 4.10%	LB Agg 4.34%	LB Agg 2.43%	LB Agg 4.33%

Figure 3: The Periodic Table of Investing
S&P 500 Index - A market weighted index of 500 large-cap U.S. stocks.

77

S&P 500 Value - The stocks that comprise the S&P 500 index that are considered to be value-style.
S&P 500 Growth - The stocks that comprise the S&P 500 index that are considered to be growth-style.
Russell 2000 Index - A market weighted index of 2000 small-cap U.S. stocks.
MSCI EAFE - Morgan Stanley Capital International index comprised of stocks traded in Australia, Asia, and Europe.
LB Agg - Lehman Brothers Aggregate Bond Index comprised of U.S. government, corporate and mortgage backed securities with maturities at least of one year.

Number One

Since the statistics presented in the above Periodic Table of Investing always depend on the performance of broad-based indexes, it may appear that small cap value stocks outperformed small cap growth stocks one year when reality actually may be that the three best growth stocks crushed the performance of the three best value stocks. Therefore, if we employed a profoundly exceptional stock picker to manage our portfolio, the returns of our portfolio may directly oppose the numbers presented by charts like the one in Figure 3. Likewise, as these charts are also utilized to justify industry diversification, it may appear one year that consumer retail stocks outperformed biotech stocks when again, the reality may be that the three best performing mid-cap biotech stocks crushed the performance of the three best mid-cap consumer retail stocks.

Number Two

These investment strategies assume that there have been no advancements in technology that make it easier to predict which industries, and specifically which stocks within which industries are more likely to outperform in today's world than half a century ago.

To illustrate point Number Two with an analogy, if we had to choose the higher scoring team between two NBA teams, we simply would choose the team that averages more points 100 times out of a 100. But if now our task changed, and we had to choose the player that scored the most points every game, our decision-making process would radically change. If the team that has the higher average score does not possess a single player that scores over 20 points a game, but the lower scoring team has someone named Kobe Bryant that scores 37 points a game, we would undoubtedly select the player on the lower scoring team, Kobe Bryant.

This is what investment firms never explain to us. Radical changes in our information landscape have enabled us to identify the Kobe Bryants of all the different asset classes, and thus, our returns could double, triple, or even be six times greater if we took the time to identify the Kobe Bryants of each asset class. Instead, investment firms 100% of the time allocate our portfolios to the Atlanta Hawks of the world (for those of you that don't follow professional basketball, the Atlanta Hawks are a perennial loser). In doing so, the returns of our managed portfolios are always full of potential but never deliver.

The reason that there are hardly any financial consultants that ever attempt to discover the Kobe Bryants of each investment asset class is because the employment of such intelligent strategies detracts from the time financial consultants can devote to gathering assets. If you are a financial consultant, you'll never climb the corporate ladder at a large global investment firm unless you gather massive amounts of assets regardless if you are achieving 40% returns for your clients every year. Ask any investment firm branch manager to name the most successful financial consultants at his branch, and he or she will readily rattle off the names. Now let's rephrase that question *to fit our definition of success* versus the firm's definition of success. Ask the same investment firm branch manager who his top financial consultants are in terms of average portfolio performance for his clients (this is a very different question than who the top money managers at the firm are). Though this should be among the highest priorities of any branch manager if client returns were valued, I can almost guarantee that this rephrased question will be met with a blank stare of ignorance.

Large-Cap Value	13%
Large-Cap Growth	17%
Large-Cap Subtotal	30%
Mid-Cap Value	8%
Mid-Cap Growth	12%
Mid-Cap Subtotal	20%
Small-Cap Value	10%
Small-Cap Growth	10%
Small-Cap Subtotal	20%
High-Yield Bonds	7%
Low-Yield Bonds	3%
Bonds Subtotal	10%
Emerging Markets	15%
European Markets	5%
Foreign Subtotal	20%

Figure 4. A Hypothetical Asset-Allocation Model
Copyright 2008. SmartKnowledgeU™

Once investment firms have convinced us of the faulty deductions they draw from periodic tables of investment, they develop asset-allocation models similar to the one presented in Figure 4 to guide the allocation of our portfolios. Such asset allocation models are usually labeled on a scale of aggressive to conservative, with more conservative models overweighting bonds and the more aggressive models overweighting stocks.

As we near the end of this decade, such a strategy is truly archaic. Today, given our access to information, we all can have a portfolio comprised of 100% stocks that possesses a better risk-reward structure than any mix of stocks and bonds determined by an asset allocation model. Especially if you are an American, as of the beginning of 2008, investing in U.S. bonds of any maturity is one of the worst places you can park your money going forward. Forget about laddered bond portfolios and any other type of bond strategy. If you are in U.S. dollar denominated bonds, get out.

Today, unparalleled access to information allows us to formulate stock portfolios that are solely driven by a low-risk, high-reward set up. The low-risk, high-reward characteristic of a stock should be the only determinant of whether the stocks you purchase are value stocks, growth stocks, foreign stocks, domestic stocks, biotech stocks or finance stocks, and not vice versa. Use this model and you will no longer have the guaranteed losers of archaic stock portfolio models, but a portfolio comprised only of stocks that ALL have very high probabilities of being significant winners.

BIG MYTH #2: Foreign Stocks are Risky

If firms consistently lost money for their clients they would undoubtedly lose the majority of their clients. Even if firms return 10% annually to clients, I still believe that they should lose the vast majority of their clients for these underwhelming performance figures. Remember, earlier in my book, I stated that Henry Ford once said, "It is well enough that people of the nation do not understand our banking and monetary system, for if they did, I believe there would be revolution before tomorrow morning." The very same holds true not only of our banking and monetary system, but also of our investment system. In fact, the best investors in the world like George Soros and Jesse Livermore have turned their back on the mainstream schools of investment thought, and in doing so, were able to build fortunes. However, most of us have not been as fortunate. Investment firms have insulated themselves from such client revolt by spending the last half of a century setting your expectations in line with the inevitable underperformance that results from the faulty strategies they continue to utilize.

Consequently, they have successfully hedged against an expectation greater than exactly what they deliver. During the first half of 2006, when most private wealth management assets (in developed markets) shrunk as clients' portfolios shrunk, many firms responded not by working harder to earn positive returns for clients, but by raising fees and commissions to make up the lost revenue from a shrinking asset base.

I am telling you that you can change your luck in investing not one month for now, not one year from now, but starting TODAY if only you have the courage to break away from the mainstream schools of investment thought that drive the thundering sheep herd of investors.

Today, investment firms unfortunately present retail investors with a double-edged sword, the worst of both worlds. They employ both the concepts of diversification and concentration in manners that harm your portfolio returns the most.

For the rest of this decade and possibly well into the next decade, you'll still find Chief Investment Officers of very well known investment firms making ridiculous claims that investors need to invest at least 50% of their stock portfolio in U.S. stocks if they wish to grow their portfolios exponentially. To disprove such egregiously poor objectives, you need only ask the following questions:

How are firms going to grow your portfolios exponentially with more than half of their stocks in a stock market (the U.S.) that has NEVER been the best performing market in the past 25 years (even among developed stock markets)?

How can firms grow your portfolios rapidly by buying stocks in a market that trades in what will be quite possibly the worst currency on earth among developed markets (the U.S. dollar) in 2008 and well into the future? For those of you that don't understand why a U.S. firm would make such a statement as their bottom line would seemingly not be affected by a decision to invest greater proportions of its client portfolios into foreign stocks, there is a definite marketing slant to such claims. Years ago, I left a Wall Street firm in the U.S. to start my own businesses. Acting as a friend, I continued to advise a former client on how his portfolio should be allocated. I told him that a minimum of 50% to 70% of his portfolio should be invested in stocks outside of the United States.

Though the reason for my recommendation had more to do with the development of certain global markets as I believed that many Asian markets would truly start to take off in 2005, the retort by the financial consultant that took over my client's account was far more revealing. When I ran into this former client about a month later and asked him how his portfolio was now being managed, he told me that he relayed my recommendations to his new financial consultant but that his new consultant told him that anything more than 30% invested outside the United States was "too risky".

Though this story occurred within the offices of a U.S. investment firm, it truly could have happened anywhere. If your portfolio is managed by a London investment house, your portfolio may have a focus on U.S. and U.K. stocks but rarely will you have exposure to Canadian, Mexican, Brazilian or Singaporean stocks unless through a mutual fund. If your portfolio is managed by a firm in Singapore, most of the stocks you most likely own trade in Singapore or other nearby regional markets like China and Hong Kong.

The reason why the U.S. consultant told my former client that investing outside the U.S. was "too risky" most likely had nothing to do with risk itself but was probably attributable to a deficiency in the consultant's knowledge about foreign stocks and/or the firm's inadequate coverage of foreign stocks. There could only have been one reason why investing more than 30% in markets that would have put the returns of U.S. markets in 2006 to shame would have been deemed risky- the inability of the financial consultant and the firm to identify foreign stocks with low-risk, high-reward characteristics.

The irony in the myth propagated by investment firms that "foreign stocks" are risky is that someone's domestic market is always someone else's foreign market. Consequently, then by nature of this perspective, every market in the world must be risky. Of course we know that is not true.

BIG MYTH #3: It's Impossible to Time the Markets

To build wealth with stock investing, you need to buy the right stocks in the right industries in the right countries at the right time. If you ever wonder why the Goldman Sachs or the Citigroups (if these firms are still around by the time you read this book) of the world will tell you that timing the market is "impossible" and a "waste of time", I'll tell you why here.

Financial consultants and the economists hired by large commercial investment firms always claim that since timing the market is impossible, clients need to be fully invested in the market the majority of the time. They claim that people that periodically jump in and out of the market always perform much more poorly than those that just park their money in the market and weather all the ups and downs. Again, firms are able to produce these conclusions because the sample population in these studies is comprised of the average Joe and Jane retail investor. If we already know that the majority of retail investors are failures at building wealth through the stock market, then of course sampling a population chock full of failures will tell you that a methodology used by failures has failed.

But what if firms conducted studies that actually sampled the less than 1% of investors that actually knew what they were doing? What if they sampled people that jump in and out of markets like George Soros? The results would be drastically different. The information investment firms spread about the impossible nature of market timing is akin to asking a sample of 6-year olds to run a mile in less than 5 minutes, and then, after all 1,000 fail, to claim that running a mile in less than 5 minutes is impossible.

The only thing I believe that is truly impossible about timing the market is buying at EXACT bottoms and selling at EXACT tops. Other than that, I think that it's extremely feasible to predict near bottoms and near tops as well as the behavior of certain asset classes. In fact, just ask my clients at SmartKnowledgeU™ about the information I have sent them about short-term market tops and bottoms in the gold and silver stock sector. For an entire year, I was right about almost every single call. If this was impossible to do, what would be the odds of that? One in a million? The secret that many of the greatest individual investors in the world have utilized to build great wealth is to find and buy asset classes that are ignored by the masses of investors before they explode in price. In essence, they time the market. Their very ability to accomplish this proves that market timing is very possible.

For example, gold stocks provide a prime example of when just entering the market blindly because "market timing is impossible" is a horrible strategy. Since there are definite historical patterns of volatility within this class of stocks that should be used by every savvy investor, I have never purchased gold stocks anywhere near their peak during spurts higher (even when adding to existing positions) nor have I ever sold gold stocks near their bottom during corrections (unless I was unloading what I had determined to be a poor pick to buy another pick that I thought could appreciate more quickly than the offloaded pick could rebound). In fact, employing such a strategy of waiting for significant dips to buy significant positions and selling down positions during times the market seemed frothy has enabled me to earn tens of thousands of additional profits over time with dozens of gold stocks.

This is not extremely difficult to do nor does it even require a great deal of time; however, given the extreme pressure placed on financial consultants by their firms to consistently gather assets every month, the ability to time markets does require more time than financial consultants have. The fact is that all of my proprietary, blue ocean methods of finding low-risk, high-reward stocks utilize proper timing to some degree (to discover more, refer to the description of our Platinum Membership levels at http://www.smartknowledgeu.com/modules.php).

The only reason firms tell you that market timing is impossible or only possible by the best investors in the world is because they remain entrenched in archaic methods of evaluating stocks. Just as a six year old will tell you that running a mile in less than 5 minutes is impossible, a financial consultant may tell you that market timing is impossible simply because they are incapable. However, incompetence is hardly the equivalent of impossible. Quite simply, you could transform yourself into one of the best investors in the world if you merely embrace the information in this book and abandon all the widespread accepted beliefs about investing.

BIG MYTH #4: The Safest Way to Invest in Foreign Markets is Mutual Funds

It's time to finally deconstruct the last of the big 3 investment myths – the benefits of mutual funds as an investment vehicle. If you have ever heard of an extremely successful investor that held mutual funds in their portfolio, that would be one more than I have ever known. This alone should be ample anecdotal evidence to prevent you from ever buying mutual funds. What do mutual funds sound like to you? If you answered the mother of all poor diversification strategies, you would be correct. However, from the perspective of an investment firm, an answer of a "time saving strategy" would be just as accurate.

A mutual fund is just an invention of the investment industry that saves them tons of time when selling you into the stock market. Buying a mutual fund in China or Japan or Singapore or Australia or Germany takes perhaps 1/20th the time it would take to research and find much better individual stocks in all those markets. Diversifying a portfolio across six different industries with a single mutual fund purchase requires perhaps 1/10th the time it would take to determine the best three industries of those six industries and to find the best individual stocks within those three industries. This is why the mutual fund myth as a "safe way to invest" is so widely propagated by the commercial investment industry.

There are additional reasons why I'm not a fan of mutual funds. Mutual funds have so many hidden fees that it's often difficult to know exactly what are your costs. Besides upfront costs that can be upward of 5% or more for some funds, there are 12b-1 advertising, marketing and distribution fees that range from 0.25% to 1.0%, administrative fees that range from 0.20% to 0.40% and of course management fees paid to the mutual fund manager of 0.50% to more than 1.0% annually. Furthermore, these fees don't include undisclosed "soft" costs of trade commissions that can add another 2.0% to 4.0% in costs. And yes, many mutual funds charge you 12b-1 expenses that they incur from advertisements and commercials that urge you to buy their funds. Ironic isn't it? If you think that you're saving on these exorbitant fees by purchasing only no-load funds, think again. If you're buying no load funds, chances are that your 12b-1 fees are higher than average, so don't let the moniker of "no load" fool you either. In no-load funds, the fees are just hidden from you and subtracted from the fund's performance. Retail investors are suckers for advertising and marketing, but make sure that you aren't one of them.

If all the costs above sound like a lot, brace yourself, because there are further intangible costs associated with buying mutual funds versus individual stocks. All mutual fund managers sacrifice a certain level of performance to maintain the necessary liquidity to satisfy share redemption. For a fund that turns over 100% of its assets annually, Roger Edelson of the University of Pennsylvania Wharton School estimates that the intangible cost of sacrificed performance amounts to approximately 1.5% of returns annually[17].

If I haven't already given you enough reasons to NEVER own mutual funds, here's one more. Can you imagine losing money in a mutual fund, and on top of that, having to pay taxes? Fund managers in losing funds frequently sell their biggest winners to meet liquidity needs, generating a capital gains income tax, thereby presenting the possibility that in any given year, **you may lose money from a mutual fund investment and owe capital gains taxes.** Believe it or not, add all the costs of mutual funds up and they can easily approach 5% to 10% or more. Yet, during my years working for a Wall Street firm, I encountered many clients that refused to pay management fees of 1.8% of assets because they deemed them excessive, yet would gladly invest in mutual funds in which they paid 4%, 5% or more in hidden fees. Who was the sucker in that equation?

Given the obvious drawbacks of mutual funds, can you believe that my negative list about mutual funds is not yet finished? If your financial consultant is among the many consultants that merely try to jump aboard hot emerging markets by buying mutual funds in China, India, or any other country, I advise you to exercise extreme caution. When pullbacks happen in these economies, and they will inevitably happen, you are at high risk of losing money very quickly.

Why? If you invest in a mutual fund, you are at the mercy of the thundering sheep herd mentality that dominates the mindset of mutual fund investors. More often than not, if an emerging market's economy experiences a correction, the thundering sheep herd will panic and head for the door in droves, causing millions of a specific mutual fund's shares to sell off over a short period of time. When this happens, the share price of your mutual fund will plummet before you've had a chance to figure out what even hit you. In mid-2006, this exact behavior drove down the value of two of the best-performing mutual funds in the market year-to-date (in Russia and Turkey) by 70% and 50% in a matter of weeks.

So now that you know that mutual funds are poor investment vehicles, what makes individual stocks better?

If you take the time to uncover the best stocks in the best industries versus buying mutual funds, your stock prices will be much more insulated and less volatile during market corrections.

While these stocks may still decline, they will most likely decline a lot less than a mutual fund in the same asset class. Strong companies' stock prices tend to weather countrywide economic downturns much better than fund prices. Furthermore, if you own strong individual stocks, they are far more likely to rebound more rapidly from a correction than a mutual fund. Why? Savvy investors will view a strong company that has corrected sharply as a opportunity to pick up the stock "on the cheap" and will often drive the share price right back to its pre-correction price in a matter of weeks. However, since a once strongly performing mutual fund can hardly present the same compelling story, investors when presented with a rapidly declining mutual fund on "sale" will be far less likely to re-purchase the fund.

To illustrate the one instance out of 100,000 when a mutual fund might be a better option than owning individual stocks, let's consider the current state of the Vietnamese stock markets. In 2007, Noritaka Akamatsu, the World Bank's lead financial economist in Hanoi, declared the Vietnamese stock markets as "the wild, wild West," and for good reason.[18]

During 2007, in Vietnam, an estimated 150 to 200 stocks publicly traded on the Ho Chi Minh Securities Exchange, a tiny market no matter how you slice it. In addition, an estimated hundreds of additional unlisted stocks were exchanging hands via Internet chat rooms and back alleyways, both figuratively and literally. These figures marked the intermediary stage of a rapid expansion from only 30 listed stocks in 2006 to a government-targeted figure of over 1,000 listed stocks by 2010. Still, in early 2007, the total market capitalization of ALL legitimately listed stocks in Vietnam was a miniscule $14 billion.[19] In comparison, in 2007, one global company, General Electric, possessed a market capitalization more than 25 times this size.

Due to its infancy, the Vietnamese stock market remained highly unregulated in 2007. In fact, thousands of listed shares still traded via unofficial "grey markets". Despite a very illiquid market where demand greatly outweighed supply, the Vietnamese State

Securities Commission still remained inadequately staffed to handle its responsibilities. In 2007, Vu Bang, the commission chairman, acknowledged the inadequacy of his 10 officers in monitoring the activities of approximately 200 listed companies as well as thousands of unlisted companies. Bang stated, "In 2007, we can't expect too much. We are considering how legal or illegal those websites are [chat rooms where unethical investors spread false rumors to inflate Vietnamese stock prices for personal gain]. In time, we'll consider it more."[20] According to Mike Temple, a director at securities-trading company Dragon Capital in Ho Chi Minh City, most retail investors conducted their stock research in the following manner: " My grandfather's uncle's cousin's wife works at this company and says it's a good buy."[21]

When there is opportunity in a rapidly growing emerging market but it is overrun with disarray and being driven higher on speculation alone, this is the one case out of 100,000 where I would advocate a mutual fund as a better choice over individual stocks. However, even with all these shenanigans, if you lived in Vietnam or had the time to travel to Vietnam to distinguish between fact and fiction, then I would once again advocate individual stocks. This is how strongly I believe that mutual funds are an invention of the investment industry explicitly designed to sell and gather assets with no intention of ever maximizing the returns of your investment portfolio.

6

WHY INVESTMENT FIRMS' FEE STRUCTURES NEVER FAVOR THE RETAIL INVESTOR

Last chapter, I exposed the biggest, most widely used investment strategies as nothing more than pure sales strategies. In this chapter, I'll expose the grave disadvantages that most investment firms' fee structures also present to us as retail investors. Contrary to commercial investment industry claims, fee-based services are not in our best interest. Large investment firms pat themselves on the back for making the transition in recent years from a transaction-based system to a fee-based system and cite that the major reason for charging you 1.35% to 3% of assets under management is to re-align their interests with yours. Over the past decade, as the retail investor became smarter and refused to be goaded into commission-based trades that were never good for him or her, the investment industry became smarter as well.

In recent years, investment firms unveiled fee-based products in a huge marketing campaign designed to convince us that clarity and disclosure in their industry have greatly improved. With the introduction of fee-based services and products, the investment industry finally admitted, that in the past, they may have sold us a crappy product just to reap the commissions. Fee based products, they ensured us, now fully aligned their interests with ours. It's a good sound bite but it's still not true. In fact, using a quick illustration, I'll demonstrate why I've never encountered a fee structure offered by the commercial investment industry that was truly favorable to the retail investor.

Financial advisors all over the world claim that by charging a percent of assets under management, if you make more money, then so do they. If you make less money, then so do they. Thus, they conclude, "Our interests are now aligned with yours." On the surface, this appears to make sense, but here's the scenario they never broach with you. If a fee-based system really aligned a firm's interests with yours, then both parties should be affected the same way under all scenarios. To illustrate why this is far from the truth, let's look at three possible scenarios and their outcomes.

Scenario 1: Your portfolio returns 15% one year.
A. Large investment firm – WIN
B. You – WIN

Scenario 2: Your portfolio loses 8% one year.
A. Large investment firm – WIN
B. You – LOSE

Scenario 3: Your portfolio loses 20% one year
A. Large investment firm – WIN
B. You – LOSE BIG

Obviously, this fee structure helps align the firm's interests more with your interests than they have been in the past, but it is still a gross misrepresentation for global investment firms to assert that a fee-based structure aligns their interests with yours. Whether or not you make or lose money, the firm still earns money. If your account is large enough, a firm can still demand substantial fees from you even when they are destroying substantial percentages of your wealth. What would truly align a firms' interests with yours is if they only took a percent of the profits they earned for you. Consider if a firm charged you 15% to 20% of the profits on your account. If you had a USD $1,000,000 account and your financial consultant earned 8% returns for you, then as a basis of comparison, a management fee of 1.80% a year would actually amount to a higher fee than 15% of profits.

For this equation to work out for the investment firm, they would have to earn you somewhere in the range of 12% a year or more. And if they earned you less than 10% a year under such an arrangement, then 15% of your profits would save you substantially more than paying a 1.80% management fee. Furthermore, if the investment firm managing your portfolio lost money, then you wouldn't have to pay them anything, because 15% to 20% of nothing is nothing. Thus, this type of fee structure would truly motivate an investment firm to perform for you as opposed to the current arrangement every commercial firm offers. Let's consider the table below.

Table 1

Portfolio Size	Annual Returns	1.80% Fee	Profit Sharing Fee Structure	Fee Difference
USD $1,000,000	8%	$19,440	$12,000	- $7,440
USD $1,000,000	25%	$22,500	$50,000	+$27,500
USD $1,000,000	-20%	$14,400	$0	-$14,400

Here's what we can conclude. While a fee of 15%-20% of profits will cost you more fees if your financial consultant is earning you 20%, 30%, or 40% a year, you would pay practically nothing if your consultant earned you less than 15% a year. From the above table, we can see that if we earned 25% and paid 20% of profits to our financial consultant, we would net from a $1,000,000 account (before taxes), ($1,000,000 * 25%) – ($250,000 *20%) = $200,000. However, if we only earned 8% from a $1,000,000 account and paid a firm 1.80% in management fees, we would only net (before taxes) ($1,000,000 * 8%) – ($1,080,000 * 1.80%) = $60,560. So if someone could consistently earn you 25% a year in returns and could net you an additional $139,440 ($200,000 - $60,560) every single year for every $1,000,000 invested, I don't know any investor that wouldn't gladly pay higher fees to net an additional $139,440 in pre-tax profits.

On the contrary, if your consultant underperformed and only earned 8% annual returns, under the proposed profit sharing fee structure, you would save more than $7,440 a year in fees in the above example. Finally, if your manager truly had a lousy year and lost you 20% one year, on a $1MM account, you would still pay most commercial firms a fee of about $14,400 despite the fact that they lost you an additional $200,000. Under my proposed profit-sharing fee structure, in a year a manager lost you 20%, you would pay them nothing because there are no profits to share in, and thus save $14,400 in fees. I don't know anyone that would not like to save a lot of money when his or her firm is underperforming.

I truly believe that if an investment firm's interests were really aligned with yours, then they would employ my proposed tiered profit-sharing plan instead of their fee-management plan. Instead, the fee-based structure of every large investment firm is still heavily skewed towards their interests and not yours. In essence, every major global investment firm's fee plan mimics what we find in Las Vegas or Macau where the odds of every casino game is with the house. In fact, the fee structure of the commercial investment firm industry is most similar to casino slot machines that are purposefully rigged to guarantee up to minimum takes of 20%. Likewise, with the current fee-based plans utilized by investment firms, they win in every single scenario whether you win or lose. Under my proposed profit-sharing fee structure, your financial consultant would truly share your pain during years of underperformance while truly reaping the rewards of great years.

This structure, and NOT the current fee structure overwhelming employed by all commercial investment firms, truly presents a win-win, and perhaps as importantly, a lose-lose structure for everyone. Any financial advisor or investment firm worth their weight in salt would be happy to arrange a profit-sharing fee structure similar to the one illustrated in this chapter. The sole criticism against this fee structure lies in the fact that people say it encourages portfolio managers to take huge risks in search of the big payout. This is a valid argument for hedge funds but not for stock portfolios, and here's why. Hedge fund managers, on average, charge their clients 20% of profits plus a 2% management fee.

In a year that a consultant earns 30% on a $2,000,000 account, 20% of profits would yield the consultant $120,000. However a hedge fund manager would take on average roughly $172,000 in fees from comparable performance, or 43% more than the profit sharing fee structure I proposed above. Though at first glance my proposed fee structure may sound very comparable to the fees hedge funds charge, it is far cheaper and extremely fair to all parties involved.

Secondly, there is a huge difference between managing a $9 billion hedge fund and tens of millions of dollars. HUGE. The reason I use tens of millions of dollars is because any independent consultant that is earning 25% to 40% a year for his clients is unlikely to be capable of managing much more than tens of millions of dollars while still earning those types of returns for his clients. In the upper range of what is capable, perhaps a consultant could manage a few hundred million dollars and still earn those returns.

Many people claim that Brian Hunter, the manager of Amaranth hedge fund who lost USD $6 billion in a couple of weeks in September, 2006, lost that money because the profit-sharing structure of hedge funds encouraged him to make unwise bets. Again, if you're managing billions of dollars and are compensated at hedge fund payout rates, the temptation of shooting for the stars is undeniable. Given the profit-sharing fee structure I proposed in this chapter, this shouldn't be nearly as big a concern.

In conclusion, profit-sharing fee structures similar to the ones I have presented are the only ones that you should ever agree to when it comes to the management of your investment portfolio. You should never continue to pay someone 1.5%, 1.7% or 2.0% every year if they only earn you nominal 8% returns, or worse, lose money for you. Reward them when they reward you and don't reward them when they don't reward you. At the very minimum, insist on a capped fee of perhaps 1.00% of assets when your financial consultant doesn't earn more than 5% a year for you. Such a structure drastically reduces your fees for poor performance as well as your risk.

If a firm is unwilling to make these concessions, in essence, they are unwilling to concede that they will be able to perform for you. Consequently, why should you trust them with your hard-earned money? If you can't find a large firm willing to concede such a payment structure, seek out an independent financial consultant that has 100% liberty to negotiate payment structures with you. If an independent financial consultant won't negotiate a similar payment structure with you either, then this is clearly an admission of a lack of confidence in his or her own abilities. In this life, you know by now that you cannot get something for nothing. Yet, investment firms have been able to do so with millions of investors worldwide. Even when they lose your money, you still have to pay them fees. And that is getting something for nothing.

Risk management is one of the most important aspects of every large financial institution's business plan. As it is now, the fee structures of most commercial investment firms are hardly aligned with the investor's interests despite what they might claim. All fee structures utilized by any global investment firm that I've ever encountered still cleverly push all the risk of underperformance on to us, the client.

This is precisely the reason why Private Wealth Management groups of large commercial investment firms continue to be the top profit margin divisions year after year. Frankly, it will be extremely difficult to find any consultant or firm willing to negotiate the profit-sharing structure I have illustrated in this chapter even though I have clearly demonstrated that such a structure is the only structure that aligns a firm's interests with yours. And this is precisely the reason, why in the end, you best serve your wealth-building interests by learning how to manage your own money.

7

THE 8 LESSONS NECESSARY TO BUILD WEALTH THAT SCHOOL NEVER TAUGHT YOU

In many styles of martial arts, it is said that a master will often divulge the most highly developed and deadliest of techniques not to his entire school but only to his top student. Likewise, regarding the highly guarded secrets about wealth accumulation strategies, there is a silent war being waged as well, a war that the upper class is winning by leaps and bounds as the rich get richer and the poor become poorer. I once had a gung fu master that trained under a traditional Chinese master, and he used to say that even though he had been under this master's tutelage for over 20 years, because he wasn't Chinese, he still wasn't offered the opportunity to learn all the gung fu "secrets" that his fellow Chinese students were granted.

This same cloak of guarded secrecy exists among the wealthy elite regarding the secrets of building wealth as well. Given that the wealthy elite founded all the prestigious universities in the world, they ensured that the secrets to building wealth would never be taught to the common person. In fact, they purposely excluded this subject material from being taught to the masses. There are 8 such courses necessary to build wealth that are not taught in traditional institutions of education. They are:

(1) A New Investment Paradigm
(2) How to Properly Interpret the Financial News
(3) Gold and Precious Metals
(4) How to Leverage Time
(5) Debunking Widespread Investment Myths
(6) Networking
(7) Corporatocracies: The Relationships of Governments, Banks and Corporations
(8) Major Currencies and their Effects on the World Economy

If you were wondering when I was actually going to delve deeper into the realm of wealth literacy, I will begin to do so in this chapter. For the previous 6 chapters, just like Musashi's apprentice, I have had you chop wood and carry water to build up your investment mind and body. Now for the payoff.

A New Investment Paradigm

In the early 1900's, J.P. Morgan formed U.S. Steel Corporation by buying Andrew Carnegie's steel company and many others. It promptly turned a profit of USD $400 million by selling stocks and bonds worth $400 million more than the combined worth of all the companies, from which it drew a $150 million fee.[22] Since then, profits at the expense of the individual investor have never ceased.

Most people know that incredibly wealthy millionaires and billionaires always seem to get richer every year, no matter if a good or bad economy exists. However, the average investor always seems to struggle with the standard investment cycle of average years, bad years and good years.

Wealthy people almost always perform well on their investments simply because their access to information is better than everyone else's. They have powerful connections that tell them in what direction interest rates are likely to head, where the prices of commodities are going, what industries will outperform, what legislation is likely to be rejected and what legislation is likely to pass – all before it actually happens. The information they receive is highly reliable and highly predictive because they are friendly with the most powerful financial individuals, legislators, and top managers at the top institutions and banks in the world.

During the past five years, I have developed proprietary, new investment strategies that leverage the flattening of the vast sea of information to give you access to very similar information that only millionaires and billionaires possess. If you still believe that Fundamental Analysis is a viable process to make your investment decisions, just remember the words of the famous British playwright George Bernard Shaw - "Telling the truth is a revolutionary act." Accountants lie, CEOs lie, analysts lie, the major financial institutions lie, and banks lie. In fact, so many people in the financial world lie that it's impossible to sort out good financial numbers, data, and analysis from the junk.

In 2001 and 2002, here are just a few of the companies involved in major accounting scandals where numbers had to be restated because they had been "cooked" to reflect better than actual performance:

Adelphia, AOL Time Warner, Arthur Anderson, Bristol-Myers, Squibb, Freddie Mac, ImClone, Citigroup, General Electric, JP Morgan, Lucent, Parmalat, Duke Energy, Dynergy, Enron, Global Crossing, Halliburton, K Mart, Merck, Qwest Communications, Reliant Energy, Tyco, Worldcom and Xerox. In the past couple of years, General Motors, AIG and Hyundia are just a few major companies that have also significantly restated earnings after disclosing accounting errors.

In addition to the partial list above, it seems that every other month a major company announces that they will have to restate their earnings for the past several years due to accounting inaccuracies (you should note that these announcements almost always happen *after* the company in question has released quarterly earnings statements that investors use as buying or selling guidelines). With inaccuracies regarding companies' financials as widespread as they are today, we just cannot rely upon their accuracy in our investment decision-making processes anymore.

Before I developed my proprietary investment strategies, I, like many other people, used to make my decisions based upon fundamental and technical analysis. Eventually, I tired of constantly having to sell shares due to decisions that were based upon faulty, misleading financials released by companies. In one year, I received at least five letters asking me if I would like to participate in class-action suits against companies whose shares I had once owned to recover money lost due to unethical behavior of said companies. And all five companies were NYSE or AMEX listed companies. Despite the lip-service corporations have given to recent corporate transparency legislation like Sarbanes-Oxley, in reality not much has changed.

Given that this is the sad state of affairs of big corporate _____ (fill in the name of your country here), the only thing you can 100% trust today is the money trail. By following the money trail in currency, commodities, stocks, and precious metals, we gain access to information that is virtually as good as the information that millionaires and billionaires use to make their investment decisions. And this is the basis behind my proprietary strategies. We send pings out to the information world and see what comes back. Sometimes the information is not so good, but often, the information that comes back to us from our MoneyPing™ strategies is so good that we're 90% confident that certain investments will yield at least 25% in the short term (one year) while possibly yielding 100% returns or more in the long term. We have consistently used our proprietary MoneyPing™ strategies for the past couple of years to uncover handfuls of stocks each year that return more than 100%, and sometimes even more than 200% to 300% in just a year's time.

Leveraging Information to Build Wealth

I invented three unique MoneyPing™ strategies each that separately could yield enough stock picks every year to earn every investor 25% annual returns or more in his or her stock portfolio. Let me elaborate a little further. Everyone of you, I'm sure, has heard of the concept of leveraging money, right? If you use a $100,000 down payment to buy an $800,000 house, then charge a monthly rent that covers your mortgage payments and consequently save for another down payment to buy another $800,000 house, this illustrates the concept of leverage. Leverage allowed you to turn $100,000 into $1.6 million in assets. In uncovering stock opportunities you can use leverage as well to multiply the stock opportunities you find.

Only instead of leveraging money, you leverage information. By leveraging information, I have uncovered some of the best performing stocks of my lifetime, stocks that have returned 50% to 100% in less than a year. In fact, many of these stocks incredibly have been large cap stocks! *And the great thing about leveraging information is that it requires less and less work the more we utilize the strategy to uncover great new investment opportunities.*

Because these counterintuitive techniques require time to learn, 25% to 60% annual returns may not be a realistic goal for someone in the first year of using them. However 15-25% annual returns is not only a realistic goal within the first year of using these techniques but a pretty darn reasonable one. If you are a quick learner, more than 40% returns is not out of the question, especially if you concentrate your asset allocation only in the asset classes most likely to outperform each year. And don't worry, a reasonably bright high school teenager could use my MoneyPing™ strategies to uncover many incredible opportunities with little difficulty.

Why? Because the strategies I teach require time and a curious intellect and nothing more. My MoneyPing™ strategies do not require knowledge of complex options trading strategies, sophisticated modeling software, or sophisticated economic formulas and theories. Just time and an internet connection! Furthermore, they are based solely on long positions, though the use of options can certainly be employed to provide additional returns. My SmartKnowledgeU™ curriculum is an investment curriculum, not a trading one. But more on this later. Let's move on to the other seven wealth-building topics.

8

HOW TO PROPERLY INTERPRET THE FINANCIAL NEWS

The second course of my wealth-building curriculum involves separating the wheat from the chaff when it comes to evaluating the usefulness of mainstream financial news in building wealth. I can sum up the best way to properly interpret mainstream financial news in two words : Ignore It! The advice of the overwhelming majority of the financial media, spokespersons and representatives should be avoided at all costs. To better describe the financial media, I have come up with some alternative descriptions. Of course, there are stellar financial journalists that provide cutting, insightful analysis of stock markets and central banks' actions. However, they are few and far between. The descriptions below are apropos for the majority of the financial media that cover the commercial investment industry.

Financial journalists: Media-paid sensationalists.

Simply put, many financial journalists are paid to generate sensationalistic headlines in order to attract a large readership base that will generate substantial advertising revenues. To illustrate my point of the general worthlessness of many financial reports in the major media, I tracked the online headlines at martketwatch.com during a span of a couple of weeks in October, 2006. Though that was several years ago, you really could replicate this experiment any year and you'll find that the headlines are still as useless today as they were back then. Here are the headlines from back then below:

Oct 12
Morning:
Bulls on the Comeback Trail

Afternoon:
Dow Hops to New Highs

Oct. 13
Morning:
Bulls hope pause refreshes
Dow's at record, within hailing distance of 12,000

Afternoon: Stock Rally Runs Out of Gas

Oct 16
Morning:
Downgrade Damage on the Dow

Afternoon:
Dow Tiptoeing toward 12,000

Oct 17
Morning:
Inflation Jitters Shake Street

Oct 18
Morning:
Dow Pierces 12,000 Level

Oct 19
Morning:
Wall Street Weighs Apple, Citi. Stocks Stroll South at Start

Afternoon:
Stocks Reverse Course, Rise

Oct 20
Morning:
A Case of Slowdown Jitters, Cat's (Caterpillar) Scratch Damages Dow

Oct 23
Morning:
Tiptoeing into a New Week
Ford Dents Street Sentiment

Afternoon:
Ford Dent Repaired on the Street
Wal-Mart Powers the Dow

When I examined headlines during another period of time (May, 2006) during which dramatic dips in the U.S. stock market indexes occurred, almost every financial newspaper screamed that a bear market was upon us. When markets rallied shortly thereafter and oil dipped to $50 a barrel, many financial newspapers screamed that 16,000 for the Dow and $20 oil was imminent. Then when oil bolted to $70 a barrel, $100-a-barrel oil became the new mantra.

Such bold headlines attract new readers and advertising fees but they hardly constitute complex analysis capable of intelligently guiding any long-term strategic investment plan. Instead, the great majority of media investment headlines are tantamount to watching the waves roll in on the beach and reporting on their activity, i.e., they add nothing to your ability to invest intelligently.

Now let's consider some other alternative job descriptions for other investment media.

The talking heads on TV: Overpaid cheerleaders of the investment industry.

Chief Investment Officers: Really overpaid cheerleaders of the investment industry.

Commercial Investment Firm Spokespersons: Government pawns or really, really overpaid cheerleaders of the investment industry.

In conclusion, almost all mainstream financial media is driven by an ulterior political or corporate agenda and consequently no attention need be paid to most of their reports. Discover and actively seek out those stellar journalists that seem to be reporting a different story than their colleagues and follow them.

GOLD AND PRECIOUS METALS

The third of my eight course on wealth building, is by far the most timely and important of all my 8 courses as of 2009 and into the foreseeable future. When gold broke through the $500 barrier at the end of 2005, the consensus among many of the most followed and respected investment firms was that gold was sitting on a bubble highly probable to burst. Frankly, I'm not astounded by the deluge of poor advice disseminated by the mainstream media about gold for three reasons.

(1) Gold is the most misunderstood asset class of all time - period.

Ninety-nine % of the advice that is freely given by the media posers on Wall Street and financial journalists about gold constitute terribly misguided and poor advice based upon a consensus of misinformed people. While some of the erroneously-reported relationships between the price of gold and the price of oil and the price of gold and interest rates tend to hold up short-term, they are quite simple to disprove. For example, even a cursory review of past gold bull runs would expose any direct relationship between gold and interest rates as completely erroneous.

For example, in 1978, 1979, and 1980, interest rates soared after Egypt and Syria's attack on Israel resulted in a punitive oil embargo imposed by the OPEC nations on the United States. According to the deluge of media reports in 2006 that falling interest rates always support gold and rising interest rates always hurt gold, then gold during 1978, 1979, and 1980 should have plummeted in price. Yet during this time, gold prices soared. In 1987 and 1988, interest rates and gold once again moved higher in tandem with one another. Even during this most recent gold bull run, which began in 2001 with gold trading at about $250 an ounce, there most definitely have been times when interest rates were rising, yet the price of gold continued to rise.

As with interest rates, the price of gold is erroneously linked directly to the direction of the dollar in a similar manner. Frequently, we see multiple headlines in newspapers that blare, "Gold declines on dollar strength" when the dollar rallies and "Gold rallies on dollar weakness" when the dollar falls. So why the deception? There are numerous reasons ranging from politically motivated futile attempts to save the U.S. dollar to attempts to shake out most investors from a monumental run in the price of gold and gold stocks so that only the elite interests that manipulate these markets will benefit. Trust me, there will come a time in the future, when the dollar will experience mini rallies but the price of gold will continue to rise.

I'm not saying that this relationship isn't important, because it is. It's just not a 100% purely inverse relationship as it is often reported in the news. Further adding to the confusion about the relationship between the dollar and gold and the relationship between interest rates and gold is the overwhelming evidence that the establishment and the U.S. government purposefully engage in misinformation campaigns about gold. This information is so extensive that it easily could provide enough material for a completely separate book (for those who are interested, I provide much of this further evidence in my Platinum Membership level and during my one-on-one consultations). With respect to the limited space in this book and with a desire to stay on point, let's just analyze one such piece of evidence - the formula that the U.S. government uses to determine inflation statistics in the United States.

Here are some of the more important manipulations and changes in the CPI formula since 1996 that enable the government to produce a fantasy CPI (Consumer Price Index) every month. Sometime after 1996, the formula to calculate the cost of the basket of goods (used in the determination of the CPI) was changed from a fixed-weight basket to a basket of substitutes. In simple terms, the government decided to assume that when the costs of living increase, EVERYONE substitutes cheaper, inferior goods for the more expensive goods that they normally buy.

For example, if the costs of beef rose, then people would eat more chicken. If the costs of orange juice increased, then people would substitute cheaper apple juice. And if car prices rose, then people would ride a horse and buggy or something to that effect. However to assume that all people engage in substitution behavior is ridiculous. There are significant percentages of people whose real costs of living rise because they do not downgrade their quality of life when inflation occurs. They will continue to eat beef despite rising costs and will not trade in their 7-Series BMWs for a horse and buggy. This manipulation of the CPI formula was just one of many changes that were instituted to make many components of inflation magically disappear.

In 1996, in order to further artificially depress the real CPI, the government switched from an arithmetic weighting in their basket of goods to a geometric weighting. In other words, the goods that fell the most in price were given the greatest weights and the goods that rose the most were given the smallest weights in the calculation of the index. Obviously, this manipulation also makes real components of inflation magically disappear as well. In addition, there are numerous variations of the CPI that are calculated, some that exclude food and energy from the calculation (the core CPI), others that include food and energy prices, and even others that allow CPI to be steady in the face of soaring rents and mortgages. In essence, many variations exist of the CPI that grossly underestimate true rates of inflation. The CPI statistic that does the best job of understating real inflation is generally the one that is emphasized in press releases.

In 2006, inflation was reported as being largely non-existent during the same month that default rates in mortgages in the state of California increased over 67%. I am sure that those Californians that defaulted on their mortgages disagreed with the government's official assessment of the CPI as increased costs in food and fuel (along with ARMS resetting at higher interest rates of course) severely crimped their ability to make their mortgage payments. If you wonder why the U.S. government so grossly misrepresents real inflation, simply put, it is because inflation represents the loss of purchasing power. If people realized how much the purchasing power of their U.S. dollars has eroded, then more money immediately would move into gold and gold prices would be driven much higher.

Thus, the CPI reported in the United States has not come close to approximating the real rate of inflation for more than a decade now. In recent years, the real rate most likely has been closer to 5.5%- 10% a year, or possibly even higher. In 2007, the U.N. Food & Agricultural Organization (FAO) reported that global food prices increased by 40% in over the previous year.[23] With oil over $90 a barrel at the end of 2007, a real inflation rate of 8% to 12% in the U.S. would not surprise me despite the much lower officially reported statistics.

If and when the U.S. Federal Reserve starts increasing interest rates, this will be the time to truly worry about the fate of the dollar. If this happens, this will be a bullish indicator for gold though the initial reaction most likely will be detrimental. With housing markets in severe trouble in the U.S., any decision to raise interest rates would indicate a last ditch effort by the Feds to prevent the world from dumping U.S. dollars.

(2) Gold is one of the most politically manipulated assets of all time.

Various comments regarding the price behavior of gold, even by the biggest players on Wall Street, are often politically motivated and are largely out of sync with reality. In turn, the reactionary short-term movements in the price of gold sadly shake many investors out of the market. Because most investors have zero understanding of how and why Central Banks (primarily in the European union along with the United States) conspire to manipulate the price of gold, these comments often successfully move markets in the short-term. Listen to mainstream advice about gold, and you will always make the wrong decisions.

As I stated earlier, too much importance is always attributed to the relationships between *temporary* strengthening of the U.S. dollar and declining gold prices (or vice versa) and the relationship between falling oil prices and subsequent declines in gold prices (or vice versa). While these relationships have considerable merit, they are not absolute. Furthermore, many behind-the-scenes actions critical to the price behavior of gold are never reported by the mainstream media.

For example, in December 2007, the Gulf nations publicly stated their support of the U.S. dollar, maintaining that they would not break their pegs to the U.S. dollar. Despite this public announcement, my investigation into their actions reveals a different reality. For example, though Saudi Arabia was among the Gulf nations that officially pledged to maintain their peg to the U.S. dollar, they "unofficially" broke the peg in October, 2007 when they opted not to slash interest rates in line with the actions of the U.S. Federal Reserve. By refusing to keep their local currency pegged to the dollar, the Saudi Riyal strengthened considerably in November and into the end of 2007. These actions that occur well below the radar of the thundering sheep herd and that are subsequently misunderstood by the investment media are what makes the overwhelming majority of analysis regarding oil, gold, and the U.S. dollar so flimsy and terrible.

Much of the rising price in oil throughout 2006 was directly attributable to severe weakness in the dollar, not shortages of oil supply and other reasons. Since oil is still priced in U.S. dollars in most markets, had the U.S. dollar not fallen so much in the past decade, perhaps the price of oil at the beginning of 2008 would still have been at $50-$70 a barrel instead of more than $90 a barrel. The high prices of oil have a lot to do with the weak currency in which it is priced, period. Yet, we will continue to receive very poor analysis of what exactly is driving the price of oil and gold. The U.S. Treasury Department will never reveal to the masses that much of the climb in the price of oil is directly attributable to the monumental decline in the dollar. If they ever did, this declaration would expose the irresponsible and foolish monetary policy embraced by the U.S. Federal Reserve over the past couple of decades (actually since its formation in 1913). And this brings me to my next point.

I believe that statements by huge players such as the Gulf Nations and Goldman Sachs are often made at the behest of the U.S. Federal Reserve. The Feds know that statements by such entities can and DO move markets, due to the nature of the willing and gullible sheep herd that wait with bated breath for these players to reveal their opinions before making their investment decisions. Irrational behavior abounds everywhere in financial markets, much of it created by an absolute lack of understanding about the fundamental outlook of commodities and currencies and the factors that truly drive their long-term behavior. However, every investor needs to understand that short-term movements in markets that are created by deceptive reports will always be short-lived. In the end, true north will always be revealed in the stock markets.

As for 2008 predictions, I said in the first two editions of this book that it was irrelevant to me that Goldman Sachs had called shorting gold one of their top 10 tips of the year in 2008.[26] That prediction was either made for political reasons, for self-serving interests, or for both. If you want my honest opinion, I think that Goldman's reasons were more Machiavellian than anything, or perhaps they were also performing another favor for their ex-CEO that heads the U.S. Treasury Department. No matter what you believe, one thing remains certain. Firms like Goldman Sachs know that the minute they say gold is going to fall that millions of people worldwide listen to them. In fact, gold dropped $15-$20 an ounce down to $783 almost immediately after their announcement. In any event, true north for gold will be much higher in the years to come despite anything Goldman Sachs may have to say.

Again, if one needs short-term validation of my above assertions, one need look no further than the subprime crisis of 2007. Markets were calmed and much confidence was injected into the system back in March of 2007 when U.S. President Bush and U.S. Secretary of Treasury Hank Paulson assured the markets that the subprime crisis was already "largely contained".[27] After these announcements, many financial stocks actually rallied much higher for the next several months. But just look what happened shortly after on the following pages. At the end of 2008, again, due to an engineered temporary collapse in gold/silver prices during the third quarter 2008, we had the same misinformation spread by the same people about the collapse of gold and a new bear market for gold being upon us. I'll explain exactly what I mean by this in one of the last chapters of this book.

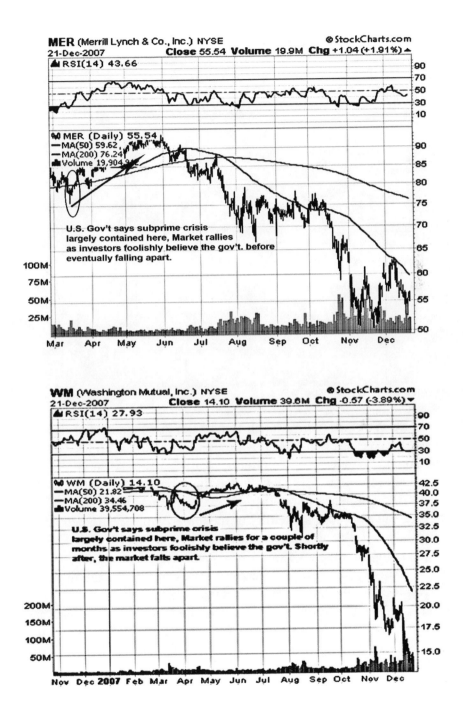

115

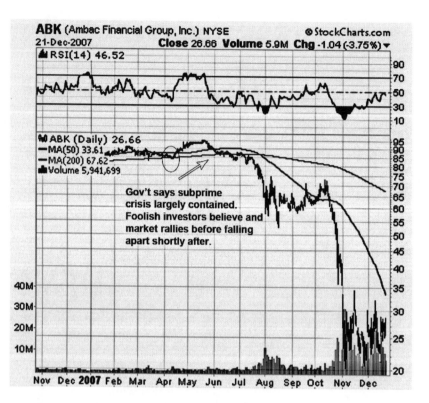

The share prices for Merrill Lynch, Ambac Financial Group (one of the largest bond insurers in the United States) and Washington Mutual all rallied quite significantly based upon assurances from our government that the subprime problem was "largely contained" in mid-2007. However, things fell apart just months later because the reality of the underlying situation could not be denied. We all know by now that both Merrill Lynch and Washington Mutual have since gone bankrupt.

Likewise, when we inevitably receive comments from the government or the media about "strong" U.S. markets that are "fine" in 2008, a strong dollar in 2009, or a bottom in the economy in 2009, those comments will be just as laughable as the comments about the subprime problem being "largely contained" in March of 2007. Whether the U.S. markets climb higher or stay together when these comments are made are irrelevant. Following the subprime comments made by Paulson, the U.S. markets climbed higher for several months before falling apart. What is important to note will be that these comments will not reflect even an iota of reality.

(3) Telling the truth about gold would severely negatively impact the bottom line of the commercial investment industry.

Although an investment in gold bullion in September, 2007 would have returned more than 20% just a few months thereafter, better than any return on any major currency, investment firms emphatically do not want you to invest in gold as part of your currency strategy. First of all, managing bonds is more lucrative for commercial investment firms, even if U.S. dollar-denominated bonds are one of the worst financial instruments you could have purchased in 2007 and in 2008. Secondly, even if commercial investment firms charge you a hefty commission for buying gold through their commodity desks, anyone with access to the internet can buy gold bullion much more cheaply via the internet. Once any investor discovers this, there essentially is no reason to buy gold bullion through an investment firm. Goodbye gold commissions, goodbye assets, and goodbye fees.

In addition, most commercial investment firms, even the big players on Wall Street, employ financial consultants that possess only a very superficial understanding about gold stocks. As proof, during 2000, 2001 and 2002, three-years that marked the worst performance of U.S. stock markets since the Great Depression, only 1% of all stocks invested in the U.S. stock market were invested in gold stocks. Yet, an investment in gold stocks equally divided among the components of the HUI (the unhedged gold mining stock index that trades on the American Stock Exchange) would have outperformed the S&P 500 by more than 120%.

Obviously, commercial investment firms in 2000, 2001 and 2002 failed to mention the enormous outperformance of gold stocks to their clients during this period, for almost all of their clients lost great amounts of money. Thus, since most commercial investment firms do not retain any financial consultants with the expertise to invest in these markets (as evident by the non-existent percentage of the U.S. market invested in gold in 2000, 2001 and 2002), if these same firms were to reveal the truth about gold to you, they would in essence be instructing you to move your money out of their firm and into a precious metals boutique investment firm or an investment firm in Canada. Again, goodbye assets and asset-based management fees.

Telling the truth to investors about gold and gold stocks would NECESSSARILY mean that commercial investment firms would lose assets; therefore, it should be easy to understand why misinformation is the name of the game when it comes to this asset class.

10

HOW TO LEVERAGE TIME

The fourth critical lesson in wealth literacy involves understanding how to leverage time. Time is one of the most valuable yet most underappreciated commodities ever when it comes to building wealth. If we utilize time properly, we can build proper networks that will assist us in building wealth as well as ensure ourselves of the greatest possible chances to create great wealth. Though time is free, many of us waste too much of it. When it comes to investing, we often tell ourselves that we simply "do not have time" to manage our own money. In life, we all fall into one of two categories: Spectator or Participant. In every pursuit we deem to be of significant importance, we all know that our chances of success multiply exponentially if we choose to be a participant versus a mere spectator.

Yet inexplicably, when it comes to investing, the vast majority of us choose to be a spectator. We simply hand our money to someone else to manage, and then sit on the sidelines. If we, as investors, leveraged our time properly to further our education, we all could double, triple or even quadruple our investment returns every year with a minimal investment of time. I have no doubt of this. Just three hours per week for half a year spent learning an investment system could dramatically improve not only our portfolio returns but also our quality of life. Yet again, the vast majority of us are unwilling to make such a small commitment to garner monumental gains. When it comes to leveraging time, those of us that refuse to leverage time to learn an investment system simply must face up to the fact that we are not serious about our commitment to increase our wealth or our quality of life.

Learning a valid investment system, not the one propagated by commercial investment firms, is just one way to leverage time in the creation of wealth. Obviously by committing time to learning a valid investment system now, we will build wealth at a much more rapid pace, and thus earn much more leisure time in the future. As an example of another of the many ways in which we can leverage time, here is an exercise you can perform. Most of us waste much too much time with the process of finding individual stocks to buy. We think that researching stocks will take hundreds upon hundreds of hours and that's why we all exclaim, "I don't have time to manage my own portfolio". This is truly one of the most ludicrous statements regarding the determination of personal wealth ever. Instead of wasting time, we all should look for strategies to leverage time. Here is one example of how to do so.

There's a technique that I've invented called "Riding the Same Stock to Multiple Winnings" that I've used many times to make easy 25% to 50% profits after initially taking triple-digit profits from the very same stock. After you finish reading this book, you will realize that it is not at all difficult to identify stocks that appreciate by triple digits in a 12 to 24 month timeframe. You will realize that your belief in the difficulty of achieving this was solely limited by the myths and poor investment advice that you have received throughout your lifetime. The "Riding the Same Stock to Multiple Winnings" strategy works as follows.

Any time that I've locked in a triple-digit winner, I don't mentally place that stock in stock heaven and forget about it. 99.9% of us make the mistake of completely forgetting about the stock after we have sold it, content with our returns. Instead, we should understand that easy additional gains from the same stock are often available. This is what I do:

(1) Keep a list of these stock(s) on a simple word document. Save it somewhere where you will remember to look at it everyday, perhaps even saving it on your desktop.

(2) Go to http://www.stockcharts.com and take two minutes everyday during market hours to check on the stock chart.

(3) If the stock falls rapidly (20% to 35% over a period of a couple of months) AND displays a floor of resistance (i.e. the 200 day Simple Moving Average, or a price level that it has tested multiple times over several weeks but failed to break below), then move on to step (4).

(4) Quickly perform a Google search (or alternate internet search engine) for all news about the stock during the period of time it tanked. If you can find no justifiable reason why the stock corrected strongly other than a country-wide stock market correction or simple profit taking (in other words, no significant change in the company's fundamental operations, management or strategy), then re-buy an equivalent amount to your initial position and place a tight 10%-12% stop loss on your position.

Often, stocks that run up very quickly correct quite rapidly due to simple profit taking or general market weakness but not because of any specific company weakness. Since you've already performed the initial research regarding the stock in question upon your original purchase, there truly is no need to perform any additional due diligence on this stock other than the check mentioned above. This is how you leverage the time that you've already invested conducting research. By performing the above five steps, you have set up a low risk-high reward scenario in which you are highly likely to reap another 25% to 50% gain in a condensed period of time with almost zero additional effort. And this is exactly what I've done several times, earning 120% gains on a stock initially, then earning an additional 70% a second time, and an additional 50% a third time.

Finally, if the risk-reward setup is compelling enough, I'll even re-buy options instead of the underlying stock. In a real-life example, let's take a look at the chart for Chinese Internet stock Baidu in mid-April of 2007. In fact, this is a play that I actually gave away for free on my investment blog, The Underground Investor (http://www.TheUndergroundInvestor.com).

After making a phenomenal run from $60 a share in May, 2006 to over $131 in January, 2007, a 118% increase in half a year's time, Baidu's stock plummeted during the first quarter of 2007 by almost 35%. At that point, in April, 2007, I used the 4-step process of "Riding the Same Stock to Multiple Winnings" to identify a near perfect setup for a strong rebound. The set-up was so compelling that I decided against buying back the underlying stock and instead bought call options that eventually produced gains 10 times as much as the quick 25% to 30% gains that would have been possible by just buying the underlying stock.

When building wealth, it is paramount to always leverage time as much as possible. As it applies to investing, the absolute best way to leverage time, hands down, is to use time to learn how to manage your own portfolio. If you do, I guarantee you that 20% or higher returns every single year is not only possible, but also highly probable.

11

DEBUNKING MORE INVESTMENT MYTHS

Throughout this book, I have continually debunked many of the most widespread investment myths. Not falling victim to the mass of misinformation is a critical lesson in wealth literacy. I have already debunked the 4 biggest investment myths of all time, but in this chapter, I will specifically address several more widely-accepted investment myths that inflict incredible damage to your ability to build wealth. These additional myths include the following:

(1) Markets are 100% efficient;
(2) Volatility equals risk;
(3) Foreign stocks are risky;
(4) Professional money management assures ownership of the best stocks; and
(5) Large accounts receive lots of attention.

Markets are not 100% efficient.

Markets are not 100% efficient. Not even close. The information technology revolution has ensured this. Next to the myth that constantly hangs like a dark cloud around international stocks, this myth has been part of one of the most widely disseminated misinformation campaigns orchestrated by Wall Street firms and the global investment industry, and one embraced by 99% of financial consultants. In the past ten years, technological advances have changed the information landscape, granting the individual investor access to information that was previously only accessible from the inside of boardrooms. This change has made it possible to find information before the general public knows about it, due to how information filters through media channels.

When I was earning my double masters in Business Administration and Public Policy, I wrote my graduate thesis about how media filters work, so I know that it is extremely possible to find information online well before the masses of investors learn about it. This makes the markets inefficient. If you only learn one secret about how to build wealth from this book, make sure you read this one as many times as you need to understand. This secret is the one that is essential for you to discover stocks that present low-risk, high-reward opportunities and can return 50%, 80%, and even 300% returns to you in a single year.

By definition, if markets were truly 100% efficient, then a stock's price at any given point in time should have incorporated any positive or negative news by the time you have read or heard about it. I know this to be patently false because I have achieved short-term gains of 30%, 60%, 100% and higher in stocks based upon information that I have uncovered, that other investors were not searching for, and that had not yet been incorporated into the prices of these stocks. At first glance, better information technology would seem to make the markets more, not less, efficient. But if you understand how media filters operate, then you will understand that positive and negative information can be uncovered about a company before it reaches millions of other people through the filtered distribution channels of Bloomberg, Reuters, the BBC, and other major media. It's only when millions of other people discover this information that stock prices start rallying or retreating significantly.

As unique human beings, we all possess passions for different topics and those are the areas that we should strive to become experts in. We are much more likely to understand how information translates into stock buying opportunities if we already have some fundamental level of understanding about a subject area because of prior interest. For example, I graduated from the University of Pennsylvania with a degree in Neurobiology and worked in healthcare for several years before returning to school to earn my MBA in finance. Therefore, medical applications and biotechnology interest me, and when I regularly track medical websites for biotech information, I understand the potential of developments I read about. Other readers may not, but that's ok because the opportunities to leverage our flattened world of information are limitless.

Even if you do not consider yourself an expert in any area, you will still have incredible opportunities to uncover stocks that will experience rapid price appreciation. Just apply logic in your thinking. In early 2006, there was an explosion in renewable, alternative and clean energy stocks. Was this really that hard to predict, given skyrocketing oil prices and the leading world powers publicly stating their desires to not be so dependent upon the Middle East's oil supply? So research the leading solar energy and wind energy companies in the world. Even at the end of 2007, you probably still have time to benefit because we are still probably several years away from experiencing any truly significant changes in patterns of global energy consumption. Think about other global problems that have not yet been solved, and the topics are numerous. Cancer, global warming, a global shortage of clean water supply, better medication delivery systems, better communication systems and so on. I can not emphasize enough that mastering this one tip will unfailingly give you better returns than you ever dreamed of.

Now let's say you've identified a company that has excited you. You go online and research this stock further. It has a low P/E compared to its industry competitors, a substantial float and no liquidity issues, and insiders have been quietly accumulating numerous shares steadily over the last several months. Still, the stock price has traded fairly flat or just slightly higher over this time period (by the way, there are numerous free sites you can check insider trading patterns including Yahoo Finance). Would this be a stock you may consider adding to your portfolio? You bet, because you've just discovered a company with loads of positive information, that insiders are buying with considerable sums of their own money, and whose stock has yet to react to any of this positive information!

In addition, every now and then, the public lives up to its lowest common denominator label. For reasons I can't really explain, sometimes the public simply fails to understand the implication of certain highly public positive news. Consequently, the company's stock price lags until the general public finally grasps the significance of this news, engages in a buying frenzy, and drives the stock's price higher. One just has to know where to uncover this information and then be able to understand its implications. For example, if you understand that pending litigation against a pharmaceutical company has depressed a company's stock price for fear of massive potential losses but can find information that gives you confidence that the company will overcome any outstanding litigation issues, you can buy this stock when everyone else is selling and benefit from the bounce that will happen when the issues are cleared.

Still not convinced that markets are sometimes inefficient? Then consider this simple exercise. I currently spend most of my time in Asia. There are lots of Asian pop stars and movie stars, Korean, Thai, Japanese, Indian, etc. that hundreds of millions of Asians know. How hard is it for you to name five Hollywood stars?

Ok, if you live outside of Asia, now name five Asian movie stars (not including any ones that have crossed over to Hollywood). Or if you live in Asia, name five famous French movie stars and pop stars? Or if you live in Europe, name five famous Hong Kong pop stars? Can't? How can you not even name two stars loved by millions of people in their native countries? This is all you need to know to understand that media filters do exist, whether it relates to entertainment or business.

Volatility Equals Risk?

Most financial consultants, when they speak of investment portfolios, mention a low beta as a positive attribute. In fact, we often hear many wealth managers stress the need of having a beta close to 1.00. Beta, in simple terms, is the measure of an individual stock's or a portfolio's volatility as compared to the volatility of the stock market index as a whole. If you own a stock with a beta of 1.30, it would be about 30% more volatile then the market index. I've often seen the beta coefficient used interchangeably with the word risk to define a portfolio's composition. For example, if the beta of your portfolio is much greater than 1.00, then many advisors will interpret your portfolio as an aggressive, risky portfolio. If the beta of your portfolio is much less than 1.00, then many advisors would state that you have a conservative portfolio. This is nonsense.

First of all, the beta coefficient is determined using the domestic stock market index as the constant. For example in the U.S., the beta coefficient will be determined by comparing the volatility of a stock or stock portfolio versus the volatility of the S&P 500 or another major U.S. index. But we are already starting off on the wrong foot by doing so because nobody should have a stock portfolio that is concentrated in his or her domestic market only. Chances are that many of the best performing stocks you will own will be in a foreign stock market. What if the beta of your stock portfolio is high compared to your domestic market index but low compared to a regional market index? What does that mean?

What if the situation is reversed? What if your portfolio has a low beta compared to your domestic market index but a high beta compared to a regional market index? This could happen if your domestic market is particularly volatile one year while the rest of the world markets are significantly less so. If your domestic market index is up 35% one year and your portfolio is up 33% the same year, because your beta is less than 1.00, does that still mean that you have a conservative, low-risk portfolio?

Investment firms will almost always tell you a high beta is bad, and that to have higher volatility is a great risk to your portfolio. If you live somewhere where the stock market index has returned on average 3% for the last five years and has moved within a very narrow range, I would say that to have a low beta would be extremely risky because it would mean that your portfolio was going nowhere. On the other hand, if your portfolio had returned 20% on average over this same time span, your beta will be off the charts. As you can see from this example, not at all, a high beta can in fact, be very healthy.

VOLATILITY IS NOT THE SAME AS RISK. FAR FROM IT.

Personally I want volatility to be a trait of many of the stocks I own. If a stock is to return 50% or more in one year, then by nature it has to be fairly volatile. Virtually no stock will rise steadily higher without experiencing some significant corrective actions to the downside. Therefore, stocks with significant gains are going to experience wider fluctuations in price than stocks that make small gains every year. It simply is not possible to build wealth without having some huge winners in your portfolio, i.e., stocks that have appreciated by 70%, 150%, 350% or even a 1000%. According to the theories propagated by most investment firms, almost all investors that have built substantial wealth through their stock portfolios have engaged in highly risky behavior. Again, the commercial investment industry would like you to believe this, but this simply is not true. I own stocks today that I'm fairly certain will return 40% or more by this time next year. Yet I would much rather own these stocks than stocks like IBM, McDonalds, or Best Buy.

Those of us that always possess huge winners in our stock portfolios make calculated intelligent decisions to identify asset classes that are poised to boom before the public considers them. We invest at troughs in price and sell when mania sets in, allowing us to reap huge gains. In contrast, the average investor will only identify these stocks after everyone else becomes aware of them or some talking head on TV marks it as a screaming buy. Thus, the average investor that purchases the stock during the mania phase will only earn average money from this stock or quite possibly lose money at a time when the wealthy investor will have already earned phenomenal returns on the very same stock.

If you ask most people, they could care less if they owned four stocks that lost 40%, 30%, 25% and 35%, if they also owned eight stocks that rose 80%, 100%, 130%, 300%, 287%, 200%, 184%, 65%, and 658%, and their overall return, given the average performance of their remaining portfolio, was 45%. At the end of the day, people only care about the total return of their portfolio. Investment firms have always stated that such a strategy is risky. If you have stocks that have performed that well, you must be taking huge risks, right? Again this is nonsense. Uncovering volatile stocks that prove to be huge winners requires time, a commodity that financial consultants do not have. Earning the types of gains I speak of above is possible without assuming much risk if you perform your due diligence and discover solid assets at rock-bottom prices and invest in them before the general public discovers them. In fact, I would argue that many stocks that earn 150% or more are less risky than the market index in which they trade in.

Just as there is dumb diversification and smart diversification, there is also dumb volatility and smart volatility. Dumb volatility is chasing penny stocks and pipe dreams of quick returns from companies that spend more money on marketing and PR campaigns to promote their stock than on the operations of their company. Of course building an entire portfolio comprised of extremely volatile stocks would not be intelligent either. But building a portion of your portfolio with such stocks to boost returns is smart.

Volatility is not the same as risk as much as most global investment firms want you to believe this. Low volatility, high diversification, and mediocre returns are time minimization/ asset gathering maximization sales strategies. Volatility is undoubtedly your friend when building wealth.

Foreign Stocks are Risky?

I'm going to illustrate the point of this section with a couple quick questions. In 2007, what company was the leading ready-to-mix concrete supplier in the world? What company possessed the largest natural gas reserves in the world? What internet search engine was on its way to having the most users in the world? The answers are Cemex, a Mexican company, Gazprom, a Russian company, and Baidu, a Chinese company. If I asked you what company is one of the largest soft drink manufacturers in the world, almost all of you would name Coca Cola. Most of you have probably heard of all of these companies, since they are among the largest companies in the world. However, there are dozens of companies like Gazprom, Cemex and Baidu that you most likely have NOT heard about. The same holds true for your Financial Consultant if you currently employ one. Simply stated, you will never hear about great buying opportunities outside of your native country without doing some serious digging.

The myth disseminated about foreign markets by the major investment firms of developed nations is one of my biggest pet peeves. The myth of course, is that investing outside of one's domestic market is much riskier than keeping your assets at home. Because this myth is repeated so many times by even the most experienced financial consultants, it consequently used to puzzle me a lot. Quite literally for decades now, developed foreign markets have outperformed U.S. markets though many U.S. investment firms continued to portray foreign markets as risky.

Many financial consultants who live in the U.S. tell you that you shouldn't ever invest more than 25% to 30% in international stocks, even during times when the U.S. market is turning your investments into dust and other parts of the global economy are thriving. Most financial consultants in other countries also don't purchase a large number of stocks outside of their domestic markets because their firms do not provide decent coverage of foreign stocks.

To recite a true story, when I left the U.S. in 2004 to move to Asia, one of my client's accounts was assigned to a new financial consultant. I advised my former client that he should have at least 50% of his stock portfolio invested outside the United States. I just didn't foresee much growth coming from the United States over the next several years.

After he spoke with his new financial consultant, he informed me that she had advised him that 50% or more was way too risky, and that the maximum amount that should be invested outside the U.S. was 30%-35%.

When it comes to investing, nothing kills good returns more than nationalism. And nationalism rules at large, commercial investment firms.

To illustrate the above point, the overwhelming majority of clients at large investment firms don't hold some of the leading, most innovative, most well-managed and fastest growing companies simply because these stocks are not traded on their domestic stock markets. For example, Samsung, a Korean company that is a world leader in high-end electronic goods, and LVMH, Louis Vuitton Moet Hennessy, a French company that is a world leader in luxury brand goods including Pucci, Fendi, Tag Heuer, Sephora, Dom Perignon, Moet & Chandon, Givenchy, DKNY, and Hard Candy *do not even trade on the major American stock exchanges.* Most times, large, commercial investment firms ignore companies that don't trade on their major domestic stock exchanges.

As long as I've been in this business, I have heard financial consultants tell their clients that foreign markets outside of their country are riskier. Riskier than what? Enron? Worldcomm? JDS Uniphase? Some American companies have held the highest bond ratings just months prior to going bankrupt. Even strong Morningstar financial ratings provide no guarantee that your investments are safe. Want to try a fun experiment? Next time your financial consultant tells you to cap your exposure to international markets at 25% to 30%, ask him or her how they determined this magical number? His or her response, to say the least, will be interesting.

In investing, it is imperative to remain flexible. That means if foreign markets are outperforming the domestic stock market in your country, then you should have no qualms about putting 80% or more of your money in foreign markets. And just in case your financial consultant gives you a pre-packaged response to the question above, I've decided to provide you with some ammunition below that will blow the misconception of risky foreign stocks right out of the water:

In terms of numbers of companies and stock listings, the U.S. no longer dominates the global stock market. According to a 2006 Forbes Online Report:[28]

(1) During the past 25 years, a blended portfolio of 60% U.S. stocks and 40% international stocks was less volatile than an S&P 500 index fund (so much for the myth that international stocks are too risky);

(2) In the past ten years, the U.S. stock market has never been the top performing global market even among developed markets. Let me repeat this. In the past ten years, the U.S. stock market has NEVER been the top performing global market even among developed markets. In fact, it's highest ranking during the past ten years has been fourth;

(3) More than 75% of all publicly traded companies are located outside the U.S.; and

(4) Growth rates in emerging markets are often multiple times higher than the U.S.

There is a simple reason why many investment firms in different global locations outside of the U.S. have also spouted the same nonsense that foreign markets are risky. The reason is because they don't have the expertise or requisite knowledge about foreign markets. Because they don't know enough about foreign stocks to intelligently recommend more than a handful to you, they simply resort to telling you that they are risky, even though this is a bold-faced lie. In the United States, up until 2006 or 2007, the majority of firms on Wall Street continued to tell their clients that foreign markets were risky. However, as it became increasingly clear that growth in Asia and the Pacific Rim would outpace growth in America, and when clients started to demand ownership of international stocks, U.S. firms finally began to address this issue. Despite a client base that is becoming more educated, many U.S. financial consultants still gain exposure for their clients to foreign markets in the form of the worst investment vehicle possible – mutual funds.

With all major stock markets performing terribly in 2008, the myth of foreign markets as risky has now been replaced with the myth of commodities as risky. Commodities in 2008 and 2009 have become the new "foreign stock." Just be aware that the lies of the commercial investment industry will never cease due to their ulterior motives. Also be aware that in 2009, as this monetary crisis deepens, few stocks in few asset classes in any stock market anywhere in the world will perform well. Concentration in only a few select asset classes as well as non-paper assets will be necessary to profit from this growing monetary crisis.

Professional money management assures ownership of the best stocks in the world?

There are many rules that regulate research at commercial investment firms that make it nearly impossible for firms to buy you the best stocks in the world.

Let's start with the numbers. There are an estimated 75,000 stocks that trade globally, approximately 15,000 of which trade in U.S. markets alone. Of these 15,000 stocks, there are about 6,000 micro cap stocks and there are several thousand more small cap stocks. According to the University of Chicago Center for Research in Securities Prices (CRSP) study, during a 79-year period, micro cap and small cap stocks outperformed large cap stocks by 437% and 165% respectively. Investing in small companies also became safer in the U.S. in 1999 when the Securities Exchange Council (SEC) passed stricter regulations for small publicly traded companies.

However, most investment houses, even the largest corporate giants, only have the resources to track about 1,500 stocks. Commercial investment firms have no choice but to track and provide research for the most popular stocks that most people want to own. Consequently, most of the stocks they research are large cap stocks such as General Electric, Microsoft, Home Depot and so on. And this is true no matter what country you live in. This limits the number of other stocks they can research. Can you imagine if you lived in Mexico, wanted some research on Cemex, and your consultant said, "Sorry. We don't cover that stock."

In fact, of all the stocks analyzed by ALL the Wall Street firms in the United States, this number amounts to only about one-third of the 15,000 stocks that trade solely in the U.S. markets.

Add to this mix another 60,000 foreign stocks, and you can begin to see how many mid, small, micro and foreign stocks are completely ignored by Wall Street firms. Since Wall Street firms typically have the largest research divisions of all commercial investment firms in the world, just imagine how much less coverage you probably receive if you utilize commercial investment firms anywhere else in the world. For this reason alone, your stock portfolio will almost never experience the returns it deserves. I would estimate that more than 95% of financial consultants at large investment houses do not follow small and micro cap stocks simply because their firms do not provide adequate analysis of these types of stocks.

So why exactly are small caps necessary? The answer is as simple as it is logical. An Ibbotson Associates study demonstrated similar results over a 71-year period, from 1926 to 1996, to the University of Chicago study. Ibbotson Associates discovered mall cap stocks returned 12.6% annually while large cap stocks returned 10.7% annually.[29] While this difference doesn't sound huge at first, the compounding effect ensures that this difference is huge. Without taking taxes and inflation into consideration for the sake of simplicity, $1,000 invested in a small cap stock index in 1926 would have grown into about $7,251,143 by 1996. $1,000 invested in a large cap index in 1926 would have grown into just $1,909,225 by 1996 in comparison.

Furthermore, remember the discussion about volatility where I emphasized the need for every investor to own some stocks that will spike 125%, 280%, 350% or even 1000% in a year or two year's time? Where do you think these types of returns are going to come from? Large cap stocks? Possibly a handful but not loads. Most of these types of returns will be achieved by the portion of your portfolio that contains small and micro cap stocks. Again, remember that it is a myth that small caps and micro cap stocks are risky. Leveraging information gleamed from relationships that provide the foundation of corporatocracies, it is possible to find low-risk, high-reward stocks among small and micro cap stocks, and not just among large-cap stocks. As Warren Buffet once said, risk comes not from volatility and not from investing in small cap stocks. Risk only comes from not knowing what you're doing.

Large Accounts Receive Lots of Attention?

To conclude this chapter, I will quickly eviscerate one final investment myth – the myth that commercial investment firms directly allocate more time to the management of your portfolio the larger it is. For a Financial Consultant to make a decent living at a large commercial investment firm, due to the payout grids most firms utilize, he or she has to gather, more or less, about a minimum of $40 million of assets under management. With $40 million of assets under management, this figure will help a Financial Consultant earn slightly north of U.S. $100,000 annually before taxes, just barely enough to eke out a living in Los Angeles or New York. Consequently, most financial consultants will strive to gather at least U.S. $50 million of assets or more under management.

Using this figure as a benchmark, let's break down what this figure means to you as a client. It's highly unlikely that a financial consultant has clients that all have accounts of $1 million or more, so let's assume that he or she does not accept clients with less than U.S. $250,000. This could create a hypothetical tier of clients as follows.

# of Clients	Account Size	Cumulative Assets
20	U.S. $250,000- $500,000	$ 7,000,000
50	U.S. $500,000- $1,000,000	$32,000,000
7	U.S. $1,000,000 +	$11,000,000
77		$50,000,000

Thus, it's fairly reasonable to assume that a successful financial consultant has 77 clients with about U.S. $50,000,000 of assets under management. Now let's calculate how many hours a year this financial consultant will devote to your account if you are a top tier client with more than a million dollars. There are 52 weeks a year * 5 days/week * 8 hours a day, or 2,080 hours a year that a Financial Consultant can devote to his/her accounts, assuming that he/she takes no vacation or holidays. Let's now assume that a minimum of

30% of a financial consultant's 2,080 hours a year is spent in corporate meetings, account maintenance, meetings with clients, pitching products to clients and prospects, and paperwork.

This leaves 70% of his or her time to focus on the management of accounts. By the way, to illustrate how generous we are being in all of our estimates, 30% is an extremely low estimate of actual time spent in sales activities. Most firms will tell their consultants to spend about 70% of all of their time engaged in sales activities. So assuming that your financial consultant is the lone financial consultant in your entire city that actually spends 70% of his time managing his accounts and not gathering assets, the time dedicated to managing accounts now become 1,456 hours (2,080 hours * 70% = 1,456 hours).

Every financial consultant will categorize their clients into different tiers depending on how much money is invested with them. The U.S. $1,000,000 or more clients would be "A" clients, the U.S. $500,000-$1,000,000 clients would be "B" clients, and the less than $500,000 clients would be "C" clients. Financial consultants universally devote the most time to the accounts of A clients, then B clients, then C clients. To simplify this example, let's say that the financial consultant spends twice as much time with his A clients than he does with his B and C clients.

If 1,456 hours is divided in this manner, his 7 "A" clients each receive 34.66 hours of personalized attention a year, and his 70 "B & C" clients each receive 17.33 hours a year. So on average, as an A client, you would receive an average of 4 days a year with personalized attention to your account and as a B or C client, only 2 days a year. Remember that our calculation of 4 days of time devoted to an "A" client utilizes numbers that represented a best case scenario illustrated by a Super Financial Consultant that ignores management's directives to concentrate his or her time on sales-generating activities. In a worst case scenario, you may have $5 million of your money at a commercial investment firm and receive only 2 days of personalized attention per year from your financial consultant.

Basically, the point of the above illustration is simply to demonstrate that every financial consultant has many, many clients and only a finite number of hours to devote to your account every year no matter how large your account may be. Given the large numbers of clients every successful financial consultant manages, it should now be self-evident that it is next to impossible for a Financial Consultant to add substantial intrinsic value to your relationship.

12

CORPORATOCRACIES: THE RELATIONSHIPS OF GOVERNMENTS, BANKS AND CORPORATIONS

While networking is the sixth critical component of wealth literacy on my list, and while my take on networking is very different than traditional outlooks on networking, because there are so many books devoted to this topic, I am going to bypass discussing this subject in depth. As well, I fully cover this topic in my online investment course available at my website (http://www.smartknowledgeu.com).

So let's move on to Wealth Literacy lesson #7, the topic of corporatocracies. When I was employed by the major investment firms in the U.S., there were so many scandals happening in the financial services industry that some of my prospects would immediately tell me right away that there was no way they would consider doing any business with anyone that was employed by my corporation. Our defense, not a particularly solid one that elicited confidence, was that there wasn't a single major U.S. investment firm that wasn't plagued by scandals.

Earlier in this book I informed you that JP Morgan, Morgan Stanley, Goldman Sachs, Credit Suisse First Boston, Lehman Brothers, UBS Warburg and U.S. Bancorp Piper Jaffray each were required to pay fines in the early 2000's between $32,500,000 (Piper Jaffray) and $400,000,000 (Smith Barney)[30]. Merrill Lynch also had to pay a $200 million fine for issuing fraudulent research during this same time period (PBS.org, October 10, 2003). In addition, one of Merrill's analysts, Henry Blodget, was fined $4 million and supposedly banned from the securities industry for life for his fraudulent recommendations (Bloomberg.com, November 3rd, 2005) after internal emails revealed that he was recommending stocks that he described to his colleagues as "crap" and "junk".[31] One of Smith Barney's analysts, Jack Grubman, was fined $15 million and permanently barred from the securities industry for egregiously unethical stock ratings as well.[32]

UBS, Switzerland's largest bank was fined $100 million after transferring $4 to $5 billion to Libya, Iran, Cuba and the former Yugoslavia (New York Federal Reserve, June 2, 2004). In 2005, Citigroup paid a $20 million fine and Putnam Investments, one of the largest mutual fund companies in the U.S., paid a $40 million fine to resolve federal regulator's accusations that they did not disclose to clients that brokers were being paid to recommend certain mutual funds to clients (SEC, March 23, 2005).

During the early 2000's, the CEO and founder of Strong mutual funds (one of the largest U.S. mutual funds), Richard Strong, was personally fined $60,000,000 and permanently barred from the industry after revelations he illegally traded his firm's mutual funds for a net profit of U.S. $1.8MM. Strong's illegal trades basically cut into the profits of long-term holders of the funds (basically, he was stealing from his own clients). At the time Strong was caught, his net worth was estimated to be U.S. $800,000,000.[33]

Though I could easily fill up this entire chapter with the fraudulent activities of the commercial investment industry, I hope I have made my point with the above examples. Greed is what drives the investment world and this cycle will never stop. In fact, the investment industry appeared to learn no lessons at all from all the fines that were imposed upon them by the SEC (Securities Exchange Council) in the early 2000's. Given the billions of dollars of revenues earned every year by the companies involved, the imposed fines amounted to little more than a slap on the wrist, and perhaps that was the problem.

The imposed penalties were hardly harsh enough to cause any real pain. Stricter regulations, after all the revelations of greed and excess in the early 2000's, could have been imposed upon the global financial and investment industry that would have prevented the current subprime crisis from developing. But they weren't. The fact that regulations did not become any tighter after all the scandals in the early 2000's should provide ample proof that governments and corporations are practically the same entity.

Despite the disheartening nature of ruling corporatocracies all over the world, it is exactly this development that has allowed me to devise groundbreaking, new investment strategies. By exploiting the relationships of these corporatocracies, I discovered that I was able to develop an investment methodology that would consistently identify stocks that would return 25% or better annual returns without the use of financial or technical analysis as primary screens.

When I tell people that my Master in Public Policy was far more integral to the development of my MoneyPing™ investment paradigm than my MBA in Finance, most people look at me in disbelief. Today, most of us still believe that the more book smarts we have, the more success we will have in stock picking. Consequently, we waste our time and our money taking all kinds of left-brain intensive courses with limited utility in building wealth such as corporate valuation classes, accounting classes and advanced degree courses such as CFAs.

When I used to work at a Wall Street firm, I overheard a guy that graduated from Harvard continually sell prospects with the notion of his trustworthiness by stating that he was smart. In today's investment world, just being smart doesn't cut it anymore. In fact, being much "smarter" than the next guy doesn't even guarantee that you'll be able to achieve better returns than a high school graduate. I finished advanced calculus by the time I was 14 years old, achieved a perfect score on the math portion of the SATs and could perform complicated statistical calculations in my sleep, but all of that never once helped me become a better investor later in life. Today, the determinants of successful investing have shifted into the creative arena of the right hemisphere of the brain.

Anybody can crunch numbers with a calculator so being a "numbers whiz" will never give you an edge against your neighbor or Wall Street broker when it comes to performance. Although the information world is "flattening", at the same time, it is ironically becoming increasingly non-linear. Yet Wall Street firms continue to approach this non-linear world with an outdated and inefficient linear process. Numbers in, numbers out is the process that they most often use, using linear statistics like P/E to growth ratios, earnings growth, working capital, dividend growth, etc. to funnel down a large pool of stocks into the small pool that becomes a stock portfolio.

The technological advancements that have allowed powerful software programs to whittle down a pool of thousands of stocks to just a handful in a matter of seconds based upon the above parameters is irrelevant. It is irrelevant because when using the wrong, inefficient linear parameters as the information funnel, the output, though it can be produced in seconds, is still going to represent garbage.

It is possible to take two people with almost the exact same position in life – similar job, similar salaries, similar material wealth, similar leisure time – yet one will view the glass as half-empty while the other will view the glass as half-full. Why? The answer lies in how one processes information. In the vast sea of information that exists today, how an investor processes information will be the difference between earning 6% or 30% annual returns. No longer does the average investor have to wait for the Wall Street Journal or the Bloomberg Report to learn what is happening in the investment world. He or she can grab this information long before it hits the pages of the Wall Street Journal or the television screen. In fact, changes in securities laws in some countries are granting the average investor information that he or she couldn't dream of accessing just several years ago. However, grabbing this information long before it reaches the masses is just a tiny fraction of the entire picture. What completes this picture is knowing what additional information has strong correlations to achieving 25% or better gains.

A new information funnel, one that is right-brained, and one that depends upon identifying non-linear relationships between stocks and share price performance, is what works best today. As I mentioned earlier in this book, the best portfolio managers in the United States, hands down, year after year are powerful U.S. Senators that have access to some of the best information in the world. A cynic may say, "Sure, these Senators have inside information and that is why they can outperform the average investor by 20% a year" (this is the actual outperformance of the market index by U.S. Senators in a five year study performed by Ziobrowski, Cheng, and Boyd between 1994-1998)[37].

Though the average investor may not have access to the exact high level of information that U.S. Senators possess, and though this information may not be handed to him or her as freely, comparable information highly predictive of stock price appreciation is available. It just takes using your right brain to find it. In Appendix Two, I'll review some of the returns from our inaugural year of my Global Stock Picker newsletter, because I have used these right-brained techniques to select the stocks I discuss within my model portfolio.

Why Low-Risk, High-Reward Investing Strategies are Always Better than Value or Fundamental Investing

As investors, we all should always seek low-risk, high-reward opportunities for the composition of our stock portfolios. Despite the proven effectiveness of such a strategy, I continually hear of alternate strategies that just don't make a lot of sense to me. For example, I am aware of one investment newsletter that employs a "buy high, sell higher" strategy. While certainly momentum in certain markets or even specific stocks can be utilized to achieve returns, such a strategy limits upside and depends on consistently identifying tops to lock in gains.

To me, it makes a LOT more sense to consistently seek stocks that have considerable upside left and offer low-risk entry points rather than to seek out stocks that have already achieved most of their gains. Perhaps more of us don't employ a low-risk, high-reward approach to the selection of stocks because we don't understand how to do it. That is why understanding the relationships among corporations, banks, and governments is paramount to our ability to grow wealth rapidly. If we can understand this, then we should be able to find a very healthy supply of stocks that fit the low-risk, high-reward criteria.

Whenever I broach this subject with investors, the questions that inevitably surfaces are:

How do you identify such stocks? Are these stocks value stocks, growth stocks, micro-cap stocks or large-cap stocks?

I contend that all of these asset classes offer low-risk, high-reward opportunities and that instead of the traditional investment strategy of dividing one's portfolio into value v. growth, large cap v. small cap, and domestic v. international that all stock choices should instead be driven by the low-risk, high-reward paradigm. The problem with today's most widely used investment strategies is that when they are able to identify a single low-risk, high-reward opportunity, people truly get excited. Instead, every single stock in a portfolio could have low-risk, high-reward characteristics if the proper strategies are utilized. The low-risk, high-reward paradigm alone should drive decisions to buy value, growth, small cap, large cap stocks or mid cap stocks and whether we are purchasing stocks that trade in Canada, China, Brazil, Australia, Vietnam, or Russia.

In today's world, there are unprecedented links among governments, corporations and banks. Though many of these links cannot be fully validated because of the general ire that would probably result among the general public were they revealed, the circumstantial evidence of their existence is so overwhelming that any rational person would be hard-pressed to deny the complexity and depth of such relationships.

To prove my point, I'm going to illustrate two major recent anomalies for you. The GSCI, or the Goldman Sachs Commodities Index, influences the positions of fund managers worldwide as many fund managers directly peg their portfolios to any changes in the weightings of the GSCI. In July, 2006, with U.S. mid-term elections quickly approaching in November, unleaded gas accounted for 8.45% of GSCI's dollar weighting. By late September, 2006, Goldman Sachs had slashed the GSCI's dollar weighting for unleaded gas by 72.66% from its July position to a measly 2.31%.[38] Such a drastic cut in the weighting of unleaded gas in the GSCI index created enormous selling pressure on gas futures, and unsurprisingly caused the price of gas futures to decline dramatically. So why would this happen? Let's put 2 + 2 together.

When Bush assumed his office of Presidency in the United States, he appointed his friend Henry Paulson to one of his most important cabinet positions, the U.S. Secretary of Treasury. Up until then, Henry Paulson had been the CEO of Goldman Sachs. As mid-term elections approached in November, 2006, President Bush and the ruling incumbent Republican party in Congress were widely believed by many political analysts to be in serious danger of losing control of Congress.

Coincidentally, several studies performed during President Bush's tenure demonstrated that his approval rating was strongly correlated to the price of gas (petrol) in the United States. Of course, a multitude of other factors also affected President Bush's approval rating, but various polls demonstrated a significant link between the price of gas and his approval ratings. When the price of gas came down, his approval ratings went up and vice versa. Goldman Sachs is perennially one of the largest contributors to the Republican Party's war chest. In November of 2006, Hank Paulson was in a position to directly help his friend Bush. So when Goldman Sachs dumped 72.66% of its position of unleaded gas in its GSCI just prior to mid-term elections, was this action only a mere coincidence or was it blatant manipulation of the markets? You decide. In fact, my online blog, The Underground Investor (http://www.theUndergroundInvestor.com), was one of the very first sources to report this story, trumping the New York Times by more than a week.

Further evidence of a strong unspoken and unreported government-corporate link is provided by the Working Group on Financial Markets. For years, may Americans have hotly contested whether or not the Working Group on Financial Markets actually directly intervenes in U.S. stock markets.

On Monday, October 23, 2006, reporter Deborah Solomon wrote in the Wall Street Journal:

"Mr. Paulson is chairman of the Working Group, which coordinates government policy on financial markets and includes the heads of the Federal Reserve, Securities and Exchange Commission, and Commodity Futures Trading Commission. Mr. Paulson has insisted that they meet about every six weeks. Before his arrival, the group met every few months and sometimes as infrequently as once a quarter."

Years ago, the very existence of the Working Group on Financial Markets used to be contested. Today, most everyone agrees that it exists, and the debate is instead over what is its exact purpose. Due to Congressional testimony, we now know that the Working Group on Financial Markets consists of the U.S. Secretary of Treasury, The Federal Reserve, the SEC, and the Commodity Futures Trading Commission. The Working Group is also known in other circles as the Plunge Protection Team (PPT). The PPT has been accused of a widespread number of actions, from buying massive amounts of futures to prop up stock markets and prevent further panic during market corrections as well as coordinating Central Bank rumors about gold sales to artificially depress the price of gold and thus keep the dollar's heartbeat, however feint, still alive. I, for one, believe that the PPT has manipulated markets in the past and will continue to do so in the future to serve its own agenda.

To what extent they manipulate markets is anybody's guess however. If I had to guess, I would say it's somewhat more than the disbelievers think but less than what the believers presuppose. Certainly we can conclude that the government is not forthright about its participation (or others may say, interference) in the markets.

If we follow this transcript of dialogue from a recent Congressional hearing between Senator Ron Paul and U.S. Federal Reserve Chairman Ben Bernanke, it's extremely hard to believe the Chairman's claims of ignorance in response to Senator Paul's hard-hitting questions. Note that Bernanke's comments about how often the Plunge Protection Team meets directly contradict the Wall Street Journal's report above. This is not to say that the WSJ is infallible, but it seems incredulous that Bernanke would not even be aware of how often the PPT meets. Note that below, Bernanke generally remains vague and evasive in his answers to Senator Ron Paul, an approach that would lead me to suspect that the PPT is much more proactive, rather than just advisory, in its role in the U.S. and global stock markets.

Here is the exact transcript of their conversation from the Hearings on Monetary Policy and the State of the Economy before the Committee on Banking and Financial Services, U.S. House of Representatives, 109th Congress, second session, on July 20, 2006 (for the full transcript of this session, Google "FRASER", the Federal Reserve Archival System for Economic Research)

MR. PAUL: Good afternoon, Chairman Bernanke. I have a question dealing with the Working Group on Financial Markets. I want to learn more about that group and actually what authority they have and what they do. Could you tell me, as a member of that group, how often they meet and how often they take action; and have they done something recently? And are there reports sent out by this particular group?

MR. BERNANKE: Yes, Congressman. The President's Working Group was convened by the President, I believe, after the 1987 stock market crash. It meets irregularly, I would guess about four or five times a year, but I am not exactly sure. And its primary function is advisory, to prepare reports. I mentioned earlier that we have been asked to prepare a report on the terrorism risk insurance. So that is what we generally do.

MR. PAUL: In the media you will find articles that will claim that it is a lot more than an advisory group you know, if there is a stock market crash, that you literally have a lot of authority, you know, to impose restrictions on the market. And we are talking about many trillions of dollars slushing around in all the financial markets, and this involves Treasury and, of course, the Fed, as well as the SEC and the CFTC. So there is a lot of potential there.

And the reason this came to my attention was just recently there was an article that actually made a charge that out of this group came actions to interfere with the prices of General Motor's stock. Have you read that, or do you know anything about that?

MR. BERNANKE: No, sir, I don't.

MR. PAUL: Because they were charging that there was a problem with General Motors, and then there was a spike in GM's stock prices. But back to the issue of the meeting. You tell me it meets irregularly, but there are minutes kept, or are there reports made on this group?

MR. BERNANKE: I believe there are records kept by the staff. These are staff mostly from Treasury, but also from the other agencies.

MR. PAUL: And they would be available to us in the committee?

MR. BERNANKE: I don't know. I am sorry, I don't know.

By the way, for those of you unaware of what Senator Paul was specifically referring to in his comments about GM stock, very curious behavior surrounded GM stock around August and September of 2006. As negative report after negative report was being released about the general state of affairs at GM, a star analyst at Goldman Sachs (which coincidentally happens to be the firm where U.S. Secretary of Treasury Hank Paulson was formerly CEO) upped his price target for GM. His buy rating on GM stock was based on some ludicrous rationalization that GM could potentially enforce sizable wage and benefit cuts during negotiations with the United Auto Workers for a new labor contract. It didn't matter that across the board, GM was hemorrhaging financially. This one piece of news that GM could potentially stem its financial woes based upon expense cuts was somehow strong enough for the analyst to up his price target a whopping 31% from $29 a share to $42 a share.

I read that analyst's report about GM and couldn't find one solid fundamental reason that backed his whopping upgrade of the stock. Do you want to guess what price GM's shares topped out at after the Goldman Sach's upgrade? GM's stock made a monumental run right after the release of this upgrade in less than a month's time from $29 a share to about $39 a share. Again, during this time, there were many accusations that Goldman Sachs was being used as a pawn by the U.S. government to increase consumer confidence in the U.S. economy during troubled times (due to the old school maxim, "as GM goes, so goes the U.S. economy).

No matter what your beliefs are regarding the two above stories, we can gleam a crucial point from them. Political intervention has historically created great anomalies in stock market performance, and in fact, intimate relationships between banks and corporations and between corporations and governments can be exploited to achieve huge gains in the stock market. Instead of being a victim to such shenanigans, the ability to uncover them and understand their implications allows an investor to reap huge profits from the stock market. That is precisely the information that my proprietary investment strategies leverage and the reasons why understanding how corporatocracies function is critical not only to building wealth, but also to preventing significant losses as well.

**13**

A NEW INVESTMENT PARADIGM IS BORN

While books like Vijay Singal's <u>Beyond the Random Walk</u> tackle investment strategies that deviate from traditional fundamental and technical strategies, these books predominantly focus on timing and trading strategies that take advantage of very short-term pricing anomalies and market inefficiencies. While <u>Beyond the Random Walk</u> is a groundbreaking book, it still focuses on trading tactics, not long-term investing tactics. My desire for a long-term investing system that radically departed from every known system today led to my quest to develop a proprietary system.

Three major recent developments in the investment industry have necessitated the use of alternate means of analysis for stock picking:

(1) The consolidation of power in the investment industry through merger and acquisition activity that has given the largest players the power to move markets;

(2) The outward signs of growing corporate greed that make reliance on financial statements suspect as a means of evaluating a stock's fair value; and

(3) The growing interconnectedness between corporations and governments that has produced a greater concerted effort to spread economic misinformation through the media.

In addition, 3 major events have created perfect conditions for the first new investment paradigm in over half-a-century.

(1) The flattening of the world through a rapid expansion of the information highway;

(2) The growing interconnectedness between corporations and governments that allows the average investor to predict the best low-risk, high-reward stocks in the world with stunning accuracy; and

(3) The combination of (1) and (2) that has created exploitable market inefficiencies in the pricing of stocks.

Morihei Ueshiba, the founder of Aikido, once stated, "Martial arts must undergo constant change. Budo develops in an evolutionary manner together with the movements of heavenly bodies and must not stop even for an instant...Its form must be continuously renewed." The same applies to anything in life. Relationships, friendships, technology, and yes, even investing. Nothing remains static. It is either progressing or devolving. Yet commercial investment strategies have remained static for half a century. Modern portfolio theory, the grandfather behind diversification principles, was founded in the late 1950's. More than half-a-century of progress later, it remains the predominant strategy of investment for the commercial investment industry all over the world. So the question we must ask ourselves is this: "In more than half-a-century of technological progress, why has the predominant investment strategy disseminated by the commercial investment industry not improved?"

The answer to the question I pose above is simple. It has not changed because investment firms have invested a substantial amount of time and money to convince the public masses that diversification is the only way to invest money responsibly. In order to maintain a unified front on this massive charade, no firm can break the ranks and reveal that diversification, as an effective investment strategy, is a huge load of junk. I actually worked at a firm once that employed managers that would encourage us to read the annual report from Warren Buffet's company, Berkshire Hathaway, at the same time they encouraged us to push diversification strategy onto our clients.

Though I'm sure my colleagues at the time failed to see the irony in this, I did not. Warren Buffet, at times, has had the vast majority of his stock portfolio in just a handful of stocks. Warren Buffet, at times, has multiplied the growth of his stock portfolio by employing heavy concentration, not diversification, in his company's stock portfolio. Thus, managers at commercial investment firms are careful only to discuss those very concepts that ultimately serve the firm's needs.

The Goal of Investment Houses is to Gather Assets

Again, remember that the goal of investment houses is to gather assets. Your goal, to maximize portfolio gains, is entirely different. Because theses two goals do not converge, different strategies must be used to realize these two different goals. Modern portfolio theory is a great strategy for asset gathering. To maximize returns, it leaves much to be desired. And that's an understatement. Like diversification, buy and hold for 10 years as an investment strategy is also officially dead. Just as I'm certain that you've heard that past performance does not guarantee future results, the past behavior of stock markets is certainly no way to gauge how you should regulate your investment behavior today, especially given the clear and imminent dangers present in global stock markets at the start of 2008. Due to explosive growth in financial derivative markets that inextricably link developed, developing and emerging markets, stock markets today are much more dynamic than they have ever been in years past. The best countries to invest in as well as the best asset classes to invest in may shift every three to five years now as opposed to lengthy timelines in decades past.

In martial arts, buy and hold is like being engaged in a sword fight. If two skilled masters are engaged in a sword fight, once one party has engaged the other, one person will make a mistake within eight seconds and die. It's extremely rare that a sword fight involving at least one skilled master would last any longer than eight seconds. That's why a master will often remain motionless and wait until his opponent commits to a strike before counter-striking. And though the fight will end in death within eight seconds of either party commencing an attack, masters have been known to stand motionless for massively long periods of time before committing to a course of action. This is all good if you have all the time in the world to wait. If it is a matter of life and death, a master can stand motionless for an hour waiting for his opponent to commit. But in investing, if you want to build wealth, can you really afford to wait ten years just to gain 20% over those ten years? Global investing has changed so much today that this is not the path of the sage. Today global investing is all about being able to identify opportunities before anyone else does.

Most Investors Don't Realize How Financial Markets are Linked All Across the World

Little-understood developments in stock markets such as the unregulated explosive growth of derivative markets (i.e. hedge funds) and the future explosive growth of "dark pool" trading has put the individual retail investor at an even greater disadvantage than years past. For those of you that don't know what derivatives are, here is the Wikipedia definition: "Derivatives are financial instruments whose value is derived from the value of something else. They generally take the form of contracts under which the parties agree to payments between them based upon the value of an underlying asset or other data at a particular point in time.

The main types of derivatives are futures, forwards, options, and swaps. The main use of derivatives is to reduce risk for one party while offering the potential for a high return (at increased risk) to another. The diverse range of potential underlying assets and payoff alternatives leads to a huge range of derivatives contracts available to be traded in the market. Derivatives can be based on different types of assets such as commodities, equities (stocks), bonds, interest rates, exchange rates, or indexes."

According to the Bank for International Settlements, the notional amount outstanding of OTC (over the counter) derivatives as of June 2006 grew to $370 trillion, a rapid increase from just $220 trillion two years prior. To put this number in perspective, $370 trillion is a figure that **represents almost nine times the size of the market capitalization of the entire 2006 global stock market**. By mid, 2007, the Bank for International Settlements estimated that the OTC derivatives market had grown to a whopping $521 trillion, an incredible 41% growth rate over just the prior year. Now in 2009, this market is estimated to be more than $600 trillion! In other words, there has been little damage done to this little-understand market of complex financial derivatives but the damage is coming. With the destruction of $30+ trillion in wealth in global stock markets as of the beginning of 2009, imagine the havoc that would be created on the world's economy of only 30% of the derivatives market melted down? 30% of this market translates into $180 trillion, more than six times the losses suffered in the world's stock markets at the beginning of 2009.

Furthermore, OTC derivatives only include financial contracts that are traded and privately negotiated between two parties. There is also another class of derivatives called exchange-traded derivatives that include contracts such as gold futures that only trade through specialized exchanges. Include the figures for these derivatives, and the total derivative number becomes one enormous, gigantic financial gorilla.

The reason that the immense size of the derivatives markets is so important to understand is because derivatives can include contracts for mortgages as well, specifically subprime mortgages. Derivatives are exactly the reason why the impact of the sub-prime mortgage debacle that originated in the U.S. was heavily felt in Europe and will eventually be felt in Asia too. How does this happen? Remember that one of the main purposes for derivatives is "to reduce risk for one party while offering the potential for a high return (at increased risk) to another." Thus, when a financial institution purchases a derivatives contract from another institution, they in turn, often generate another derivatives contract to offset their risk and sell it off to another institution. Often, these transactions take place across global borders. In fact, it is estimated that the effects of bad U.S. subprime debt will be felt more strongly outside of U.S. borders than within U.S. borders due to the global nature and the immense size of the global derivatives markets.

During speeches I gave in Asia in 2007 regarding the imminent dangers inherent in the U.S. market and the potential for a huge correction in 2008 despite the best inflationary, money creation policies of the U.S. Federal Reserve, most investors that were not heavily invested in the U.S. that attended my speeches seemed indifferent to this news.

Most investors today seem to believe that Asian or European markets are insulated from problems that originate in the U.S. and that stock markets in other global regions will continue to soar even if U.S. markets suffer huge problems. I believe that this is a mistake. Given the difficulty of determining exactly where the risk of this 2009 $600+ trillion derivatives market ultimately resides as contracts are bought, repackaged, and resold over and over again all over the world, it should be evident that despite problems originating in the United States, they could come home to roost in any market in the world.

The Impact of Dark Pools

Dark pools are pools of stocks listed on private or proprietary electronic exchanges that allow a buyer or seller to move large blocks of stocks anonymously without even causing bumps in the price of a particular stock as would happen if an investor were to buy or sell a large position of a stock in a publicly followed exchange. As was the case with all the other fiascos and shenanigans of commercial investment firms discussed previously in this book, regulatory agencies again (surprise, surprise) seem to be firmly taking the side of the institution and not the consumer. Erik Sirri, Head of the Division of Market Regulation for the U.S. Securities Exchange Commission, stated that "while the increasing use of hidden orders may be troubling,"[34] the SEC plans to do nothing until it is clear that the use of hidden orders in dark pools is damaging the individual retail investor's ability to buy and sell stocks at a fair price.

By the end of 2006, it was estimated that UBS, Goldman Sachs Group and Credit Suisse Group executed 12 percent of their U.S. stock trades on their internal systems instead of through the New York Stock Exchange or NASDAQ. This figure is expected to increase to 18 percent by 2010.[35] In 2007, it was estimated that the percent of shares listed in the NYSE that traded in dark pools was 17% to 25%, obviously a significant percentage of the total market. In Europe, the trend towards trading in dark pools is the same. Citigroup, Goldman, Deutsche Bank, Merrill Lynch, UBS, Morgan

Stanley and Credit Suisse have formed an internal continent-wide equity trading system that will challenge traditional European stock exchanges like London Stock Exchange Group and Euronext. The problems with these dark pools is succinctly summarized by NYSE President Catherine Kinney, who stated that every single share traded in the dark was a share that would not assist the market in determining a fair price for that share. In other words, without the benefit of knowing the amount of buying and selling volume occurring in these dark pools, retail investors would indeed be purchasing and selling the same shares without critical market information, aka, "in the dark".[36]

While Kinney's comments are sure to be self-serving to some extent as these dark pools degrade commission income for traditional stock exchanges such as the NYSE or Euronext, her comment is still 100% valid for the retail investor that is trying to buy or sell $10,000, $30,000, or $50,000 blocks of shares. Dark pools obstruct transparency in the markets and severely harm the ability of the retail investor to know what type of real-time trading volume is happening in the stock markets. For the higher net-worth investor that may be trying to move a $2,000,000 block of shares, however, dark pools may certainly offer the best place to move such blocks as this type of investor may be willing to sacrifice a little in share price for the guaranteed full execution and anonymity of the trade.

The explosive growth of derivative instruments and dark pools have undoubtedly further eroded the value of traditional investment analysis. With the introduction of dark pools into the market, how does the retail investor purchase or sell a stock with incomplete market information, unsure if one is receiving a "fair" price? With the explosion of the financial derivative market into a $600+ trillion market, how does one know what amounts of "difficult-to-value" financial instruments are being held on the balance sheets of corporations and if they are even being valued by management within a ballpark range of what is truly reasonable? Often, these "difficult-to-value" financial instruments are valued by corporate executives with the use of internal valuation models. The huge problem with this picture is that often these executives' year-end bonuses depend on the value they decide to assign to these derivative products. A greater conflict of interest could not exist than this.

Thus, these are just several more reasons why anyone that sticks to the use of traditional financial and technical analysis as their sole and primary means of stock picking will never develop great wealth. Far too much deception and misinformation is reflected in these traditional means of stock analysis for them to be of great utility.

Sample Representatives of MoneyPing™ - Like Strategies

Note that this section is entitled MoneyPing™-*like* strategies, **NOT** MoneyPing™ strategies. In this section of my book, I will present some strategies that utilize concepts similar in nature to the proprietary strategies I have invented. However, what you'll find on-line at http://www.SmartKnowledgeU.com are absolutely new strategies unlike the ones I will discuss here. The reason I have chosen not to reveal any of my proprietary MoneyPing™ investment strategies in this book is because it would be redundant to cover a topic that I have spent hundreds of pages covering online. However, I have no doubt that in five years, the rest of the world will realize what I have already realized – that information technology has killed investing through Fundamental and Technical Analysis. Though every single investment institution as well as online course continues to stick to "advanced" fundamental and technical analysis courses, remember that I have already revealed the motivation for doing so earlier in this book.

The strategies I am presenting below are either broad-based or seasonal strategies or require active trading; thus, please understand that these strategies are not truly representative of my proprietary

MoneyPing™ strategies. My MoneyPing™ strategies are much more specific in that they identify specific stocks and assets to buy versus broad indexes, and in general are for holding terms of six months to several years, and therefore constitute investment strategies versus trading strategies. I will discuss some unique strategies below only to give you an idea of what my MoneyPing™ strategies are about.

STRATEGY #1: Buy a country's iShares (a fund that tracks the country's major stock market index) in the year preceding a re-election year for an incumbent President or Prime Minister.

I know that you must be scratching your head now after I just dumped on the ineffectiveness of mutual funds right? But iShares are different than most mutual funds. There are no sales fees or redemption charges and their fund expenses are a fraction of the average comparable mutual fund. And again, we are listing this strategy to provide a concept conceptually similar to my MoneyPing™ strategies. This is NOT one of my MoneyPing™ strategies, nor do I advocate anything but the purchase of individual stocks and other non-stock assets in our much more specific and detailed MoneyPing™ strategies (to learn more about the origins of my strategies please visit http://www.smartknowledgeu.com).

Historical patterns of global stock markets have revealed that the performance of a country's stock markets tends to be considerably higher in the years preceding a re-election date for an incumbent President or Prime Minister. The reasons for this are quite logical if you think about it. Generally speaking, with few exceptions, the most important factor in whether a President or Prime Minister will be re-elected is the state of the economy. A Prime Minister or President may even have presided over several lousy years in the economy, but as long as a strong economy exists in the year leading up to the re-election date, then most times he or she will be re-elected.

In general, this strategy works extremely well because the sheep-herd of investors tend not to care if a short-term strong economy is artificially produced, even when such political shenanigans are to the detriment of the long-term economy. The overwhelming numbers of sheep-herd investors have very short-term memories, tend to associate the most recent economic strength with the incumbent Head of State, and overwhelmingly believe that these conditions will continue as long as he or she remains in office. Governments know this as well, so they artificially produce strong economies in the year prior to re-election years to give the incumbent the best chance of winning. The only thing that supercedes this factor is war. Depending on the status of an ongoing war, war can become the most important re-election campaign issue.

My conceptually similar MoneyPing™ strategy: I've delved deep into the financials of the world's central banks and the U.S. Federal Reserve to understand the loosening and tightening of the global U.S. dollar and gold reserve supply. By understanding as much as I possibly can about how this works, I can predict with strong accuracy the price movements of certain commodities, currencies, and stocks. Again, the specific details of this particular strategy are reserved for our online customers at SmartKnowledgeU™.

STRATEGY #2: Buy companies a couple of days immediately before they are added to a major index such as the London FTSE 100, or the U.S. S&P 500 and sell them a couple of days after they've been added. Buy companies that have been dropped from major indexes in the week after they've been dropped and hold on to them for six months or longer.

Again, for purposes of clarification, note that this trading strategy is not reflective of my proprietary MoneyPing™ strategies, all of which are investment strategies. Again the purpose of discussing this particular strategy is merely to provide a conceptual framework.

Decades of historical data have demonstrated that almost all companies receive a major boost in share price, usually in the range of 2% to 4%, as soon as they are added to a major global stock market index. Again, the reason for this pattern is quite logical. Studies illustrate that more than 90% of all professional money managers in the world peg their portfolios to the major indexes in their country, only cherry picking a few stocks outside of the index in an attempt to add some additional returns to their portfolios. In addition, nearly all mutual funds contain most of the components of the major stock indexes in their country. This means that as soon as a new stock is added to a major index, huge sums of institutional money will automatically flow into that stock. This "automatically guaranteed" large additional buying volume immediately gives the stock's price a nice bump, though it usually does not last.

On the other hand, buying stocks a couple of weeks after they have been dumped from a major index often leads to six-month to year-long gains of 30% or more. The reason for this phenomenon is not as intuitive, but certainly as logical as anything else I've discussed here. In some years, as many as 50 or 60 new companies may be dropped from or added to each of the world's major stock market indexes. Sometimes the subtractions and additions seem arbitrary, and may be even unjustified at times. In any event, when a company is dumped from a major index, many investors perceive this act as the ultimate low point for a stock. Therefore, as long as there are no material concerns that plague the company, they feel that the stock has nowhere to go but up, and in a self-fulfilling prophecy, they buy into the stock and push shares significantly higher.

My conceptually-similar MoneyPing™ strategy: As investors, what we must understand about the above two strategies is that they experience a lot of success because of the "self-fulfilling prophecy" factor. There is a large enough volume of investors out there that have studied and strongly believe in such historical trends, and in essence, it is their beliefs, and their willingness to act on these beliefs that make these beliefs come true.

My MoneyPing™ strategies peel back an additional layer of this onion and delve deeper by following the investment patterns and money trails of the most powerful institutions and people in the world. If one day, people stopped believing in the historical trend explained above, then the strategy of following stocks added to and subtracted from the major indexes would fail to work. This is not the case with my MoneyPing™ strategies. Because my MoneyPing™ strategies dig down to the core investment habits of the wealthiest persons and institutions in the world, they should work until the end of time.

As an example, I have discovered a company so influential and so powerful that you are almost guaranteed to earn 50% annual returns from individual stocks if you invest in the same companies that they invest in at the same time they do. Until 2005, this strategy, for reasons we explain inside our membership area, was impossible to use. And it's a little tricky to use too. It's not nearly as simple as downloading this company's annual report and looking at its corporate holdings. But inside the hallways of SmartKnowledgeU™, I teach you exactly how to find these companies. However, this particular MoneyPinging™ strategy is merely an offshoot of one of my three core strategies, none of which are this specific.

Hopefully, in this chapter, I've given you just a tiny bit of insight into how technology has revolutionized the world of investment strategies. I hope to have opened up your eyes into how an entire blue ocean of investment strategies exists that remains vastly unexplored despite offering high probabilities of achieving returns multiples of those typically offered by large commercial investment firms.

14

THE COMING DOLLAR CRISIS. WE'RE AT THE TIPPING POINT NOW.

The last three chapters of my book are dedicated to explaining the dangerous fulcrum on which global markets are balanced as we enter 2009. The eighth and last lesson in my curriculum on wealth literacy is entitled "Major Global Currencies and their Effects on the World Economy." This particular lesson is paramount to building wealth because without an understanding of how decades of monetary policy mismanagement by the U.S. Federal Reserve has now caused an impending dollar crisis and Peak Investment Crisis as of 2009, one cannot understand the best opportunities to build wealth rapidly that are available as we end 2008 and enter 2009.

All dedicated martial artists eventually develop a sixth sense, an ability to sense impending danger. The ability to sense things before they happen is critical to a martial artist's ability to defeat an attacker, even if it merely translates into an ability to sense an impending kick or punch before one is thrown by an aggressor. Likewise, in the investment world, many times investors are caught off-guard and financially "knocked out" by crises that seemingly materialize out of nowhere. In reality, every historical financial crisis has always produced numerous warning signs of their imminent occurrence many months, and sometimes even years, before they materialize. The crisis that has reached its tipping point today is no different. The reason why stock market crises catch millions of investors off-guard is not for lack of evidence, but for lack of curiosity, lack of independent thinking, and an inordinate amount of misplaced trust in the investment industry.

Let's start with the last point. Millions of investors are blindsided whenever pullbacks, corrections, and crises afflict stock markets because investment industry insiders are notoriously known for being perpetual bulls and for always recommending that their clients remain fully invested at all times. We need not look any further than the 2007 subprime fiasco to confirm the fact that commercial investment firms will never have the best interests of their clients at heart. In July 17, 2007, according to Investopedia, "in a letter sent to investors, Bear Stearns Asset Management reported that its Bear Stearns High-Grade Structured Credit Fund had lost more than 90% of its value, while the Bear Stearns High-Grade Structured Credit Enhanced Leveraged Fund had lost virtually all of its investor capital. The larger Structured Credit Fund had around $1 billion, while the Enhanced Leveraged Fund, which was less than a year old, had nearly $600 million in investor capital."[39] A couple of weeks later, both funds were declared bankrupt and Bear Stearns chose to liquidate all holdings in the fund and close them out. In the end, investors lost close to $1.5 billion.

Incredibly, when a third fund holding about $900 million experienced great difficulties the following month, Bear Stearns chose to freeze all redemptions, not allowing investors to pull out their money even if that is what they desired. "We believe the fund portfolio is well positioned to wait out the market uncertainty", Bear Stearns spokesman Russell Sherman told The Wall Street Journal back then. "And we believe by suspending redemptions, we can ensure the best long-term results for our investors, he said. We don't believe it's prudent or in the interest of our investors to sell assets in this current market environment."[40] Regardless of whether Bear Stearn's assessment was correct or not regarding this third fund, the fact was that they never gave their clients a choice to withdraw their investment if that was the course of action they desired. In essence, after having two funds fall apart, Bear Stearns essentially demanded that their clients trust them with their money, an incredibly arrogant maneuver given the huge losses investors shouldered in the two prior funds that went belly up.

One need not dig very deep to understand why I still remain extremely skeptical of the motives of the investment industry when they say they act with clients' interests in mind. In response to many of the scandals that plagued investment firms in the early 2000's, the investment industry agreed to self-regulate itself and separate their investment banking divisions from their brokerage houses as far as compensation and bonuses were concerned. Many believed that this separation would create greater honesty in the analyst ratings of these firms. This is how much the separation of investment banking from brokerage house fees improved ratings: In 2003, before this step was implemented, 89% of all stocks covered by Wall Street firms were rated a "buy or hold", with only 11% rated a "sell". In 2007, of all stocks covered by Wall Street firms, 93% were rated "hold and buy" and only 7% "sell". Although the figures are not out for 2008, given that 2008 was a horrendous year for US stocks, it would be interesting to know that these stats were for 2008.

In other words, the number of stocks rated a "sell" by the Street declined in what was generally a difficult investing environment in 2007. The reason for these counter-intuitive results is simple. If analysts rate a company's stock as a "sell", he can generally kiss his access to top corporate management goodbye. In order to remain in favor with top corporate management, analysts continue to rate companies as a "hold" or "buy" even when they know they should be rated a "sell." For this very reason, no credibility should ever be given to analysts' ratings. Basically, we should follow Warren Buffet's advice that we should only read industry analysts' reports when we want a good laugh.

Proof that Our Governments Try to Shield Gold's Value From the Public

There is much literature that challenges the official U.S. reserve figure of over 8,000 tonnes of gold as there is a lot of circumstantial evidence that the U.S. either sold or leased much of their gold reserves during the late 1980s and 1990s in order to manipulate and depress the price of gold during this time. Understanding Central Banks' attempts to mislead the public about the amount of global gold reserves as well as their attempts to artificially set prices much lower than what free market forces would dictate is crucial, because these manipulations serve to conceal the dollar crisis from the public. What allows figures of the world's gold reserves to remain so murky are strange, non-GAAP conforming practices allowed by the U.S. Federal Reserve (GAAP stands for the Generally Accepted Accounting Principles that all publicly traded companies use when stating balance sheet assets and liabilities).

In essence, the U.S. Federal Reserve still reports leased gold no longer under their ownership as an asset on their books. Other central banks, particularly those that belong to the European union, also engage in murky accounting practices when it comes to reporting their gold reserves. Thus, their official numbers are also questionable.

The reason the above shady practices are so important to the gold market is because of the Central Bank Gold Agreement that covers about 85% of the world's central banks' gold reserves. Many futures traders closely follow gold sales through the lens of this agreement to gauge the probabilities of future sales throughout the course of each year.

Basically, this agreement stipulates four items:

1. Gold will remain an important element of global monetary reserves.

2. Gold sales already decided and to be decided by the undersigned institutions will be achieved through a concerted program of sales over a period of five years, starting on 27 September 2004, just after the end of the previous agreement. Annual sales will not exceed 500 tons and total sales over this period will not exceed 2,500 tonnes.

3. Over this period, the signatories to this agreement have agreed that the total amount of their gold leasings and the total amount of their use of gold futures and options will not exceed the amounts prevailing at the date of the signature of the previous agreement.

4. This agreement will be reviewed after five years.

Obviously, any allowances by governments that allow central banks to lease gold and thus increase market supply, yet report that same gold as an asset on their books, allows central banks a "secret" window to circumvent the Central Bank Gold Agreement annual sales quota of 500 tonnes. For example, if one year Central Banks have already reached their 500 tonne sales quota but still wish to flood markets with supply in order to depress soaring gold prices, they would be able to do so without anyone knowing of their actions due to this strange accounting anomaly.

Theoretically, they could release an additional 300 tonnes onto the market while still reporting it as an asset on their books. Thus, to any investor attempting to understand a spike downward in the price of gold, Central Bank involvement would appear to be non-existent. This is why I believe that this shady accounting practice almost undeniably proves that Central Banks have acted to depress the price of gold in the past. If Central Banks were not trying to conceal their true actions, then why not subtract their leased gold from their official reserve numbers as good accounting practices would dictate? Why continue to commingle leased gold with actual gold reserve numbers? The only reason to continue this practice would be to purposefully deceive the public.

Despite the uncertainty about the reliability of "official" gold reserve figures, we can still utilize central bankers', finance ministers', and commercial investment firms' actions and words as an accurate and indicative proxy for where the dollar is heading if we understand how to interpret this information properly. Why? Short-term behavior of the global stock and currency markets are spurred by the reaction of the thundering sheep herd to the manipulations of central banks and other large financial institutions that have ulterior motives. However, the masses of individual investors that act irrationally ultimately have no power over true monetary policy change. Because the thundering sheep herd always reacts to what it hears or reads through mainstream media, governments and central banks utilize this knowledge to purposefully manipulate the masses of investors to lead them down a disastrous path.

The "powers that be" recognize that sheep find it mentally daunting and extremely frightening to take a stand against the herd even in instances when following the herd can be financially disastrous. Thus, if the U.S. Federal Reserve can convince an icon like Goldman Sachs to announce shorting gold as one of their top 10 tips for 2008, then the gold market is almost guaranteed to correct immediately in the short-term (as it did in early December, 2007) and cast enormous quantities of doubt into the minds of any investor that had been considering an investment in gold. Those investors, however, that can recognize these short-term manipulations will instead identify any significant downturns in gold and precious metal stocks as buying opportunities. By adding to existing positions at even cheaper prices, these investors will wind up making a fortune from their insight.

How Inflation Statistics Are Manipulated to Also Shield the Truth About Gold and the U.S. Dollar

A review of the formula used to calculate inflation in the United States provides additional evidence that the establishment and the U.S. government engage in misinformation campaigns about gold and the dollar. In determining what enables the government to produce a fantasy CPI (Consumer Price Index) every month, here are some of the more important changes to the calculation of the CPI that have occurred since 1996. I could probably fill an entire book just with a discussion of how inflation statistics are manipulated but for fear of putting you to sleep, I will merely discuss just a couple of the manipulations that I deem to be the most important.

In the mid-1990s, the formula used to calculate the cost of the basket of goods (used to determine the Consumer Price Index) was greatly tinkered with to hide real rates of inflation from the general public (see pp.108-109 for an explanation of some of the specific changes). In addition to outright tinkering with the CPI formula, the U.S. government calculates numerous inflation figures, some that exclude food and energy (the core CPI) and even others that allow CPI to be steady in the face of soaring rents and mortgages. But this is precisely why so many different inflation statistics are calculated. The multiple CPI calculations ensure that there will always be at least one deceptive inflation statistic that can be reported to the public to state that inflation is under control even as it is soaring.

One of the main reasons that real inflation is so misrepresented by the U.S. government is because inflation represents the loss of purchasing power. If people realized how much the dollar has devalued and how much the purchasing power of their U.S. dollars has eroded, then more money immediately would move into gold and gold prices would be driven much higher much more quickly. At the end of 2007, when gold soared higher from $670 to $790, even at $790, I stated on my online blog, the Underground Investor, (http://www.theUndergroundInvestor.com) that one day, we would look back at $790 in gold and reminisce with amazement at how cheap gold used to be. I made that comment because I understand how much the U.S. Federal Reserve has truly devalued the dollar versus the public mumbo jumbo they feed to the masses that suggest otherwise.

If Americans truly understood how stock markets are manipulated by the release of false and deceptive information, again, there would be revolution by the crack of dawn the next day. In the Spike Lee movie, "The 25th Hour" (a great movie by the way starring Edward Norton, Rosario Dawson, Barry Pepper, and Philip Seymour Hoffman), Barry Pepper plays the role of a Wall Street big shot. In the movie, he makes huge bets on derivative products that depend on unemployment figures.

There is a scene in the movie in which he waits for the monthly unemployment figures to flash on his screen because he is betting that they will come in lower than the general consensus on the Street. The reporting of this one figure will literally determine whether he will earn or lose millions of dollars for his clients, and whether he will be promoted or fired by his firm. In reality, the market often plays out exactly like this. The markets for certain stock and derivative products are frequently and significantly moved higher or lower based upon certain reported government statistics. The reason that these relationships are so ludicrous is that, as I have demonstrated with inflation above, most government statistics do not reflect the true nature of the economy and are manipulated to serve political and government interests. Thus, huge market movements often occur on bogus statistics that never reflect the true nature of the economy.

Thus, due to all the changes in the various measurements of the core inflation rate and the CPI over the years, the CPI has not come close to approximating the real rate of inflation for more than a decade now. The reason this is such an important concept to understand no matter where in the world you live is because if inflation statistics in your country are not honestly reported, a truly significant question you must ask yourself AND take the time to answer is the following: "What is all this inflation doing to my quality of life?"

For example, during the last real estate market boom in the U.S., which again was manufactured by the Feds to compensate people for trillions of dollars that were lost during the stock market crash that began in March of 2000, if your real estate property was worth $800,000 in 2001 and then soared to $1,000,000 in March of 2005, consider this very real conundrum. If, during that time, the increase of your property value was only attributable to severe inflation of the dollar, then did your real wealth really increase? For example, how did that increase in real estate value translate into purchasing power? If you had taken that $800,000 and purchased a basket of goods in 2000 and that exact same basket of goods in 2005 cost $1,300,000, then your true wealth actually diminished. However, if the government told you that inflation was only 2.5% when in reality it was 12%, you may actually be fooled into believing that your wealth had increased (because after all, who is going to check the basket of goods example that I just presented?). In a nutshell, this is why the U.S. government hides the true rates of inflation from its people.

A real way of looking at this picture in an adequate fashion is to measure things in a true currency – gold. Consider if you were to buy a prime piece of real estate in New York City that seemingly has remained immune from the U.S housing crisis because its value has increased in dollar value from $1.8 million to $3.1 million over the past seven years? Then consider if you were paying for this piece of property in gold. In 2001, you had to spend 7,200 ounces of gold to buy the property (using $250 an ounce gold as the exchange rate). Now, in 2008, you would only have to spend 3,333 ounces of gold to buy the property, even at its increased $3.1 million sales price (using $930 an ounce gold as the exchange rate). In conclusion, did ownership of this property just make you 72% richer (the appreciation percentage in dollar terms from $1.8

million to $3.1 million) or did you just lose 54% of your wealth (the depreciation of the property value when measured in gold)?

Because we clearly have been in a severe inflationary dollar environment for many years, I would argue that the only reasonable manner in which to evaluate the above scenario is to look at the value of property in terms of real currency. Even with gold's temporary decline to $850 an ounce in 2009, you would have still been much better off holding gold than holding this property because of gold's superior ability to hold purchasing power over the US dollar. To answer which one is real currency, let me ask you the following question: If I were to offer you $8,500 or ten ounces of gold at the start of 2009, and you would then have to stash this money away and without any access until three years from now, which one would you take? If you answered dollars, then you would be 72% richer in the scenario I illustrated above. If you answered gold, then you would be 54% poorer.

More Political Shenanigans and Their Effects on the U.S. Dollar

We only need to look at the below comment made in 1966 by a very powerful man to understand how a fortune can be made today from the impending dollar crisis:

"This is the shabby secret of the welfare statists' tirades against gold. Deficit spending is simply a scheme for the confiscation of wealth. Gold stands in the way of this insidious process. It stands as a protector of property rights. If one grasps this, one has no difficulty in understanding the statists' antagonism toward the gold standard."

Do you know who made this comment? Take a guess before reading any further.

The person that made the above comment, well before he became Chairman of the U.S. Federal Reserve, was Alan Greenspan, in an article he scripted called "Gold and Economic Freedom." The article was first published in 1966 in Ayn Rand's "Objectivist" newsletter and reprinted in her book, Capitalism: The Unknown Ideal, in 1967. It should be well noted that Mr. Greenspan, during his long tenure as U.S. Federal Reserve Chairman, became exactly the man that he warned us against in 1966.

Earlier in December of 2007, the Gulf nations publicly stated their allegiance to the U.S. dollar, vowing that they would not break their pegs to the U.S. dollar. Though Saudi Arabia was among this group of nations, in my opinion, they have already "unofficially" broken their peg by refusing to slash domestic interest rates in line with the actions of the U.S. Federal Reserve at the end of 2007. Because of their refusal to keep their peg, despite their official statements, the Saudi Riyal strengthened considerably at the end of 2007, thus helping to curb inflation in Saudi Arabia that no doubt would have become much worse had they kept their peg to the dollar. The actions that go on below the radar of the investing sheep herd and the statements that are made in the media for the purpose of maintaining "appearances" are what makes the overwhelming majority of analysis regarding oil, gold, and the U.S. dollar so flimsy and terrible.

Given that I travel so much for work, I have noticed that the information that is reported by the Asian media is drastically different than the information being reported in different parts of the world. This is precisely why neither your focus in investing nor your focus in information gathering can be limited to your own country. While Goldman Sachs and other investment firms in Europe were busy at the end of 2007 manufacturing nonsense about a dollar rally in 2008 (and I'll reveal later in this book how these firms can spin a still weakening dollar into the appearance of a rally), other parts of the world, like the Middle East, were reporting stories about grave concerns in their own countries about a dollar collapse. Now that 2008 is over, we have the same disingenuous stories being spun again by the same players about a monumental US dollar rally in 2009.

Even stories about other commodities that influence the price of gold are spun to deceive investors. If oil had been priced in a strong Euro instead of the weak dollar for the past five years, the rise in the price of oil would have been drastically reduced.

Yet, very poor analysis of what drives the behavior of oil and gold prices continues to plague the mainstream financial media, some of it simply driven by the misunderstanding of analysts and some of it driven by a purposeful misinformation campaign waged by powerful interests. Of course, the U.S. Treasury Department desires to conceal from the masses the fact that much of the climb in the price of oil has been directly attributable to the monumental decline in the dollar, for this revelation would expose the irresponsible and foolish monetary policy embraced by the U.S. Federal Reserve over the past couple of decades (actually ever since its formation in 1913). And another significant portion of oil's rise from $50 to $147 a barrel that was driven by speculation was also concealed from investors in 2008 through fudged futures numbers that were inaccurate.

In concluding this section, I want to repeat an assertion I made earlier in this book. Statements by huge players such as the Gulf Nations and Goldman Sachs can and DO move markets. Just by the nature of the willing and gullible sheep herd that make their decisions based upon their statements, markets are sure to follow their predictions in the short-term. For this reason, gold and gold stocks from time to time receive unreasonable corrections as those investors influenced by such talk take profits when they shouldn't. Irrational behavior abounds everywhere in financial markets, much of it created by an absolute lack of understanding about the fundamental outlook of commodities and currency, the factors that truly drive their long-term behavior, and historical precedent that predicts future outcomes. However, let me be clear about one more thing.

Know that any short-term movements in markets influenced by the statements of prominent players that attempt to pool the wool over the collective eyes of investors can only be short-lived. In the end, your investment decisions should never be influenced by these short-term shenanigans for true north will always be revealed. For this very reason, oil, gold and silver should experience very strong years in 2009 just based upon the massive, continuing devaluation of the dollar that all seems but inevitable.

The Similarities Between Conditions That Triggered Past Major Financial Crises and Today's Global Economy

Currently, any student of history can spot the writing on the wall that exists in the U.S. and other co-dependent economies as we enter 2009, and the writing is fraught with dire warnings. Let's look at three past crisis, the death of the German mark, post-WWI, the dot.com crash in March of 2000, and the 1997 Asian financial crisis. I will reveal startling similarities between these past global crises and our current economic situation in 2008. Hopefully this brief study will clear up one of the greatest misunderstandings about the instability of the global economy that exists as we enter 2009. When I released the first edition of this book in early January, 2008, I stated that too much of what had happened up to that point, including 1,000+ point drops in the Nikkei 225 and the DJIA, and multiple single day plummets between 2% to 4% in Australian markets, Taiwanese markets, South Korean markets, and Hong Kong markets were erroneously being attributed to the subprime mortgage debacle.

The crisis that grow dangerously stronger in 2009 is not a subprime crisis. It is a monetary crisis, specifically a Dollar Crisis, that will spread like the flu and afflict the Euro and the Pound Sterling as well. This Dollar Crisis would have happened irrespective of the subprime crisis. This is the biggest story that I believe investors have still failed to realize. The financial media was spinning the story of the terrible global market performance to start 2008 as fallout from the subprime crisis. The subprime crisis was merely a trigger that precipitated the onset of the dollar crisis much more quickly. But the dollar crisis would have happened with or without the subprime fiasco. Back in early 2008, I stated that the subprime crisis was merely the trigger, because given the historical (mal)function of the U.S. Federal Reserve, I believed that they would embrace a solution of monetary expansion that would elevate the Dollar Crisis. At the start of 2009, my early 2008 prediction certainly seems to be coming to fruition. Instead of addressing the Dollar Crisis intelligently, the US Federal Reserve has engaged in an unprecedented journey of US dollar monetary base expansion, an action in my opinion, that will evolve into unprecedented monetary supply expansion in 2009 and 2010.

Until investors realize that we are firmly in a Dollar Crisis, and not a subprime crisis, a liquidity crisis, or a solvency crisis, they remain at much larger risk of having their portfolios decimated during this crisis. Without realizing the greater Dollar Crisis that is at hand, investors will make the mistake of holding on for rebounds as this bear market deepens instead of completely restructuring their portfolio. So despite the fact that the U.S. Federal Reserve seems to have learned nothing from the failures of other countries, and even our own past failures, let's take a look down memory lane.

The Hyperinflation of the German Papiermark in 1922-23

In the early 1920's, inflation of the German mark evolved into hyperinflation as speculation and irresponsible Reichsbank (the German Central Bank) policy drove the value of the mark into worthlessness. In 1919 and 1920, after WWI, foreign speculators with large holdings of German marks bet on the recovery of both the German economy and its currency. Foreigners used their holdings of marks to buy real assets such as real estate and stakes in

German companies as well as paper assets such as German stocks. However, as the German government kept printing marks to pay off large punitive war reparations imposed upon them by the winning countries of the war, eventually the mark's rapid and continued devaluation discouraged foreign capital inflows and speculation soon completely halted.

As the German Reichsbank continued to rapidly devalue the German Mark, foreign countries slapped prohibitive, protective tariffs on cheap German goods to prevent German imports from taking over their economy. These actions disrupted the German export market and one of Germany's only viable sources of repayment for war reparations and consequently triggered a liquidity crunch in the German banking system. With the economy floundering, the German government along with the Reichsbank decided to solve their debt problem simply by printing ever-growing supplies of more money.

Before the war, the highest denomination of German currency was 1000 marks. By October of 1923, German printing presses working overtime had caused severe inflation and an increase in the largest banknote denomination from 1000 marks to 1000 billion marks.[41] The cost of a mere loaf of bread skyrocketed to about 200,000,000,000 marks (I wrote that figure out with all of its zeros so you can see how the German central bank created a situation of utter desperation), and 99% of government income was sourced entirely from the creation of new money. During this time, German citizens demanded payment of their salaries three times a day so they could take their morning payments and run to the grocery store to buy food items before they increased several hundred percent mere hours later. During this time of hyperinflation, gold was one of the few assets that held its value.

Today's Comparable Scenario: The U.S. Federal Reserve's decision to expand U.S. dollar supply (outside of the U.S.) from $600 billion in 1990 to more than $6+ trillion today.

The U.S. government, unable to pay off its national debt, has raised the national debt ceiling five times since ex-US President Bush took office in 2001 (most recently in October, 2007 to $9.82 trillion). This, despite the fact that "official" U.S. national debt figures don't even include multi-trillion dollars of unfunded government obligations such as Medicaid and Social Security programs. If one accounts for all of the unaccounted programs that should be included in the U.S. national debt figure, the "true" national debt rises into the stratosphere at multiples of the "officially" reported figure. For the last four years, there have been no new taxes to fund an increasingly costly war in Iraq. The cost of the Iraqi war is now estimated to be in the trillions of dollars. How is the war being funded? With printing presses that are working overtime, just like in post WWI Germany.

In 2007, a financial sector liquidity crunch hit Europe and the United States that was largely created by speculation in subprime mortgage instruments. In order to fend off disaster in U.S. financial markets, the U.S. Federal Reserve again opted not for responsibility, but to bail out irresponsible financial institutions by massively increasing the global U.S. dollar supply. Of course, the bailout plan also included bailing out their own irresponsible fiscal policies for the past couple of decades as well.

However, this strategy is a house of cards that cannot remain standing under the weight of its foolishness. Though the situation that exists at the beginning of 2009 in the United States and Europe is not yet as severe as the German papiermark crisis, the similarities of misguided fiscal policies are astounding. In addition, the growth of the $600+ trillion gorilla, the derivatives market, has linked financial markets all across the globe like at no other point and time in history. Thus, while the present liquidity crunch may not be as deep as the one that triggered hyperinflation in Germany back in the 1920's, it certainly is more widespread today.

The U.S. Federal Reserve has grown the money supply of dollars outside of the U.S. by more than tenfold since 1990. Since the US Treasury stopped printing M3 money supply statistics years ago, it is impossible to know exactly how much this money supply has grown since then, but the latest figures available before discontinuation in 2006 indicated that it had grown by more than ten times. Responsible money creation should occur at or around the rate of inflation, only 2% -3% a year (Granted the real rate of inflation, as I've explained earlier in this book, is many multiples of the officially released figure but since this is the figure the government releases to the masses, we will use it for guidance in this example). In 17 years, U.S. dollar money supply, at a responsible growth rate of 3% a year, would have increased from $600 billion to about $913 billion by 2006.

Instead, the Feds overshot that figure by $5,087,000,000,000 in growing that figure to $6,000,000,000,000. Simply put, this is why, if you are an American, your dollar is practically junk now in Europe and Asia.

Furthermore, the super-inflated dollar encouraged holders of strong foreign currency to invest in U.S. stocks that traded at super cheap valuations in the early 2000's (similar to cheap valuations in Germany after their economy was ravished by war). Thus, much of the rise in U.S. stock markets during this time was triggered by foreign, not domestic investment, and was only sustainable as long as foreigners believed that the discounts of U.S. stock prices outweighed the risk of holding assets valued in U.S. dollars. The investment paradigm for foreigners has shifted in 2009 and with huge rapid devaluations of the Euro and Pound Sterling at the end of 2008 in addition to continued US dollar weakness, faith in holding dollar denominated assets has collapsed. According to the Bureau of Economic Analysis, a division of the U.S. Department of Commerce, foreign private holdings of U.S. securities increased from 20% in 2005 to an estimated whopping 30% to 35% of the entire U.S. stock market cap of approximately $15 trillion in 2006. By the end of 2007, the total US stock market cap stood at about $19.9 trillion and private holdings of foreign private investors continued to be strong in 2007, increasing by $760.1 billion to $6.132 trillion (excluding holdings of US Treasury Securities). The figures for 2008 are not yet available but it is a fairly safe bet to assume that in 2008, foreign investment in the latter half of 2008 stopped flowing into U.S. stock markets when foreigners realized that the risk of investing in dollar-denominated paper assets outweighed the current discounts in price. Even though the situation in Germany was exponentially more severe, the steep sell-off in U.S. markets by foreign investors that is highly likely to continue in 2009 will produce the same beneficiary as the post-WWI German economy – Gold.

The 1997 Asian Financial Crisis

Prior to 1997, the Asian "tigers", in particular, South Korea, Thailand, and Indonesia attracted foreign investment in three manners: (1) The liberalization of investment policies and consequent elimination of restrictions on foreign capital inflows; (2) the maintenance of high domestic interest rates to attract capital inflows; and (2) the pegging of domestic currencies to the U.S. dollar to allay foreign investors' fears of volatile currency movements.

Extremely high 8-12% GDP growth rates in South Korea, Thailand and Indonesia in the mid-1990s created rampant foreign speculation in real estate markets and created unsustainable, inflated real estate prices. When the real estate bubble burst, a flight of capital ensued. As foreign currencies were withdrawn at record levels, the domestic currencies of the Asian tigers suffered a rapid depreciation in their exchange rates against the Western denominated currencies of the investing nations.

To provide stability to the economies of the Asian tigers, the IMF proposed a 3-pronged Structural Adjustment Package: (1) Cut back on government spending to reduce deficits; (2) Allow insolvent banks and financial institutions to fail, and (3) Aggressively raise interest rates to strengthen domestic currencies.

Historically Comparable Scenario: 2000-2009 U.S Economic Timeline

The U.S. markets, over the last nine years, have created a situation today that is very similar to the one that triggered the 1997 Asian Financial Crisis. Here is what has happened in U.S. markets during the last 9 years: (1) Dot com crash in 2000; (2) To alleviate the pain Americans suffered in stock markets after NASDAQ crashed, the U.S. Federal Reserve manufactured an artificial real estate bull and explosive growth in the subprime mortgage market by slashing Fed Funds rate 12 times in a row from May, 2000 to June, 20003; (3) As a consequence of the Fed Reserve bailout, subprime mortgage fallout from irresponsible fiscal policy rattled global financial markets in 2007; (4) 2008, 2009 and beyond – Extended real estate bear, inflation, and depression with periods of pure panic in between???

The dot com bubble collapse in March of 2000 caused the U.S. NASDAQ index to plummet from a peak of 5,038 to a low of 1,114 in October, 2002 – a decline of 78% in less than three years. Runaway valuations and frenzied buying of a hot tech sector caused the tech market to collapse as investors and venture capitalists blindly threw money at companies that had never declared a single dollar in revenue or profit, creating absurdly inflated stock valuations.

Even though revenues, earnings and cash flow were all absent, this didn't seem to matter as a rapidly rising index provided a rising tide that lifted all boats regardless of the missing components of quality, fundamental soundness, and profits (by the way, in the first edition of this book, I stated this exact sentence: "the result of this foolishness should also raise a red flag as of the beginning of 2008 to those invested in the Shanghai markets where stocks are trading at ridiculous valuations sometimes two to three times as much as they are trading in Hong Kong". In 2008, the Shanghai Stock Exchange opened at 5261.56 and closed the year at 1820.81, a whopping drop of 65.39% in valuation!)

But back to a discussion of the US tech bubble now. When the foolish actions of investors finally culminated in the tech bubble bursting, to ease the pain of losses in the stock market, the U.S. Federal Reserve cut the Fed Funds interest rates a dozen times from 6.5% to 1.25% (the discount rate was cut 13 times to 0.75%). The creation of this nearly "free money policy" spurred massive speculation in the housing market. These massive and rapidly implemented interest rate cuts achieved two simultaneous goals:

(1) They pulled the U.S. economy quickly out of a deep recessionary environment; and

(2) Fueled massive equity gains in the housing and RE market that allowed many Americans to forget the pain they had just suffered in the stock markets.

However, this foolish monetary policy in 2003 created the sub-prime crisis of 2007 as buyers jumped into the U.S. real estate market to buy houses beyond their budget (something they were able to do courtesy of the nearly free money that the U.S. Feds had created).

Interestingly enough, remember what the IMF's solution for the Asian tigers was back in 1997?

(1) Cut back on government spending to reduce deficits;

(2) Allow insolvent banks and financial institutions to fail, and

(3) Aggressively raise interest rates.

When faced with the exact same scenario in 2007 & 2008 (caused by similar conditions), the U.S.'s response was to

(1) Raise the national debt ceiling and increase deficits;

(2) Bail out insolvent banks and financial institutions by printing as much money as required; and

(3) Aggressively reduce interest rates.

Do any of you truly believe that this solution can have a happy ending? By acting irresponsibly, the U.S. Federal Reserve created a façade of economic health; however, in the long-term, their poor short-term decisions will create massive problems.

Strong and continued currency inflation will always invoke a couple of reactions:

1. Wealth will be stored not in domestic currencies but in non-monetary assets or in a relatively strong foreign currency to maintain Purchasing Power Parity (PPP); and

2. Monetary and trade transactions occur in a foreign stable currency, not the domestic currency.

Certainly condition (1) has been executed, at least among savvy investors, for many years now with the accumulation of foreign currencies as well as the accumulation of lots of gold, silver and real estate in emerging and developing countries. Condition (2), started to appear at the end of 2007. I've encountered a few U.S. owned merchants online that now request payment in other currencies other than the US dollar as the default currency of payment. In addition, at various points and time throughout 2007 & 2008, it was widely reported that US merchants in New York City routinely posted signs stating "Euros accepted" in their store windows.

This brief examination of history has led me to one conclusion: I believe that the only action that would be able to save the dollar right now is its replacement with a new currency, much like the German papiermark was replaced by the Rentenmark after the German Reichsbank's hyperinflation monetary policy caused the utter collapse of the German mark.

However, given that political deals struck between the U.S. government and OPEC back in 1973 ensured the dollar its role in international trade as the de facto international currency, replacing the dollar with an alternative American or North American currency, i.e. the Amero, would be a monumentally difficult task.

For now, the only conclusion that I can logically draw from my brief examination of history is that unless a grand scheme is hatched to replace the U.S. dollar with another currency, great fortunes in gold and gold stocks are waiting on the horizon as well as in other select commodities as we end 2008 and enter 2009 (which we disclose in our Platinum Level SmartKnowledgeU™ online membership). Even if a replacement currency scheme is hatched, if initiated by the United States, this scheme will be monumentally difficult to implement unless the new currency is backed by gold.

Thus one should interpret any short-term corrections in gold and gold stocks for the time being (as we begin 2009) only as opportunities to add to existing positions.

15

CONDITIONS THAT WILL FEED THE GOLD BULL

The continuing decline of the U.S. dollar and a loss of faith in other major fiat currencies such as the Euro, the Pound Sterling, and the Yen (especially as the European Central Bank, the Bank of England, and the Bank of Japan continue to create more Euros, Pound Sterlings, and Yen out of thin air as their solution to injecting liquidity into liquidity-starved markets) will be the major driver of the continuing gold bull run. Most bull runs occur in 3 stages. (1) The initial stage of this current gold bull run occurred from 2002 to 2005, when gold and gold stocks shot up in price and valuation very rapidly. This first stage was then followed by (2) A consolidation phase which occurred from the latter half of 2006 through most of 2007; The third stage, the stage that has yet to run its course, is (3) The mania stage, a stage that often exceeds the first stage as far as profitability is concerned. Originally I have believed that the 3rd state, the mania stage would start at some point in 2008.

However, the mania stage was temporarily delayed by the temporary interruption of the fraudulent stage (I will discuss this in more detail in Chapter 17). Certainly all the macroeconomic factors were in place for the mania stage in gold to begin in 2008 but it did not happen due to massive intervention in gold markets by the US Federal Reserve and US Treasury.

My beliefs about the mania phase in gold beginning in 2008 were partially based upon the 3-yr chart pattern formation of the HUI index that existed as we entered 2008 (the HUI is the unhedged gold mining stock index that trades on the American Stock Exchange). The HUI chart at the beginning of 2008 mimicked those that gave way to a meteoric 135% return of the HUI during the 1st stage of this gold bull run.

In addition, at the beginning of 2008, I expected money that fled a devaluing Euro as well as money withdrawn from Chinese stock markets to find its way into gold. The setup seemed almost perfect for the start of the gold mania phase in 2008 and indeed for the first three months of 2008, both the price of gold and gold stocks absolutely soared as the monetary crisis deepened. However, as the US dollar struggled for its very survival, the soaring prices of gold and gold stocks unnerved the US Federal Reserve and they intervened in free markets to engineer a temporary collapse in the price of gold and gold stocks. So at the start of 2009, though we have had a temporary setback to the bull run in gold, the gold bull is still very much intact.

An interesting point to note as we enter 2009 is that in addition to continuing strong global investment demand for physical gold (currently India and Japan are #1 and #2 in the world in private ownership), strong increased demand from Asian Central Banks should continue to manifest itself in the coming years as well.

In 2006, Central Banks in China and Japan held less than 2% of their combined USD $1.75 trillion of foreign currency reserves in gold, and instead, as of the end of 2008, still hold huge amounts of an asset that constitutes the world's biggest bubble - US Treasury bonds and dollars.

Read the above statement again, because the first time I uncovered this fact I was amazed. In 2006, the central banks of China and Japan held less than 2% of a combined USD $1.75 trillion of reserves in gold. Due to China's creation of a non-transparent Sovereign Wealth Fund in 2007, basically a private, state-owned and state-run fund, it is difficult to know exactly what these figures are today. As of the end of 2007, China had already begun the process of moving tranches of $200 billion out of its Central Bank reserves and into its Sovereign Wealth Fund.

When analyzing the fate of the U.S. dollar, the media often solely focuses on China and its massive amounts of dollar-denominated holdings, overlooking the private, non-reportable Sovereign Wealth Funds of the OPEC Gulf Nations. To do so is a huge mistake. The UAE and Abu Dhabi alone were rumored to hold more than $700 billion in their Sovereign Wealth Fund at the beginning of 2008. Obviously, if large percentages of these Sovereign Wealth Funds move into gold, or have moved into gold, as the dollar crisis grows deeper (and this would likely happen off the radar screens of the mainstream media), gold could seemingly explode in price literally overnight.

The Many Ways to Invest in Gold

There are many different ways to invest in gold so be careful NOT to be misled by the commercial investment industry into believing that gold ETFs (exchange traded funds) are the best way to invest in gold. Gold ETFs may be the easiest, most convenient way to invest in gold but as far as potential returns, gold ETFs may be one of the absolute worst ways to invest in gold, especially in a taxable account. Here is a partial list of the many different ways to invest in gold: gold coins, gold bullion, gold ETFs, gold certificates, gold futures, gold mutual funds, gold land companies, gold royalty companies, gold producers, gold developers, and gold explorers. Unfortunately, because gold still remains the most misunderstood asset class of all time, the great majority of investors will still miss out on the huge gold boom that is on its way as of year-end 2009.

To illustrate just how misunderstood this asset class is, during 2000-2003, the worst three performance years in the U.S. stock market since the Great Depression, when NASDAQ lost 78% of its value and the S&P 500 index nearly lost half of its value, only one asset class made a fortune for its investors. This asset class was gold. Still, during this time period, of the entire pool of money invested in U.S. stocks, less than 1% was invested in gold stocks. As I have explained earlier in this book, much of the lack of interest in gold and gold stocks originates from misinformation campaigns from the commercial investment industry that fear massive losses of assets under management should their clients become educated about the merits of investing in gold during financial crises. The bottom line stipulates that the commercial investment industry can still be extremely profitable even if 100% of their clients lose money. However they cannot be profitable if assets leave the firm.

If you wish to make a profit from this imminent dollar crisis, I highly recommend that you learn how to properly evaluate precious metal stocks. Precious metal stocks do not behave like traditional stocks so using traditional means of analysis like PEG ratios and so forth often have little utility in helping one determine what are the best precious metal stocks to purchase. Furthermore, precious metal stocks demonstrate seasonal patterns that must be utilized to identify low-risk, high-reward entry points. I have developed many proprietary charts and graphs only available at my website, http://www.smartknowledgeu.com, to help the savvy investor understand how best to make a fortune from this impending crisis. Furthermore, I devote a number of online courses (in my Platinum Membership) that teach you how to identify the best precious metal stocks destined for legendary returns as this monetary crisis deepens. During the coming gold mania, out of the hundreds of precious metal stocks, only a few dozen will make serious money. Thus, it is imperative to learn how to properly invest in precious metal stocks and not to rely on an investment advisor that is a newbie in precious metal stock investing and is merely jumping on the bandwagon along with everyone else.

Throughout this book, I have advocated becoming involved in your investment life as one of the sure ways to ensure that you will make a profit from this impending crisis. Oddly enough, the overwhelming majority of people in a critical aspect of wealth building, the management of their investment portfolios, actively choose to be spectators. I use the words "actively choose", because it is a choice. Many investors rationalize to themselves that it is not a choice. I've heard all the excuses. I'm too busy. I don't have any free time. I work too much. Or the worst one of them all – "I don't know how" as if the lack of knowledge is a permanent condition that cannot be altered. As investors, if we are truly serious about building wealth, then we will make the time to be active in the management of our stock portfolios instead of leaving the management of our portfolios to someone that quite frankly, probably knows little more about how to pick stocks than your next door neighbor. Let me illustrate the disadvantages of being a spectator.

If you were a spectator, you were likely to have believed the Goldman Sachs warning in November 2007 to short gold in 2008. In fact, they went so far as to call shorting gold one of their very top 10 plays for 2008, which would imply that they believed gold was likely to suffer a very steep downward spiral. Perhaps that is why I read so many analysts predicting $500 an ounce gold after Goldman issued their announcement through many media channels. After all, if the premier Wall Street firm believed gold was going to crash, then there was no way many of the world's top analysts were going to bet against this belief.

If you are a spectator, you are likely to believe commercial investment firm's analysts that still rate the best precious metal stocks in the world (as of January 2008) as "speculative" buys. In January, 2008 I read an analyst's report regarding one of the best precious metal stocks in the world and he had actually downgraded it from a "speculative" buy to "hold". Commercial investment firms, because they don't follow precious metal stocks, confuse the volatility of these stocks for elevated risk characteristics and thus, due to their ignorance, grade them as "speculative." Instead of rating them as speculative, they should be telling you to hold them as mainstays of your portfolio, despite their volatile nature, for the next several years. Despite the volatility that gold stocks underwent in 2008, if you understand this monetary crisis, you will understand that you will be rewarded in the future (2009, 2010 and beyond).

If you are a spectator, you are likely not to benefit as much as you should even if you are invested in precious metal stocks. Why? Just see the above paragraph. If you want good advice, you'll have to DIY (Do It Yourself) or seek the guidance of a firm that specializes in precious metal stocks but certainly not the guidance of a commercial investment firm.

What if you are a participant? If you are a participant, you will understand that in investing, as Warren Buffet stated, risk only comes from not knowing what you are doing. Most commercial investment firms have no clue as to what they are doing when it comes to investing in traditional stocks let alone precious metal stocks. Remember that their concern is only to gather assets, not to maximize your returns. Some of the greatest profits I have made by playing call options on precious metal stocks in the range of 300% to 500% have come after a major commercial investment firm downgraded the stock to hold or sell (call options make money when the stock rises). I probably need say no more regarding this matter.

Also, remember the chapter in which I warned you not to pay any attention to the financial media? February of 2008 provided a perfect illustration for this warning. In February of 2008, the U.S. government released a report stating that January retail sales increased by 0.3%, a performance that far outperformed analysts' estimates of a dismal -0.2% decrease. Upon this announcement, the Dow Jones Industrial Average index rallied almost 200 points that same day. Almost immediately after the release of this statistic, articles flooded the media hailing the resiliency of the U.S. economy and the possibility that this report could mark the turnaround of the U.S. economy. However, if one just took a few minutes to dig below the surface, here's what we would have discovered. According to the U.S. Department of Commerce, the savings rate in the U.S. was -.0.4% in 2005. The savings rate in the U.S. was -1.0% in 2006. As of the printing of this book, the figures are not yet out for FY2007, but you can bet the bank that they are negative and look worse than the 2006 figures. **The only other two years in American history when savings rates were negative were 1932 and 1933 during the Great Depression.** Thus, if Americans are currently spending more than they are earning, and retail spending is increasing, this can only mean that Americans are going further into debt. Is this really healthy? And should this really be spun as a "positive" development for the U.S. economy? I don't think so.

So again, be aware that almost every report regarding any key economic indicator in any country can be spun as a positive story. However, just because a positive story appears in the mainstream news, this does not mean that everything is "okay" beneath the surface. Just remember that when the Great Depression hit the United States and spread throughout the world in 1929, everything had appeared rosy on the surface. US stock markets had risen for 10 straight years and unemployment, at less than 1%, was at an all time low. Then unemployment skyrocketed to 25% almost overnight. The same scenario and fragility exists in the global economy today that may cause similar breakdowns. Today, despite all the media spin of "everything is okay", the cracks below the surface warn of us of an imminent great economic crisis. Prepare now and you can make a fortune.

Feel free to consult us online at our homepage, http://www.SmartKnowledgeU.com, for additional assistance, and good investing.

16

FALSE SOLUTIONS OF 2008 HAVE NOW FAILED AS I PREDICTED

As I prepared this book in early January, 2008 for the printing of its first edition, there was a concerted effort in the media to publicly denounce gold and to sing the praises of the U.S. dollar.

On December 17, 2007, a new U.S. Federal program, the Term Auction Facility (TAF), stated its intent to auction $20 billion of funds to U.S. banks at rates very close to the Fed Funds rate. For those of you unfamiliar with the definitions of the discount rate and the Fed Funds rate, simply explained, the discount rate is the rate at which US banks can borrow directly from the Feds while the Fed Funds rate is the rate at which US banks lend to each other. Banks normally only borrow at the discount rate as a means of last resort, for the discount rate is usually about 50 basis points higher than the Fed Funds rate. At the beginning of 2008, the discount rate was 4.75% and the Fed Funds rate was 4.25%. The monetary crisis worsened so critically in 2008 that the Fed Funds rate has been slashed and burned all the way to 0.00% to 0.25% at the start of 2009, an obvious sign of desperation on behalf of the US Federal Reserve.

Before the introduction of the TAF program, US banks could only borrow directly from the Fed through the discount window at a rate. The TAF program was initiated to allow US banks to borrow directly from the Feds at a much lower rate. At the start of 2009, with the Fed Funds rate at practically 0.00%, the borrowing rate is no longer an issue.

Still, there are several things severely wrong with this program. Number one, the TAF will allow banks to borrow from its program anonymously, thus again favoring the charlatans and greedy financial institutions over the consumer by hiding from the consumer the names of the banks that may need to take advantage of this program due to gaping holes in their financial risk management program. The US Federal Reserve has been petitioned in 2008 by several members of the US media to list the US banks that are secretly borrowing from them under the Freedom of Information Act (FIA) but thus far, have refused to cooperate and disclose the names of these distressed US banks. Secondly, the TAF will accept mortgage-backed securities as collateral for these loans, in essence providing extremely cheap credit to banks at interest rates far lower than they would be able to receive on the open market.

Making easy credit available to the worst offenders of this subprime fiasco is not a reasonable solution. It is quite possible that American banks will not learn from history and follow the path of Japanese banks during the Japanese banking crisis of the 1990s and make even riskier loans with this easy credit in an attempt to quickly recoup some of their huge recent losses in the subprime market. If American banks repeat the mistakes of Japanese banks in the 1990s, this development would plunge the U.S. into an even deeper liquidity crunch.

Intelligent monetary policy would dictate that the U.S. government and the U.S. Federal Reserve act in a manner that is almost in direct opposition to the current policies they are implementing. The proper way to fix a reeling financial system would be to weed out the worst offenders that contributed to the problem, not to bail them out and reward them for a job poorly done. Can you imagine if you, as a private borrower, defaulted on loans and subsequently had your U.S. FICO credit score drop from 750 to 510? Can you then imagine if two weeks later, you received a notice that informed you of a huge cut in your 30-year mortgage interest rate from 6.5% to 1.75%? Not in a million years, right?

However, this is exactly the type of atmosphere that the U.S. Federal Reserve is aiding and abetting right now as their preferred solution to this subprime mess. They have demonstrated a willingness to throw as much money at the problem as is necessary. Who suffers the brunt of the stupidity of this solution? You and me. Such a solution is bound to vastly devalue US dollars meaning that all dollar holders around the world should prepare for a massive loss of purchasing power in the US dollar from 2009 forward. Remember if you have $2 million that purchase less goods and services than $1 million could just five years ago, while your absolute amount of dollars has doubled, your purchasing power (and thus true wealth) has actually decreased. You merely have more dollars because the US Federal Reserve has inflated the currency into worthlessness. This is the illusion of growing wealth that almost all citizens worldwide fall for year after year after year.

From a purely anecdotal level, just this past month, two banks I utilize in the U.S. held cash wires for a ridiculous seven working days. You can read that sentence again because I was not depositing a check of any kind but cash, and two American banks still took a week or longer to grant me access to basically a no-risk deposit of money. Of course, in reality, since the entire global monetary system is fraudulent, even cash that you deposit in a bank today has counterparty risk to default of some kind.

This anecdotal story serves a more significant point than just to amuse or from my perspective, infuriate. The obvious glaring reason why Wall Street tried to convince the international community that there would be an extended dollar rally in 2008 is because much of the U.S. financial system and markets is currently propped up by foreign money. Because other major currencies appreciated so strongly against the U.S. dollar due to the U.S. Federal Reserve's penchant for printing money in the early 2000's, foreign institutions and private investors purchased large quantities of U.S. dollars as they sought to purchase American stocks and real assets such as American companies. As the monetary crisis grew in 2008 and foreigners stopped buying US dollars and dollar denominated assets, the time to run misinformation campaigns became ripe and was eventually manifested in the prediction of 2008 dollar rallies.

In the last edition of this book, I wrote, "Let's look at the dollar rally stories that originated out of the media at the end of 2007 and then I'll deconstruct **how deceptive they are even if a dollar rally appears to happen in 2008.**"

"I am confident that the dollar will have a significant rally next year, especially against the euro and the pound," said Stephen Jen, the London-based head of currency research at Morgan Stanley, who expects the U.S. currency to strengthen to $1.35 [against the Euro] by December 2008. Jim O'Neill, chief economist in London at Goldman Sachs Group Inc., one of the most profitable securities company in the world, stated last week that the narrowing trade deficit will help revive the dollar's allure [in 2008] ("Dollar Bears Poised for Reversal as Deficits Shrink", Min Zeng, Bloomberg, December 3, 2007).

These spin doctors at various investment firms make predictions of dollar rallies without any concurrent predictions of the changes that must accompany a true dollar rally, as if some magical voodoo spell can rally the dollar simply because it has fallen so much. Since these analysts with political agendas provide no analysis of the conditions that must exist for a dollar rally to happen, I will. **Low interest rates, easy credit and massive dollar supply creation have been responsible for creating massive dollar devaluation. Logically then, a reversal of these conditions**

would be necessary, mainly in the form of much higher interest rates that would cause significant money supply contraction. This is what is truly necessary to create a true dollar rally versus the illusion of a rallying dollar.

Let me explain further here because remember above, I stated, "I'll deconstruct **how deceptive the [dollar rally stories] are even if a dollar rally appears to happen in 2008.**" So now that we have seen that "dollar rally" whereby Morgan Stanley's Stephen Jen's prediction last year of the 1.35 dollar to Euro exchange rate has now materialized at the end of 2008, let me tell you why those predictions of dollar strength are full of hot air, just like every other statement any industry person declares.

The dollar rally that occurred at the end of 2008/start of 2009 was a mere illusion. Considering that both the BOE (Bank of England) and the ECB (European Central Bank) vastly increased the respective Pound and Euro money supply in 2007 due to the failures of European banks, this action guaranteed that the Euro and the Pound would weaken in 2008. In relative terms, Euro and Pound Sterling monetary supply creation may have been much greater than U.S. dollar supply creation. I say may, because like the U.S. Federal Reserve, neither the BOE nor the ECB make it easy to figure out how much they are growing money supply. The U.S. Federal Reserve has made it almost impossible to figure out how quickly they are growing money supply. In any event, all three currencies were greatly devalued in 2008. This is a race to the bottom. It is not a dollar rally, but a lesser weakening relative to the devaluation of the Euro and the Pound Sterling.

Let me explain. Money supply of U.S. dollars is measured in M0, M1, M2 and M3 figures. The definitions of these supplies are listed below:

M0: The total of all physical currency, plus accounts at the central bank that can be exchanged for physical currency.

M1: M0 + the amount in demand accounts ("checking" or "current" accounts).

M2: M1 + most savings accounts, money market accounts, and certificate of deposit accounts (CDs) of under $100,000.

M3: M2 + all other CDs, deposits of Eurodollars and repurchase agreements.

On March 23, 2006, the Board of Governors of the Federal Reserve System released this statement: "The [Board] will cease publication of the M3 monetary aggregate. The Board will also cease publishing the following components: large-denomination time deposits, repurchase agreements (RPs), and Eurodollars. The Board will continue to publish institutional money market mutual funds as a memorandum item in this release. M3 does not appear to convey any additional information about economic activity that is not already embodied in M2 and has not played a role in the monetary policy process for many years. Consequently, the Board judged that the costs of collecting the underlying data and publishing M3 outweigh the benefits."

Several things are patently very curious about this statement. If M3 had not played a role in the monetary policy process for many years and it was truly monumentally expensive to collect this data, why had the Federal Reserve continued to collect this data for so many years? Surely, with supposedly some of the brightest economic minds in the world working at the Federal Reserve, someone would have figured this out years ago, and stopped printing this number then, right? Secondly, if M3 numbers play no role in monetary policy, why did Japan dump $18.2 billion of U.S. Treasuries that very month, and why did the world's central banks become so nervous that just two months later, they dumped more dollars than they purchased for the first time in six months? And why to start 2009, has foreign purchases of US Treasury bonds dropped off a cliff?

I, again, do not buy this press release by the Federal Reserve one bit – not even one teeny tiny bit. I believe that the Feds continue to track M3 supply but that they want to keep the rest of the world from knowing. So let's take a look at what M3 supply tracks above and beyond M2 supply – Eurodollars and repurchase agreements.

What are Eurodollars? Many people confuse Eurodollars with Euros. Eurodollars have nothing to do with the Euro. It is just a generic term for all U.S. dollars held at banks outside the United States and not under the jurisdiction of the Federal Reserve. So without the release of M3 figures anymore, it's simply impossible to know exactly how many dollars the U.S. Federal Reserve is printing. The reason for this opacity is obvious. They stopped releasing the numbers because they don't want the public to know exactly how many dollars they are printing and how quickly they are devaluing the dollar. Thus, it all becomes a guessing game.

Though both the Euro and the dollar weakened in 2008, the Euro weakened at a greater clip than the dollar due to factors of monetary supply, the amount of fiat currency supply returning from member banks to the central bank, interest rates decisions, and secret agreements cut among the ECB, BOE and the US Federal Reserve. The only question that remains for 2009 is which currency will fall at a faster pace relative to the other? Thus, until I see US Fed Fund interest rates increased to 10%, 12%, 15% or higher (which of course would then cause a massive housing collapse), I will not believe any of the ludicrous stories being spun about dollar rallies in 2008 nor in 2009.

Remember in the last edition of this book, I wrote, "If this situation plays out like I believe it will, with both the dollar and the Euro losing value but the Euro losing value at a greater clip than the dollar, when smart investors finally realize that no fiat currency is safe, I believe that investors (at least the savvy one) will begin to dump the Euro and the Pound as well. Where do you think this money will ultimately be invested as it seeks a new home? My bet is firmly on gold. Even if the dollar continues to fall more quickly than the Euro, this situation will still bode well for gold." Of course, at the beginning of 2009, again, we know that this prediction of mine has since come true.

This brings me up to silly headline number two, which no doubt contributed to weakness in gold markets that occurred at the beginning of December, 2007. On November 29, 2007, Reuters in London reported that Goldman Sachs advised that "Investors should sell gold in 2008 to take advantage of falling prices as the dollar steadies, naming the strategy as one of its top 10 tips for next year…We would now use a short exposure in gold, expressed in US Dollars, to capitalize on a gradual relaxation of credit concerns in the financial sector over the coming months, and as an avenue to benefit from the prospect of a stabilization in the US Dollar." Given that Goldman Sachs is basically an extension of the U.S. Treasury, I interpreted this as a purely politically motivated statement. Now in hindsight, with the third edition of this book printed a full year after the first edition, we can see how silly that comment truly was. Goldman Sachs stated, "to capitalize on a gradual relaxation of credit concerns in the financial sector over the coming months," short gold. We all saw how much concerns about the credit worthiness of US banking institutions disappeared in 2008 just as Goldman Sachs predicted, right?

Less than one week after Goldman Sachs made this statement, Saudi Arabia's finance minister stated that no public declaration of any Gulf Nation's decision to cut its peg to the U.S. dollar should ever be made, for it might create, in his own words, a "dollar collapse". Given the disparate nature of these two comments that were made only one week apart, this begs the question, "How can finance ministers of Gulf Nations believe that a simple move such as the unpegging of Middles Eastern currencies from the U.S. dollar would cause its imminent collapse while U.S. Wall Street players are so confident that the U.S. dollar will experience significant sustainable rallies in 2008?" Politics, my friend, is the answer. Though gold immediately dropped $11 an ounce based upon that announcement, it has since risen much higher since then, even with the engineered massive correction in 2008.

In conclusion, let's take a look at some graphs that will visually expose the many shenanigans being reported today. Although I have updated my outlook for 2009 in the third edition of this book, I have left the commentary about previous years in this chapter as I believe that reviewing old commentary can remind us all of some very important lessons. Remember that before 2008, the consensus among all the industry experts, including even those based in Europe, was that the dollar had fallen too low and would experience a sustained rally all throughout 2008. Let's start by observing the 3-yr. chart of the U.S. dollar at the end of 2007/ beginning of 2008, for the bounce that existed then was the impetus behind all the dollar rally predictions.

I have circled previous dollar rallies on this chart, some much stronger and longer in duration than this current rally that was supposed to trigger gold's death and revive the dollar in 2008. As much as has been made of the dollar "rally" at the end of 2008 and the start of 2009, the "rally" is so weak that it has barely taken the dollar above the critical 3-yr floor that was broken in the latter half of 2007. At the start of 2009, the dollar rally took the USD to about 86 on the above chart and I would be surprised if it did not fizzle out at somewhere around 88 or before then.

Just Google the periods of time when dollar rallies occurred in the chart above and you will find loads of articles hailing the revival of the dollar that were very similar in nature to the propaganda being spread at the beginning of 2008. In 2008, we did not experience the sustained rallies in the USD that were predicted but instead experienced massive rallies of 16% in a few weeks that were followed by massive crashes of near 13% in a few weeks. This type of volatile behavior in the USD is indicative of the level of manipulation that is occurring in currency markets and the attempt of the Feds and the US Treasury to prop up the US dollar. Again, always remember that the big players in financial markets can manipulate markets to act accordingly in the short-term because of the preponderance of uneducated investors in the market that willingly follow their deceptive advice. However, long-term trends will always resume.

Next, let's look back at my gold predictions in the first edition of this book at the end of 2007. At that time, I included the 3-yr charts for gold futures contracts below. At the end of 2007, I noted that the chart looked extremely similar to the formations that preceded the last great gold bull run.

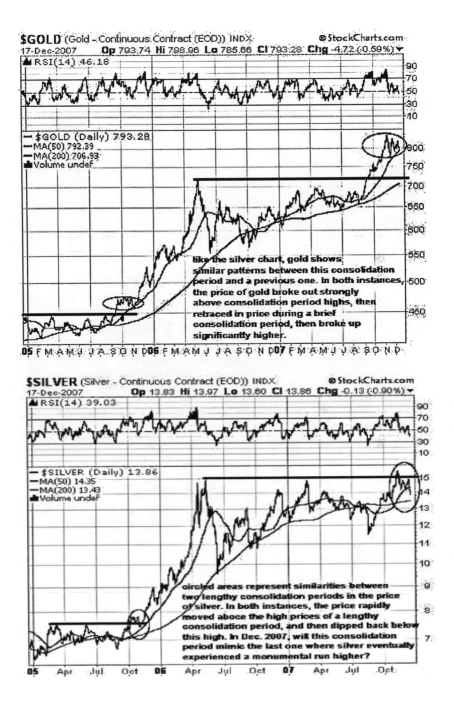

If we looked at the chart for silver at the end of 2007 (on the previous page), as was evident in the chart for gold, I again noted marked similarities between chart formations back then (that I have circled) and those that immediately preceded the last great bull run in silver. Again, as I will explain in Chapter 17 of this book, both runs higher for gold and silver were interrupted through massive US central bank intervention into the gold and silver markets in 2008 but should get back on track at some point in 2009, and firmly back on track. In the first edition of this book, I also included the chart for unhedged gold stocks, the HUI index, at the beginning of December, 2007.

Back then, we saw a picture that slightly deviated from the long-term outlook of the underlying commodity of gold. When we looked at the 3-yr chart of the HUI back then, we saw that the HUI gold stock index broke through its 18-month support level at the beginning of December, 2007, never a good sign. However, my exact words back then were that "the HUI, at this point, should experience strong support only 13 points away from its current level of 374 at the 200-day SMA of 361. At the very least, this 200-day SMA support level should be one that the HUI index will rapidly return to should it break below it (as it did last August, 2007 as illustrated in the above chart)." As this is the third edition of my book, updated as of January 2009, we now know this prediction did indeed come true, with the HUI immediately skyrocketing to above 500 over the first three months of 2008.

Even of greater relevance however was the strong continuing performance of gold and silver against the Euro. For many years, Europeans have complained that gold was not as great an investment for holders of Euros versus holders of dollars due to the Euro's relative strength against the dollar. This certainly was a valid argument. However, as we end 2008 and enter 2009, not only has gold strengthened considerably against the Euro but so has silver.

Given that the fundamental long-term outlook of gold and silver is so positive, here are some important support levels to take note of as of early 2009. Remember that just a short time ago, investors in gold were hailing the fact that gold broke above $700 an ounce. In fact, a mere 15 months ago, in September of 2007, gold was trading at about $680 an ounce when I predicted that gold would reach $850 an ounce before the end of the year (at a Dollar Crisis workshop I conducted at the Pan Pacific Hotel in Asia).

Back then, $850 an ounce in such a short time frame seemed impossible, and as such, my prediction elicited much skepticism. Although I still see $700 gold as the new "floor" for gold prices at the beginning of 2009, if gold can climb to and break above $900 for much of 2009 as I believe it will, the $900 figure, and possibly even $1,000, may supercede $700 as the new floor. Just remember, strong bouts of volatility are the norm for gold and you should expect continuing volatility in 2009 as this monetary crisis deepens. However, any strong pullback in gold from its present January 2009 $840 an ounce price will only present a strong buying opportunity.

As for silver, the upside in silver in 2009 may even be greater than that for gold. Still, gold is the number one alternative money to fraudulent fiat money in my humble opinion.

For up-to-the-date analysis of precious metal markets from 2009 forward, consider scheduling one of my one-on-one private consultations, a subscription to my investment newsletter, Crisis Investment Opportunities, or a subscription to our Platinum Membership. Details regarding all three services are available in the final Appendix of this book. Of course, you have other options other than my company, but I would strongly urge you to avoid seeking guidance from any mainstream commercial investment company. Find someone that has been a gold and monetary expert with at least 5-10 years of experience in this field and they should be able to guide you through the very trying years of 2009, 2010 and 2011 with flying colors. Having digested all the information contained in this book, I sincerely hope that you are now firmly on your way to building a fortune in the stock market in the coming years.

17

THE TRUTH ABOUT THE GROWING 2009 MONETARY CRISIS

As we head into 2009, everything I wrote in the first edition of this book still remains valid. Gold and a very few other select assets are firmly where you want your money. But first let's take a look at my predictions for 2008 and how they panned out. I stated that gold stocks should reverse on December 17, 2007 (note the date on the chart on the following page) when the HUI gold bugs index was at 375. In fact, gold stocks immediately reversed, with the HUI index soaring 38.67% to 520 by March of 2008.

I stated, "The crisis we are entering in 2008 is not a subprime crisis [as was being stated by the major world media back then]. It is a monetary crisis, specifically a Dollar Crisis, that will spread like the flu and afflict the Euro and the Pound Sterling as well...Until investors realize that we are firmly in a Dollar Crisis, and not a subprime crisis, liquidity crisis, or a solvency crisis, they remain at much larger risk of having their portfolios decimated during this crisis." When I made this prediction, those in the mainstream media ridiculed this prediction, stating that the US dollar would rally all throughout 2008 and that the Euro and Pound would retain their strength as well. However, these experts again failed to realize that we were, and still are in a monetary crisis, and that from a fundamental standpoint, the Euro, the Pound Sterling, the Yen, or any other paper currency, is no better than the US dollar. Though the Euro remained strong for the bulk of 2008, when the monetary crisis gained more steam towards the end of 2008, the Euro plunged nearly 24% against the dollar in a matter of weeks.

The Pound Sterling fared even worse, holding up for the first half of 2008, but then plunging by nearly 30% in value against the dollar during the last half of 2008.

Given that my above predictions came true, then how could the HUI possibly have collapsed in late 2008 all the way to 150 before doubling quickly to 300 to start 2009? Did the collapse in 2008 of gold signal the end of the 7-year gold/silver bull run as many US investment industry experts stated during the collapse? Hardly. All we need to do to discover the answer to this question is to look at the physical market for gold in 2008 - the real physical market, not the fraudulent paper one that was interfered with, mangled, and manipulated in the New York COMEX futures markets by the US Federal Reserve and the US Treasury Department.

In November 2008, Perth Mint sales and marketing director Ron Currie reported, "One European client purchased 30,000 ounces [of gold] for $33 million." Given that the price of paper gold was between $720 and $820 for all of November, it is interesting that an individual was willing to pay $1,100 an ounce to obtain physical gold. And stories like this were more common than rare. So how could gold stocks have collapsed (temporarily) in the second half of 2008 even as the monetary crisis was growing worse? Shouldn't the opposite have occurred? Shouldn't have gold and associated gold stocks risen strongly as US and European banks were teetering on the verge of collapse in the latter half of 2009?

One only need look no further than then $50 billion Bernie Madoff fund Ponzi scheme fraud that occurred in US equity markets for your answers. The Wall Street Journal reported on December 13, 2008 that "Harry Markopolos, who years ago worked for a rival firm, researched Mr. Madoff's stock-options strategy and was convinced the results likely weren't real. 'Madoff Securities is the world's largest Ponzi Scheme,' Mr. Markopolos wrote in a letter to the U.S. Securities and Exchange Commission in 1999. Mr. Markopolos pursued his accusations over the past nine years, dealing with both the New York and Boston bureaus of the SEC, according to documents he sent to the SEC reviewed by The Wall

Street Journal." Upon learning this information, the Wall Street Journal stated, "the SEC's failure is business as usual. The real news would be a case when the SEC did prevent a fraud."

So what does Madoff have to do with plunging gold and silver prices during the third quarter 2008? The answer is that the same fraud that has been enabled in US stock markets for years has also been enabled in US commodity markets. The CFTC's (the Commodities Futures Trading Commission) failure to prevent fraud in gold, silver and oil markets in 2008 is business as usual. The real news, in commodities, would be when the CFTC did prevent a fraud. Just as the SEC appeared to aid and abet massive fraud in the stock market, it is my belief that massive fraud has occurred for a very long time in the NY COMEX futures markets for silver and gold. As has been the case with the Bernard Madoff fraud, it is also my belief that very little is currently being done to try to end this fraud.

Fraud in the paper futures markets for silver and gold would, of course, explain why prices in the paper futures market for gold collapsed at the same time private investors were paying record prices for the real physical stuff in 2008. The perpetrators of this fraud have consistently been able to maintain their fraudulent ways by convincing the masses that all claims of fraud are made by crazy conspiracy mongers. By embarking on a constant campaign of disinformation and discrediting, the fraud perpetrators have been able to bamboozle the entire world and successfully and continually marginalize the well-researched and supported fraud claims of gold and silver investors. Label them as conspiracy mongers and you immediately discredit them. Only until recently have the fraud perpetrators such as Madoff been exposed and the "crazy conspiracy mongers" redeemed in their claims.

Though fraud in financial and gold/silver markets has been widespread for decades now, the realization and exposure of this fraud today has thankfully become so widely discussed that even mainstream financial icons are finally jumping on the "fraud" bandwagon. In the past, even when fraud was obvious to anyone with an understanding of how markets truly work, mainstream icons were always strongly hesitant to make any public accusations for fear of being labeled as a conspiracy loony and subsequently banished to investment purgatory. Today, fraud is so rampant and so obvious that mainstream icons no longer fear making such public statements.

It is my strong belief that a criminal, fraudulent scheme hatched by the US Federal Reserve and the US Treasury, led by US Treasury Secretary Hank Paulson, was solely responsible for the severe decline in gold, silver and the associated precious metal stocks during the second half of 2008. Donald Coxe, the chairman and chief strategist of Harris Investment Management in Chicago and a very well known, respected figure in the international investment scene, publicly attributed the steep gold and silver selloff during the third quarter 2008 to a deliberate destructive plan executed by western financial leaders.

"My attitude is, 'Goddamn it, they're [the US Federal Reserve and the US Treasury] good -- it was brilliant," he stated. I'll admit that the plan was devious, manipulative and certainly required a deep understanding of human psychology to execute, but was it really brilliant? To label such a fraudulent scheme as brilliant is an insult to all investors that were robbed by this fraud. Brilliance is a term I reserve for ethically and morally uplifting plans. To call such a plan brilliant is similar to calling a serial killer that has avoided capture as brilliant for his evasive skill. For manipulative and fraudulent plans, brilliant is a term that I refuse to adopt.

In any event, the steep and rapid selloff in gold and silver that induced panic among even veteran gold and silver investors was almost undoubtedly executed for two reasons. To fool the world regarding the future viability of the US dollar and US Treasury bond and to drive the prices of major US financial stocks higher. As the share price appreciation effect in financial stocks did not last very long, the fraudulent suppression of gold and silver prices was likely executed to grant the most powerful financial executives in the world a short window of opportunity to recoup massive amounts of their personal losses – in other words, it was likely fraud at the highest level.

Though Donald Coxe has stated that he has no direct proof that the US Federal Reserve and the US Treasury colluded to drive down the price of silver and gold and to boost financial stocks during the third quarter 2008, he stated that his belief was based "on conversations with hedge fund managers and on years of watching financial markets". This circumstantial evidence was so incriminating that he stated, "there's no doubt whatever in my mind about what happened." Again, because of Donald Coxe's influential position, I believe he was just being diplomatic in stating that there is no proof.

There is plenty of very damning circumstantial proof of the manipulation, and I discuss this in detail in our members-only online Platinum Modules at http://www.smartknowledgeu.com. For the sake of brevity, I won't go into the details here, but the numbers that provide evidence of fraud exist in the very numbers reported by the Commodities Futures Trading Commission (CFTC). In fact, it is my years of watching gold and silver markets, both paper and physical, that leaves no doubt in my mind that massive fraud was committed in the gold and silver markets in the latter half of 2008. If one considers that the Commercial traders have never been NET long in gold for all seven years of this current gold bull run, then these "experts" are either idiots or have an ulterior motive for their short positions other than profits.

To understand the nature of this fraudulent activity, consider if you gave money to a US equities manager that perpetually shorted the US equity markets as the S&P 500 index rose from 200 in 1986 to 600 by 1996 and did not, for even one day, maintain a net long position in your US stock portfolio during this entire time. You would think that there is no way for a human being to possibly be that stupid, correct? Well this is exactly the fraud that has been happening in US commodity markets for 7 years in a row now. The Commercial traders as a group, have not ONE SINGLE TIME, ever maintained a net long position in gold during 7 years in which gold rose from $250 an ounce to more than $1,000 an ounce. If you can believe that the industry "experts" can be this stupid, I guess I will never ever be able to convince you that massive fraud happens in the US gold and silver COMEX markets.

However, there is a lesson we need to learn from this fraud, and it is this. Because anything paper (stocks, options, futures) can be easily manipulated by the US Federal Reserve and US Treasury (as long as the institutions that aid and abet them are allowed to hold massive short positions in gold without any requirement to purchase the quantities of physical gold to back their shorts), it is imperative to own lots of physical gold. Thus, the next logical question is this. With such manipulation rampant, how can I still be so sure that gold is where your money needs to be in 2009? Quite simply, this crisis is a monetary crisis, and gold as the ultimate form of money, is the only currency that simply has zero counterparty risk. Secondly, we are coming to a tipping point where fraudulent schemes will be increasingly difficult to maintain for a plethora of reasons that I will soon discuss.

This is not to say that fraudulent schemes will lose all efficacy, however, for the majority of people can be duped the majority of the time. Consequently, volatility in gold and silver will remain the norm into the future due to these fraudulent manipulative schemes. As we get closer and closer to the tipping point of this monetary crisis, I believe that the law of diminishing returns will also take effect, as each subsequent manipulative attempt to suppress gold and silver prices, even in the easily-manipulated paper markets, becomes increasingly less effective. For example, the only people in the entire world that now believe that dollar will rally in a sustainable fashion into 2009 and 2010 live in one country only – the United States of America.

With less people believing in fraudulent schemes, their effectiveness will almost certainly wane. I am quite certain that the Federal Reserve would have been very content to see gold/silver stocks and the gold/silver futures markets remain at the artificially low prices they engineered at the end of the third quarter 2008, yet both have rebounded very nicely since these lows even though traditional stock markets around the world continued to struggle tremendously to gain any traction at the end of 2008 heading into 2009.

How to Deal with Excessive Central Bank and Government Meddling into Free Markets

In today's market, government interference in free markets has never been higher, not even since the 1930's. Thus merely studying fundamental and technical patterns will provide no advantage in predicting stock market or precious metals behavior without attempting to anticipate, understand, and predict future government and Central Bank interventions into free markets. All major global stock markets still have significant risk of either floundering for all of 2009 or further significantly declining. Despite the efforts of Central Banks worldwide to print hundreds of billions of currency out of thin air, whether it is yen, euros or dollars, and to inject great monetary supplies into their respective economies, economic resuscitation accomplished by these foolish actions will be hugely negative for the general populace. Here's why.

Any subsequent appreciation in major stock market indexes that occurs as a result of monetary supply expansions will be 100% illusory when it comes to wealth creation. As such appreciation can only be accomplished through massive inflation, even a 30% increase in your stock portfolio will have made you poorer if the currency in which your stocks are denominated has been devalued by your Central Bank by 40%. This is the MYTH of wealth creation that Central Banks utilize to control people and to keep them from revolting during economic downturns. This type of "wealth creation" is in essence pure gangland-style robbery of your wealth.

The only thing that ever matters with currency is its purchasing power. If you have 2 million US dollars in 2009 that purchase less than 1 million US dollars did in 2003, your wealth was actually greater in 2003 with only $1 million. **The absolute quantity or amount of currency you own does not determine your wealth. Ultimately the only thing that matters is your currency's purchasing power.** As I said, if $2 million 2009 dollars can purchase less than $1 million 2003 dollars, your wealth is greater with $1 million in 2003 than it is with twice as much money in 2009. This is a concept you must understand to profit from this growing 2009 monetary crisis.

The Biggest Lie in Modern History

If any of you are shocked by the $50 billion Bernard Madoff Ponzi scheme fraud, you shouldn't be, because we all partake in a much bigger Ponzi scheme that dwarfs the Madoff fraud. The Ponzi Scheme of epic proportions is our global monetary system and the fractional reserve banking system. The fact that Bernard Madoff was a former Chairman of the US NASDAQ stock exchange should not shock you either as the SEC was repeatedly warned that Madoff's scheme was a fraudulent one for nine consecutive years and chose to look the other way. Why should this not shock you? Because many people, including myself, have repeatedly written the Commissioner and staff of the Commodities Futures Trading Commission (CFTC) informing them of fraudulent price suppression schemes against gold and silver that were executed during September, October and November of 2008. While some members of the CFTC have provided written explanations to our concerns, the CFTC has still taken almost *no action* to address our concerns. My belief is that the whole system is rotten to the core and that US "regulators" either choose to aid and abet fraudulent activity for the benefit of a few or are handcuffed by those above them and not allowed to act.

According to an Associated Press report on December 21, 2008, "Banks that are getting taxpayer bailouts awarded their top executives nearly $1.6 billion in salaries, bonuses, and other benefits last year, an Associated Press analysis reveals. The rewards came even at banks where poor results last year foretold the economic crisis that sent them to Washington for a government rescue. Some trimmed their executive compensation due to lagging bank performance, but still forked over multimillion-dollar executive pay packages…Benefits included cash bonuses, stock options, personal use of company jets and chauffeurs, home security, country club memberships and professional money management, the AP review of federal securities documents found. The total amount given to nearly 600 executives would cover bailout costs for many of the 116 banks that have so far accepted tax dollars to boost their bottom lines."

But the above story just amounts to bankers' greed and robbery. There is a much bigger story than this greed and theft. When I tell people that the global monetary system is one big Ponzi scheme, most will deny it right away, even if they are not employed in the banking or finance industries. They will state that a bank is not the same as a Ponzi scheme because they take your money and they actually invest it, while it is alleged that Madoff took peoples' money, never invested it, and merely used other investors' money to pay other investors his stated returns. However, if you understand how a bank truly works, you will realize that a bank's operations are even worse than a Ponzi scheme. First of all, why should there be any risk to any money you deposit in a bank? After we have witnessed many bank failures worldwide in 2008, and with our deposits only insured up to a certain amount in the largest US banks, all of us have realized that banks are not fail-safe depositories anymore. So from where does this risk originate?

To understand the answer to this question, you must know that if you have a large amount of money on deposit at a bank, that it is no longer there. If you have $500,000 on deposit at a bank, if you walked in today, unannounced, and wished to withdraw $400,000, I can guarantee you that most banks would not be able to give it to you on the spot. I have heard stories where major US banks couldn't even provide as little as USD $7,000 to someone that walked into a branch unannounced. So if the banks don't have the money, where does it go? After all, when a large percent of the Madoff funds was called in for redemption by investors, and Madoff could not provide the redemptions, Madoff's fraud was finally revealed.

So what does happen to your money once it's deposited in a bank? The US Federal Reserve, the privately owned US Central Bank, has systematically changed reserve requirement regulations over the past decade that now free most every major commercial US banks from any reserve requirement constraints. Thus, if you deposit $1,000,000 with most major US banks and they direct that money into a money market fund, they can then lend out almost every dime of your money. So today, whether you get your deposited money back from a US bank is contingent upon Joe the Plumber or Bill the Real Estate Magnate making good on the repayment of their loans. In essence, the money that you deposited as CASH may now have counterparty risk to Joe the Plumber and Bill the Real Estate Magnate. If enough Bills and Joes default on the loans that were made to them with your money, the bank may have to take another customer's money to pay you the amount you want to withdraw. Sounds more and more like a Ponzi scheme, doesn't it?

But what happens if instead of having many Joes and Bills default on their loans, the bank invested your money in subprime mortgage backed assets that are now worthless? (1) You may lose some of the money you deposited because the US Federal Deposit Insurance Corporation (FDIC) only guarantees $250,000 of your deposit; or (2) the government may bail out the bank (as was the case with Citigroup) with billions of dollars to allow it to recapitalize its balance sheet. But where does this bailout money come from? Anyway you slice it, the answer is you. Either the money is coming from taxpayer money, which means the bank was able to gamble with house money at no risk to them, or it is coming from freshly printed new money, which expands monetary supply and devalues all money you have on deposit at a bank. As a bank customer, because this process destroys the purchasing power of the money you have on deposit at the bank, YOU are bailing the bank out with your personal money.

Still with me? Well, what happens if the bank is smart and makes money from lending and investing the money you deposited with them? Surely you must win then, right? Think again. You still only receive a measly 0.0% to 1.5% or so on your deposited money and the bank keeps all the profits they make from gambling with your money, hardly a fair deal, right? (though feasibly you could participate a little if you owned the bank stock and the stock appreciates). So what's the best case scenario? In the best case scenario, the bank takes your $1 million deposit and through the fractional reserve banking system, creates anywhere from $10 to $100 million of new money in the form of loans, and the loans are successfully repaid.

Thus, under the best possible case scenario, as a bank customer, the bank will return all of your deposited money to you at some point. However, the money you receive will have lost massive amounts of purchasing power by the time it is returned to you, considering that it is unlikely that you will withdraw all your money within one or two months. Thus, the very process that enables a bank to make profits, that of multiplying monetary supply and creating money out of thin air, actually steals purchasing power from the money that you have on deposit with a bank. If you don't understand that statement, read it again. Remember, the greater the money supply, the less money is worth. Thus, the very process of money creation by which banks earn profits destroys the very purchasing power of your money. Are you beginning to see the fraud of our "modern" banking system now?

If you wonder why you have to pay $6 for a box of cereal when you only had to pay $1.89 for that same box six years ago, it is simply due to the fact that banks continually destroy the value of the money they hold for you by the very nature of how they earn profits for themselves. Why do you think banking CEOs are always among the best paid executives in the entire country no matter what country you live in? It is because the fraudulent monetary system allows them to make easy profits at the expense of every citizen of the country. Their scheme is comparable to the oft-repeated dream, "If I could only skim a few pennies every day from everyone's bank account without them knowing, I would be a multimillionaire in no time." Guess what? Banks have figured out how to do this without your knowledge. The modern day banking system is the enabler of the most massive fraud in history through the rapid expansion of the monetary supply, an act that perpetually devalues the worth of all existing money within the system. Central banks make the policy decisions that lead to monetary base and monetary supply expansion. Inflation is a result of expanding the monetary supply. Thus, compared to the fact that banks perpetually debauch all money you deposit with them, Madoff's Ponzi scheme seems the better choice, does it not?

And that in a nutshell, is why we are experiencing severe housing, stock market, and economic downturns in major economies all over the world. The biggest bubble in the world is the US dollar and US Treasury Bonds. In order to not "pop" this bubble, Central Banks all over the world are expanding monetary supply in accord with the US Federal Reserve and devaluing their currencies as well. The US Treasury and the US Federal Reserve have greatly degraded their balance sheets as a result of this crisis and have traded enormous amounts of the US financial sector's toxic waste for US Treasury bonds.

Since 2008, when these massive bailouts were initiated by Ben Bernanke and Hank Paulson, **the US Treasury has sold about half of its $800 billion Treasury bonds,** and increased their assets from about $850 billion to $2 trillion, with much of the growth in assets comprised entirely of toxic assets from US institutions that currently have very little value in the open market. **The Federal Reserve has done the same thing to their balance sheet, increasing its balance sheet from less than $1 trillion to almost $2 trillion, with almost the entire increase of assets on their balance sheet now comprised of the risky, toxic financial assets**

of US financial institutions. With the US Treasury and US Federal Reserve balance sheets now muddled with so many dirty assets, who in their right minds would continue buying US Treasury bonds and trusting the US dollar? This situation does not bode well for the future of the US dollar.

Furthermore, the leading central banks in the resource rich nations of South America, the Middle East and Asia/the Pacific Rim already realize and understand all of the above issues. They will not continue to buy US Treasury bonds that not only have the counterparty risk of a bankrupt US government but also the counterparty risk of AIG, Fannie Mae, Freddie Mac and Citigroup. The International Business Times reported on November 9, 2008 the following story: "Argentine President Cristina Fernandez announced Thursday that Brazil and Argentina will no longer require bilateral trade to be in U.S. dollars, saying trade in their national currencies will increase regional integration and boost economic growth." Russian's PM Putin has already begun negotiations with China to also halt the use of US dollars in their bilateral trade. There are stories and rumors emanating from many other countries of the same reaction to the US dollar. These actions will eventually be devastating to the US dollar.

So if you can understand that the roots of this crisis are firmly planted in a fraudulent currency and a fraudulent monetary system, you should understand why I still heavily advocate owning physical gold. Please know that all physical gold investments are not equal, however. Physical bars, bullion coins, and rare coins are all better purchases at different points and time in the gold bull cycle. Please seek our help at www.SmartKnowledgeU.com or the help of an independent gold expert to best learn how to safely and intelligently purchase such vehicles. Always remember that it is possible to know what assets to buy during crises, to purchase such assets at the wrong time and sell them at the wrong time, and still lose money.

Inflation versus Deflation?

Remember that the same people that now argue for prolonged deflation throughout 2009, 2010 and 2011 are the very same people that told you that global financial markets were sound and that the crisis had bottomed in 2008. In fact, these are the same people that are still trying to tell people that a tremendous buying opportunity in traditional stocks existed at the end of 2008 (McDonalds, Starbucks, Bank of America, United Airlines, etc.) in the American and European markets.

This alone should tell you that they are not to be believed and that they are part of the same banking cartel that has lied about this crisis for the past 24 months in a row. I believe that this crisis was and is being deliberately manufactured to consolidate power among the Central Bankers, in particular among the families that own the US Federal Reserve, as there is a lot of historical precedent for crises being created specifically to execute "power grabs". Consider the fact that Goldman Sachs and JP Morgan have virtually eliminated all of their competition on Wall Street within the last 12 months and you should not have a hard time believing that statement.

Furthermore, if you do some research regarding the key figures and institutions employed by the US Federal Reserve, the US Treasury, and Wall Street that are intimately tied to destroying all regulations in US markets that would have prevented this crisis from happening, the deliberate planning of this crisis becomes crystal clear. For Alan Greenspan to recently state that "free markets" are the reason behind this crisis is a complete joke. Free markets do not mean lawlessness as even regulations are needed for free markets to operate efficiently. Furthermore, "regulations" that are designed and disguised to protect fraud and greed and to prevent free markets from operating are not regulations at all. This definition covers most regulations that "regulate" major markets today.

Beware, because as the discussion for the need of more "regulations" and the failure of "free markets" are shaped in the media by those in power, know that they will falsely use these arguments to pass more regulations that further degrade your liberties and serve to protect the status quo and perpetuate fraud. At the urging of his friends on Wall Street, Alan Greenspan, as Chairman of the Federal Reserve, promoted lawlessness as he systematically destroyed all regulations of the Glass Steagall act (a law enacted after the Great Depression to prevent financial crises from happening). Today, he shamefully uses "free markets" as the "fall guy" for the very crisis that he specifically played a huge role in creating.

But back to deflation v. inflation. Currently, the US is expanding its monetary base at unprecedented rates, consistently expanding existing facilities like the Term Auction Facilities by hundreds of billions of dollars seemingly every other month, and creating new facilities like the Commercial Paper Funding Facility (CPFF, created to provide support to the trillions of commercial paper that may be toxic and that need to rollover every 30-45 days); the Money Market Investor Funding Facility (MMIF), the Asset-Backed Commercial Paper Facility; and the Money Market Mutual Fund Liquidity Facility that cumulatively back trillions of dollars of their related investment vehicles. If you never have heard of these facilities, don't worry, the leading global central banks are well aware of these facilities and the possibility that trillions of dollars will likely have to be printed to fund these facilities. Even if the new money printed to fund these facilities merely replaces "bad" money and thus does not expand money supply, do you think that other countries will want to continue purchasing dollars when they see how inherently faulty the US dollar is?

Remember, the creation of all these facilities to support touted "safe" investment vehicles like Money Market Funds is unprecedented. Many analysts pointed to the strengthening dollar and the associated decline in commodity prices as proof that deflation is here to stay but again this is much more propaganda than truth. As 2009 progresses, additional money will most likely continually need to be fed to bloated carcasses like AIG, Citigroup, Fannie Mae and Freddie Mac as well as to other huge companies on the brink of failure. Does anyone even care that the original $85 billion that Hank Paulson promised to AIG ballooned to $123 billion before the end of 2008, with reports that AIG was still in serious trouble and that 75% of that bailout money was allegedly already gone?

And does anyone really believe that Hank Paulson's measly bailout estimate for Fannie Mae and Freddie Mac won't balloon into multiples of that original estimate in the near future? Furthermore, where is the US government getting their trillions of dollars to fund the still ongoing Iraq/Afghanistan war? The answer, of course, is directly from the US Treasury and their printing presses. The money to fund war is NEW money. And despite these numerous deflationary arguments, what is the REAL story? The real story is that real inflation in the US, as reported by shadowstats.com, is still growing at or above a double-digit rate annually. That doesn't seem like deflation to me.

Finally, what is most important to understand, as the global media exceedingly fails to properly explain this crisis, is that this crisis is a monetary crisis, period. Out of this monetary crisis sprung the derivatives crisis, the subprime crisis, they housing crisis and the global stock market crises. Without an unsound monetary system based upon currency that can be printed out of thin air with only cotton paper and ink as the restricting inputs, wildly irresponsible monetary expansion that created all these other crises would not have been possible. Do you really think a bloated $600+ trillion derivatives market would have been created in the presence of a sound global monetary system?

Some of the above crises that have moved away from the forefront of media attention will once again return in very unwelcome fashion in 2009. For example, remember that the Bush administration's goal that will be out of office on January 20, 2009 was to get out of dodge before this whole thing blew up as evidenced by many of their actions. US Treasury Secretary Hank Paulson froze resets on subprime ARMS until 2009. When massive quantities of subprime ARMS reset in 2009, we will have to revisit a problem that has all but disappeared from financial talk shows already – the US housing crisis. Secondly, US regulators postponed requiring financial institutions to mark their toxic assets to "market" until the end of 2009. Thus, at the start of 2009, many major US financial institutions continue to mark Level 2 and Level 3 toxic assets at fantasy valuations that they will never receive except when they are asleep and dreaming. When these institutions have to come clean and honestly report their balance sheets (and at some point they will), another crisis will arise. And how will the US Feds respond to these new "old" crises returning to the forefront again? If history is accurate, they will print and print and print more money. So is deflation likely? No.

The reason now a lot of the charlatans are claiming that deflation will overrule inflation is because they claim that the hundreds of billions, and eventual trillions of dollars the US Treasury is printing right now, while expanding the monetary base like never before, will not expand monetary supply. Why would it not be expanding monetary supply? The charlatans claim that the monetary supply will not expand because the trillions of dollars being printed are only replacing the $30 or so trillions of dollars that were destroyed in global financial markets. For example, consider United Steelworkers President Leo Gerard's analysis of US Secretary Treasury Hank Paulson's $850 billion Wall Street bailout plan here

http://assets.usw.org/News/GeneralNews/paulson-letter-final.pdf

Certainly, Mr. Gerard does a fine job of pointing out how this taxpayer money will not produce new loans that will resuscitate the economy but rather go directly into the pockets of Hank's Wall Street friends. I know the number one argument in support of deflation is the fact that $30 trillion in global stock market capitalization has just been destroyed. Thus the argument pushed forward by deflationists at the start of 2009 is the following: Who cares if the US Federal Reserve has just expanded monetary base by an insane estimated $8+ trillion dollars when $30+ trillion in stock market capital has just been destroyed? The deflationists argue that this new money will merely replace some of the $30 trillion that was destroyed and that it will not end up in the monetary supply. My biggest problem with that argument is the following.

If that $8+ trillion was given back to hard-working citizens that were defrauded out of this money, then presuming this money would have remained invested in stock markets and other financial derivatives, the addition of this money would not have inflated monetary supply. However, this is not what happened nor what will happen. The cumulative bailout money has been given to failing automotive companies, failing insurance companies, failing mortgage companies, and most importantly failing financial institutions. Continuing to support financial institutions that deserve to collapse is not only amoral because it spends hundreds of billions of taxpayers' money with zero visible benefit to taxpaying investors, but it **PROLONGS** the crisis.

Letting firms collapse that deserve to collapse is the ONLY solution that can make a weak financial sector stronger in the future. How will financial institutions that are teetering on the edge of bankruptcy raise enough capital to continue operations? As I've explained before, financial institutions make money by expanding the monetary supply through loan creation. Thus, lending the bailout money they received to the public and expanding monetary supply is almost inevitable. Thus it is my strong belief that this current massive expansion in monetary base at the start of 2009 will eventually translate into a massive expansion of monetary supply, a hugely inflationary event.

Will Obama Save the US and Global Economies?

In a simple word, no. If you believe President-elect Obama is going to come to the rescue of the global economy like a knight on a white horse, you will be sorely disappointed in 2009. Consider the following:

(1) Obama voted FOR the horrible bailout plan that accomplished less than zero in fixing the global economy while only transferring wealth from people that were defrauded to the very financial executives that defrauded them. This singular action does not bode well as Obama being a President that will champion the rights of the common man over the greed of the elite.

(2) The problems afflicting the global economy have not yet been addressed in any intelligent manner and thus, we are not on the path to recovery; and

(3) No single man, no matter how competent, can fix a monetary crisis that took more than two decades to materialize within a short period of time (with perhaps the exception of re-instituting the gold standard, but it is difficult to fathom that the US will lead the way with this solution).

As a final indicator that no one should ever expect any good to come from any government decisions regarding this crisis, consider that, according to the UK Daily Mail, Goldman Sachs utilized $11-14 billion of the bailout money ex-CEO Hank Paulson allocated to his former firm to pay 2008 year-end bonuses to its 443 partners worldwide.

So with the largest robberies in American history now taking place daily, could the deflationists be right? Most, not all, but most of the deflationists are people that work for the very firms that have been robbing people at will over the past several months. Again, this should provide you with some semblance of guidance as to how much merit you should place in their deflationary arguments. Furthermore, in times when more rhetoric exists than good solid analysis, certain logical points that substantiate an opposing argument tend to get ignored. For example, when is the last time you heard anybody speak about the costs of the ongoing Iraq/Afghanistan war to the United States? The answer was probably sometime around early 2007, a long time ago. Every war in history has been hugely inflationary to the currencies of the major participants of that war and this war has been no different.

To convince people to believe in scenarios that have very little probability of occurring, such as the one of sustained, prolonged, multiyear deflation, the engineers of this crisis even will compare apples to oranges. The deflationists point to Japan as a model of what will happen to the US, claiming that the 0.00% to 0.25% US Fed Funds rate will not cause inflation. As "proof", they state that when the Bank of Japan cut interest rates to zero, these low interest rates failed to encourage Japanese to spend more Yen in the economy and decades of deflation persisted. Yet, there are several critical points that are glossed over in this false comparison. One, the zero interest rate did stimulate growth, just not in Japan. By cutting interest rates to zero, Japan exported inflation to the rest of the world as foreigners borrowed trillions of yen to invest in foreign assets. So, yes the Bank of Japan's zero interest policy stimulated massive growth, **only it contributed to risky investing behavior and caused real estate and stock market bubbles outside of their own country.**

Secondly, all during the time of their zero interest policy, Japan maintained a trade surplus, so foreigners were not worried about a default on the yen given that all paper currencies are only backed by the "full faith and credit" of the issuing government. However, this is not the case for the US dollar. The US Treasury and US Federal Reserve are implementing massive expansions in the monetary base of the US dollar at a time when the US government is bankrupt and running the most massive deficit of any world government in modern history. These two situations are not even remotely similar, so how an intelligent person can conclude that deflation will then be the result in America by looking to Japan's history is beyond me.

Even if deflation wins a temporary battle between deflation and inflation, one battle that will not go away is the monetary crisis. Several critical issues are almost absolutely certain today.

(1) The world's top economic powers are extremely unhappy with how the US Treasury and the US Federal Reserve have manipulated commodity prices for the benefit of the US dollar and their confidence in any asset denominated in dollars is at an all time low. This lack of confidence in US dollar denominated assets has been reflected in their actions to begin 2009, and they are highly unlikely to allow the US Federal Reserve to have the same absolute control over their countries' wealth in the future that they currently maintain.

(2) This monetary crisis is beyond Barack Obama, and there is nothing he can do that will prevent this crisis from becoming worse over the next several years.

(3) This is not a once in an 80-year crisis dating back to the Great Depression, but this is a once in a lifetime crisis that may see the global monetary system as we know it collapse.

(4) This crisis is being misreported by virtually every finance journalist in the world due to an education system that teaches an unsound Keynesian economic model at every top university in the world. Anybody that believes the unsound Keynesian economic model that was educated at Harvard Business School, Oxford, or any other top education institution will have zero understanding of this crisis

(5) Great patience will be required to weather this storm and come out on top. One must remember that the attacks on

gold and silver that occurred in 2008 were the most prolonged and strongest of any during the entire 7-year gold bull run. This points to the fact that the dollar was literally fighting for its life in 2008. One must also remember, if one questions whether such manipulation can continue en perpetuity, that gold and silver always perform during monetary crises. This is undoubtedly a monetary crisis.

(6) Remember the great volatility in gold in the second half of 2008 when we witnessed $60 to $100 an ounce differences within 24-hour periods between the highs in Asian markets and the lows in New York markets. This type of extreme volatility has never before happened in the history of gold markets and it was almost certainly engineered by the US Treasury and US Federal Reserve to confuse you and to lead you into wrong decisions about the US dollar, gold and silver. Keep your eye on macro trends as is delineated NOT by PAPER MARKETS but by PHYSICAL MARKETS for gold and silver, as the physical markets tell a RADICALLY DIFFERENT story than the paper markets that are the target of manipulation by the US Treasury and US Federal Reserve.

(7) Consider the parabolic rise in the US dollar from 77 to 86 on the above chart that occurred at the end of 2008. Normally a 10% increase in a currency's strength over an entire year creates massive problems in global trade and in the global economy. **This was a 16% increase in four weeks!** Nothing short of extraordinary circumstances can create such an unprecedented massive rally in such a short period of time. The extraordinary circumstances were the simultaneous deleveraging of stock markets all around the world that was engineered by the US Treasury and the US Federal Reserve. One must understand that banks, hedge funds and investment firms all borrow US dollars when engaging in risky investment practices. They borrow

massive amounts of a low interest rate currency such as the US dollar to make investments in other foreign denominated (and even other dollar denominated) investments that pay a higher rate of return. When these investments all started to go south, margin calls occurred on hundreds of billions of USD-denominated loans.

Thus, borrowers from all over the world were suddenly forced to sell whatever assets they had, whether they wanted to or not, and they had to BUY dollars to pay back their dollar loans. **In essence, the unwinding of the dollar forward carry trade caused this massive spike in US dollar strength, and it was a forced event, NOT an event that marked the dollar's fundamental strength and a turning point.** This explained the very quick plunge that followed this rise, which again, was followed by more intervention that led to another dollar rise at the beginning of 2009. However, I am very doubtful that this rise to begin 2009 in dollar strength can break through the 88 barrier and expect a strong decline in dollar strength to occur soon at some point in the first quarter of 2009.

I have found over time that most people do not understand the massive leveraging that happens in global currency markets. Over the years, when friends have scrambled out of a plummeting US dollar, I have always advised them to hold physical gold as the best form of currency. Instead, I've often discovered that they chose to invest in whatever foreign currency was paying the highest interest rates at the time. In the past, these financial assets included Asset Backed Commercial Paper (ABCP) denominated in Icelandic Krona or Australian Dollars due to the at-the-time high interest rates of 7% to 13% a year. I often warned my friends that they had better understand the process by how these commercial paper facilities were able to achieve these higher interest rate yields.

I warned them that risky leverage ratios and risky financial investments were likely involved in the higher interest rate equation and that if they didn't understand how this short-term paper was paying such high interest rates, then they should not be buying it. Still, many investors foolishly just chase yield with no understanding of how it is achieved. Of course, as evidenced by the rapid plunge in the strength of the Australian dollar and the Icelandic Krona in 2008 in response to the deleveraging of global markets, those that chose to chase high yields of short-term commercial paper in 2008 were slaughtered.

The Strong Argument for Imminent Massive Global Inflation

Consider these signs from Central Banks all over the world in 2008 that point to imminent expansions of monetary supplies in all major global currencies. Below is a partial list of desperate monetary base expanding actions executed by the US Central Bank, the Federal Reserve, as of the beginning of 2009:

On September 29, 2008, the US Federal Reserve announced the following:

"(1) an increase in the size of the 84-day maturity Term Auction Facility (TAF) auctions to $75 billion per auction from $25 billion beginning with the October 6 auction, (2) two forward TAF auctions totaling $150 billion that will be conducted in November to provide term funding over year-end, and (3) an increase in swap authorization limits with the Bank of Canada, Bank of England, Bank of Japan, Danmarks Nationalbank (National Bank of Denmark), European Central Bank (ECB), Norges Bank (Bank of Norway), Reserve Bank of Australia, Sveriges Riksbank (Bank of Sweden), and Swiss National Bank to a total of $620 billion, from $290 billion previously."

On October 7, 2008, the Feds announced the following:

"the creation of the Commercial Paper Funding Facility (CPFF), a facility that will complement the Federal Reserve's existing credit facilities to help provide liquidity to term funding markets. The CPFF will provide a liquidity backstop to US issuers of commercial paper through a special purpose vehicle (SPV) that will purchase three-month unsecured and asset-backed commercial paper directly from eligible issuers."

On October 13, 2008, the Feds announced the following:

"In order to provide broad access to liquidity and funding to financial institutions, the Bank of England (BoE), the European Central Bank (ECB), the Federal Reserve, the Bank of Japan, and the Swiss National Bank (SNB) are jointly announcing further measures to improve liquidity in short-term U.S. dollar funding markets. The BoE, ECB, and SNB will conduct tenders of U.S. dollar funding at 7-day, 28-day, and 84-day maturities at fixed interest rates for full allotment. Funds will be provided at a fixed interest rate, set in advance of each operation. Counterparties in these operations will be able to borrow any amount they wish against the appropriate collateral in each jurisdiction. Accordingly, sizes of the reciprocal currency arrangements (swap lines) between the Federal Reserve and the BoE, the ECB, and the SNB will be increased to accommodate whatever quantity of U.S. dollar funding is demanded. The Bank of Japan will be considering the introduction of similar measures. Central banks will continue to work together and are prepared to take whatever measures are necessary to provide sufficient liquidity in short-term funding markets."

On October 21, 2008, the Feds announced the following:

"the creation of the Money Market Investor Funding Facility (MMIFF), which will support a private-sector initiative designed to provide liquidity to U.S. money market investors."

From the above cumulative actions, it is apparent that nearly every capital market in the US is breaking down, including markets previously believed to be the safest of safe markets, Money Market Funds. Through an ever expanding Term Auction Facility and a bank lending program whereby US banks borrowed an unprecedented half a trillion dollars a day from the Feds for the week ending October 12, 2008, the Feds have greatly polluted their balance sheet with all kinds of worthless junk (according to Reuters, Banks and dealers' overall direct borrowings from the Fed averaged a record **$437.53 billion per day** in the week ended October 15, 2008 topping the previous week's $420.16 billion/ day).

If we look at the 1-year chart of the 20+year US Treasury bond market I presented on the previous page, it is obvious that there have been large players buying lots of Treasury bonds at the end of 2008. Despite the recent dip, the chart still looks pretty bullish. Thus, you may wonder why I would say that the US Treasury bond market has a strong possibility of collapsing. Given the degradation in the US Treasury balance sheet that I've already discussed, people should be asking, "Who exactly would be buying these bonds and why would they be buying them?" The perception, as reported by the global media in their stories, is that the entire world was buying US Treasuries because of their "safe haven" status, an analysis that is ridiculous, especially given the preponderance of stories outside of the US of countries needing to divest themselves of US Treasuries because of the huge risk of possible default.

So who are these buyers of US Treasuries if they indeed are not major global players as was the assumption, and misinformation, propagated by the financial media? Most likely, the answer is the US financial institutions that received massive amounts of US government bailout money. I suspect that, as of the start of 2009, most US financial institutions have not loaned to the public any of the bailout money they have received because the US Treasury has directed them to buy US Treasuries with their bailout money. Thus this would account for the large spike higher in US Treasury bonds in late 2008. Furthermore, I suspect that the US Treasury has directed US financial institutions to hold US Treasury bonds in an attempt to artificially manufacture a short-term rise in US Treasury bonds in order to fool major foreign holders like China and Japan into believing that the US Treasury bond market is sound and safe. **Just as the US dollar rallies in 2008 occurred on the back of forced deleveraging, I highly suspect that the US Treasury Bond rally in late 2008 and early 2009 occurred on the back of forced purchasing by US banks as directed by the US Treasury and US Federal Reserve.**

But it is not just the US Central Bank and US government that are in deep trouble. Many other major Central Banks have also been printing money like it is going out of style since mid-2008 and at to begin 2009. Consider these stories:

On November 26, 2008, the UK Guardian reported that, "China has slashed interest rates and cut the amount of money banks must set aside as reserves, as it attempts to bolster the economy in the face of the worldwide slowdown. Today's 1.08 percentage point cut, to 5.58%, is the largest reduction for a decade, reflecting the government's increasing alarm at slipping growth rates and its keenness to ensure companies and consumers spend more. This year will end the country's half-decade run of double-digit growth and the World Bank yesterday cut its prediction for GDP growth next year from 9.2% to 7.5%, which would be the lowest rate since 1990."

On December 20, 2008, this story was reported out of Tokyo: "The Japanese cabinet on Saturday approved a 4.8 trillion yen (US$54 billion) second extra budget to finance a massive stimulus package, government officials said. Prime Minister Taro Aso's cabinet plans to submit the budget, for the year to March 2009, to parliament early next year, the officials said. The budget, exceeding the 1.81 trillion yen first supplementary budget, is intended to fund cash handouts, a job-creation scheme and other economic measures in the 26.9-trillion-yen stimulus package unveiled in October."

However, perhaps the most compelling story of them all was the one the London Telegraph reported on January 14, 2009: "The Bank of England will be able to print extra money without having to legally declare it. The government is set to throw out the 165-year-old law that obliges the Bank to publish a weekly account of its balance sheet -- a move that will allow it theoretically to embark covertly on so-called quantitative easing...The ostensible reason for the reform, which means the Bank will not have to print details of its own accounts and the amount of notes and coins flowing through the UK economy, is to allow the Bank more power to overhaul troubled financial institutions in the future, under its Special Resolution Authority...It comes after the Bank's Monetary Policy Committee cut interest rates by half a percentage point, leaving them at the lowest level since the bank's foundation in 1694...The reforms, which are likely to be implemented later this year, will make the Bank of England by far the most secretive major central in the world, experts said. 'Quite why the Bank has to keep its operations so shrouded in secrecy is a mystery to me,' said Simon Ward, economist at New Star. 'This [reform] will make it much more difficult to track what the Bank is doing.'"

I think Mr. Ward's assessment is right on target. The Bank of England has begun the process of printing money without legally declaring it so that it will be impossible to "track what the Bank is doing." This all but near guarantees that unlimited printing of money will be utilized in an attempt to pull the UK's economy out of the dumps.

All these stories bring me back to one of my former points. If Central Banks use the debasement of currency and inflation as a way to pull their stock markets out of the gutter, though the surface result may lead you to believe that all is okay, every person will have in reality, firmly lost. Here's why. By printing massive amounts of money in an attempt to resuscitate dead economies and stock markets, the value of currency in the offending country will decrease significantly as supply of that currency spirals higher. If a Central Bank devalues a currency by 30% in order to "stimulate" an economy, if you regain 20% of your portfolio losses in a rising stock market, your net result will still be a 10% loss in your wealth. And this is the trick Central Banks continually play on their citizens. They make you feel like winners while continuing to steal your wealth.

While millions of ordinary citizens may be fooled by this game, it is already obvious that other Central Banks of countries not aligned with Western economies are already onto this scam, even as they perpetuate the same scam in their own countries. Consider this commentary from the Chinese newspaper, the People's Daily, that originated out of Beijing on October 24, 2008: "The United States has plundered global wealth by exploiting the dollar's dominance, and the world urgently needs other currencies to take its place, a leading Chinese state newspaper said on Friday. The front-page commentary in the overseas edition of the People's Daily said that Asian and European countries should banish the U.S. dollar from their direct trade relations for a start, relying only on their own currencies...The grim reality has led people, amidst the panic, to realise that the United States has used the U.S. dollar's hegemony to plunder the world's wealth, said the commentator, Shi Jianxun, a professor at Shanghai's Tongji University."

Was There a Rational Solution to This Crisis?

Of course. The first rational solution was to have US regulatory agencies actually perform their job instead of acting as Wall Street lobbying groups. That meant that Alan Greenspan would not have dismantled the Glass-Steagall Act and the world economy would have been in a lot less trouble than it is today. If this happened, regulations would have been passed that would have regulated markets instead of having regulations passed into law that were designed to protect and aid fraud. But it is too late to rewind the clock by two decades. Absent of that solution, the only other rationale solution was to allow free markets to operate once the fraud had already been committed. Every greedy and weak financial institution that would have failed without US Treasury and US Federal Reserve intervention should have been allowed to fail.

An extremely ugly year would have developed after the decision to do this, but after one year, perhaps 18 months at best, a stronger, more US vibrant economy that would have been trusted worldwide would have emerged. This in turn would have helped the global economy recover as well. Instead, Central Banks and government worldwide have reacted to this crisis by manipulating markets, bailing out the worst offenders of this crisis, and assigning the creators of this crisis (the US Federal Reserve and Hank Paulson) unlimited powers to manage the crisis. These actions have resulted in the loss of US and Western credibility among global economic leaders, and has, at the beginning of 2009, guaranteed that this crisis will be prolonged and drawn out for many subsequent years.

Our current monetary crisis is one that has been deliberately created to allow its creators a ripe environment of panic and fear that they can advantageously use to consolidate their power. Henry Kissinger, interviewed on CNBC's "Squawk on the Street" by hosts Mark Haines and Erin Burnett at the New York Stock Exchange in January of 2009 openly opined of this crisis: "[US President Barack Obama] can give new impetus to American foreign policy partly because the reception of him is so extraordinary around the world. His task will be to develop an overall strategy for America in this period when, really, a **new world order** can be created. It's a great opportunity, it isn't just a crisis."

Kissinger's comment gives credence to my hypothesis that certain Central Banks have deliberately created this crisis in order to consolidate their power in the global economy and create a new financial world order. Thus, one would be prudent in 2009 not to heed the advice of the talking heads in the media but only to seek out the opinions of independent analysts that maintain zero affiliations to the mainstream investment industry. Great profits and great opportunity to make profits always exist during crises as long as you do not allow yourself to be fooled by the misinformation campaigns of the commercial investment industry and Central Bankers. Keep active in your hunger for the truth about this crisis, and if you do, you should not be among those that will be economically devastated by this growing monetary crisis.

APPENDIX I

Bamboozled! Help End the Big Money Lie

As we start 2009, I am in the process of embarking on the most important project of my life – a short documentary about the roots of this current global monetary crisis entitled "BAMBOOZLED! – End the Big Money Lie". My hope is that "BAMBOOZLED!" will become one of the most important short films you will ever watch by raising your awareness of how a fraudulent monetary system has negatively affected all of our lives since the day we were born. In fact, our current fraudulent global monetary system will continue to negatively affect all of our lives until the day we die unless we collectively stand up and take action now. This is not a film just about the banking elites that control money and how they use this power to control our lives, but this is a film more importantly about humanity, truth, and ultimately, love. In fact, I believe that the **SINGLE GREATEST CONTRIBUTION TO HUMANITY** would be the transformation of our current fraudulent monetary and banking system into a sound monetary system, and here's why.

John Maynard Keynes, the father of the modern economic system implemented by the major world economies today, once stated: "There is no subtler, no surer means of overturning the existing basis of society than to debauch the currency. The process engages all the hidden forces of economic law on the side of destruction, and does it in a manner which not one man in a million is able to diagnose."

The bankers that control our global monetary system today have consistently debauched our currency year after year, and this is the greatest single factor that has given rise to our current global economic crisis. More importantly, our current fraudulent monetary system enables the persistence of poverty, starvation, war, civil unrest, refugees, and terrorism worldwide. This fraudulent system NEGATIVELY IMPACTS US ALL, rich or poor; black, white, yellow, red or brown. We cannot reasonably expect to solve any of the world's major problems, or even its minor ones, without first putting an end to today's fraudulent monetary system. "BAMBOOZLED! End the Big Money Lie" will cite historical evidence that will illustrate how a sound monetary system will automatically contribute to solving the world's major problems, and this is why my short film ultimately is a message about humanity and love.

"Bamboozled!" will explore questions we must all answer if we want economic stability in the world today.

(1) Why do we accept operational business models employed by banks worldwide if we would deem this same business model fraudulent if utilized by any other business sector?

(2) Why do we conclude that the USD $50 billion hedge fund Ponzi-scheme fraud committed by former NASDAQ chairman Bernard Madoff is "shocking" while simultaneously concluding that the exact same scheme employed by banks is "acceptable"?

(3) Why do we accept monetary inflation and a reduction in our standard of living as a fact of life when a sound monetary system has proven to lead to price stability for hundreds of consecutive years?

STEP ONE: UNDERSTANDING

Understanding the process of money creation is the first step to ending the fraudulent global monetary system. **If you knew that every dollar, real, peso, yen, euro, krona, pound, baht, or yuan that you deposited in a bank was guaranteed to be returned to you at a lesser value, would you stand by idly and accept this fate for the rest of your life?** Even if you answer no, today we all stand guilty of accepting this fate because it happens every day to every one of us. A fraudulent monetary system based upon unsound currencies makes it virtually impossible for all of us to maintain the same standard of living year to year without accumulating debt in some shape or form.

Instead of slave masters using whips to control slaves today, bankers use the ability to deflate and inflate money at will to impose conditions of economic slavery upon the world in a manner so devious and subtle that not one in a million men understands it. Consequently, the global mass media has failed miserably in their erroneous explanations of this world economic crisis. When the media participates in the spread of misinformation worldwide due to its lack of understanding, an alternative medium of spreading the truth is needed if we are to stop supporting a monetary system that perpetually spreads, economic instability, global conflict, poverty, and war.

I am making "BAMBOOZLED! End the Big Money Lie" so that not just one in several million people will understand today's crisis, but that millions eventually will. The first step of understanding starts with psychology. Ironically, it has always been much easier to convince millions, or even billions, to believe the treachery of huge, mountainous lies versus little, small white lies.

Why? Human behavior is enormously driven by a strong need for acceptance and conformity.

Numerous psychological studies have proven that a majority of people will eventually obey ideas and actions that they know to be untrue or harmful just to avoid the discomfort of conflict and to avoid being the only person that does not agree with everyone else. The landmark 1963 Stanley Milgram shock experiment discovered that the majority of peoples' behavior was even easier to mold if a perceived "authority figure" delivered the request to conform. The Milgram shock experiment concluded that 65% of people would follow an authority figure's instructions to deliver severe electric shocks to a stranger as long as an authority figure encouraged the subject to continue and informed the subjects that they would not be held responsible for their actions.

Milgram concluded that **"ordinary people, simply doing their jobs, and without any particular hostility on their part, can become agents in a terrible destructive process."** And that is exactly what we have become today – agents for a terribly destructive and fraudulent global monetary system instructed to do so by the authoritative figures of Central Banks and global financial institution CEOs, men who end up as Time Magazine's "Man of the Year" when they should instead be bestowed with the award of "Thief of the Year".

Throughout history, bankers have consistently preyed upon our overwhelming need to conform in our behavior and belief systems. They realized that once scientific studies proved that a perceived authority figure could direct the majority of people to behave in manners that conflicted with their personal morality and ethics, that merely convincing the masses to believe a BIG LIE would be a virtual walk in the park. Consequently, bankers started spreading the **BIG LIE** that Central Banks are an institution of monetary stability when in fact the exact opposite is true. Central banks have never acted in the interest of their fellow countrymen and have always acted in the interest of the elite banking families that own them to the detriment and harm of all citizens. Though Central

Banks have committed more acts to destabilize society and countries than any other person or institution in history, they are still incredibly perceived as authority figures even today, and thus have never found it difficult to gain acceptance among masses of people of their many big lies.

And now that all of us have bought into the **BIG LIE** of a fraudulent monetary and banking system for more than a century, it is easy to direct all of us to continue our belief in these lies because of our great psychological need to conform. Asian culture even has a term to describe continued foolish, inappropriate behavior in the face of evidence that we are wrong - "saving face." It is now time for us to forget about "saving face" and time to accept the fact that our beliefs about our current global monetary system have been wrong for close to a hundred years.

If we do not take the time to understand the fact that a fraudulent monetary system is behind all global economic and social problems today, we will sentence our brothers and sisters, our nephews and nieces, our sons and daughters, and our friends and neighbors to a bleak future where their economic and social health will be subject to future cycles of devastation and destruction. The "truths" I will illuminate in my short film about the monetary system will be comparable to the discovery that the sky is really green after having believed it to be blue for your entire life. As this monetary crisis deepens, the lies will become greater and more grandiose in scope, to the point where people may actually be fooled into believing that things are getting better when they are not. Thus, it is essential that we get the word out today about how the fraudulent monetary system operates. In "BAMBOOZLED!" I will illustrate to you how these deceptions are likely to play out.

STEP TWO: AWARENESS

Upon completion of "BAMBOOZLED!", I will present my short film online and free of charge to maximize awareness of the fraudulent nature of our current global monetary and banking system around the world. For those of you currently engaged in other noble causes such as fighting poverty, preserving our environment, and providing humanitarian aid to refugees, my short film will demonstrate how a fraudulent monetary system constantly makes your battle an uphill one and how a sound monetary system can provide the foundation your battle needs to succeed.

If we wish to solve any of the instabilities that exist in society today, whether it is the lack of food, the lack of healthcare, or the preponderance of violence in our communities, these problems are all virtually unsolvable without a stable monetary system. To take a giant leap forward in our ability to solve these problems, I urge you to become more active in spreading awareness of the fraudulent global monetary system. Finally, if my travels bring me to your city, once my film is completed, I will be happy to speak about the subject matter contained in BAMBOOZLED! on a pro bono basis.

STEP THREE: ACTION

Consider that severe market distortions and grave economic crises have only happened during periods of our history when fraudulent monetary systems existed. When sound monetary systems existed, the boom/bust cycles that have become the hallmark of modern economies have never happened. In fact, most people are unaware that sustainable, stable economic periods of prosperity and growth lasted for centuries at a time in the past, a concept that is literally inconceivable under a fraudulent monetary system. The monetary crisis we face today currently is destabilizing societies in America, Mexico, Iceland, the Ukraine, China, Greece, Singapore, Australia, Russia, India, Argentina, Spain, the United Kingdom, Germany and numerous other countries; however, this crisis is not without a viable, sustainable solution. We can no longer look to our government leaders for the solutions as they only offer perpetuation of our present conditions.

Instead it is up to us to bring the change necessary to instill peace and prosperity in our world. "BAMBOOZLED!" will provide credible solutions that we ALL can act upon to build a stable, more productive society. As this crisis deepens, the progression of lies will become even greater, to the point where many people may actually be convinced that things are getting better when they are not. We are now firmly at a tipping point where **ONLY WE CAN DECIDE IF THINGS GET MUCH WORSE OR MUCH BETTER**. We can continue on our current path to a spiritually and economically bankrupt future or we can change our future by establishing a new monetary system that will bring peace and prosperity to the entire world.

I am acutely aware of the difficult financial times that exist today, but that is why the timing of my project is especially critical. Unless we make a stand RIGHT NOW against the fraudulent monetary system, we can 100% expect this crisis to get much worse. So PLEASE stand up now and contribute to UNDERSTANDING, AWARENESS & ACTION against the fraudulent monetary system.

If you believe in the importance of this project as much as I do, I urge you to visit my project's website at http://www.SmartKnowledgeU.com/bamboozled.php and to also please forward this URL to all of your friends.

WE CAN CHANGE THE WORLD BY RAISING AWARENESS OF THIS ISSUE TODAY.

Blessings, Awareness, & My Deepest Gratitude

J.S. Kim

APPENDIX II

101 Reasons Why You Should Manage Your Own Money

As I have done throughout this book, I am going to begin this Appendix with a martial arts story to help illustrate my point.

A long time ago, a young teenager who lived in the Qinghai province in China decided that he wanted to be the best martial artist in the country. After three months of begging, the young man finally convinced the best Northen Shaolin kung fu master in all of China to take him under his wing. The young man did not disappoint, training every day for six hours. After one year, though the young man was an accomplished fighter, he felt as though his master was withholding certain elements of his training that would help him master his art more quickly.

He asked his master, How long before I'll become the best fighter in all of China?

The master answered, Ten years.

Disappointed, the student started to train for twelve hours a day, sometimes even skipping meals.

After six more months, he asked his master, How long now?

The master answered, Fifteen years.

Unbelievably frustrated at his master's response, the student started training day and night.

After another six months, he asked his master again, How long?

His master replied, Twenty years.

If a student of martial arts lacks vision, he or she will never attain success within the realm of martial arts. All of my teachers have always told me that the students who come in with only the goal of earning their black belts often disappear from the dojo the moment that they earned their black belt. Why? Because they never embraced the true warrior spirit of a martial artist, even during all the years of training it took to earn a black belt. The same type of spirit and vision is necessary for an investor. Chase short term dreams and you will often end up with nothing but a series of losses. But focus down the road and dig deep enough down the rabbit hole to generate this focus and you will end up making the most intelligent investment decisions of your life.

Consider these Art of War principles: (1) If they are greedy, lure them with goods; (2) Show them a little prospect of gain; then attack and overcome them; and (3) When the enemy is confused, then you can overcome them. All investment firms continuously apply these principles. These principles are the difference between intelligent investors and the great majority of retail investors. Retail investors let themselves be deluded by poor investment strategies of firms that push the majority of risk on to them while allowing firms to minimize their risk. Intelligent investors utilize investment strategies that push the majority of risk back on to the market and minimize their own.

For instance, in 2006, we were consistently bombarded with headlines from the financial media of record highs and how we were in the midst of raging bull markets all throughout the world, many of which were provided by high level executives of investment firms. These messages all had the underlying themes of "give us more money now or you will miss out on enormous upside potential." As I had warned numerous times, caution and waiting for dips to buy was the much better strategy as opposed to blindly following the mainstream advice and jumping on board. One would have been well served to wait for dips in China, Japan and India. As for U.S. markets at the end of 2007, I have already discussed the grave dangers that exist.

Although the internet has flattened our world today and given us access to information that allows us to easily outperform the investment returns of commercial investment firms, it also has had a concurrent negative effect. The commercial investment and financial industry also realize that in today's hi-tech world, they have unparalleled reach into markets they never had access to before. As such, they have stepped up their misinformation campaigns through the internet in order to preserve and protect their profits. Currently, I see the greatest amounts of nonsense I have ever seen in my lifetime being reported in the financial media.

Furthermore, as I've stated throughout this book, courses regarding financial literacy will never make you wealthy. Throughout my lifetime, I've personally known many financially literate people that responsibly contributed to their 401 (k) plan and took great care to review their estate plan every couple of years, yet never built wealth because they never learned the concepts of wealth literacy. Because the amount of poor advice outnumbers the good advice by 1000 to 1, it is more critical than ever for us to apply a Zen like state of mind to the investment strategies we choose to incorporate into our wealth-building plan.

It is often said that Zen meditation is of no use if the mind is not clear or empty, and that without a correct orientation of the mind, all Zen practices are in vain. The same is true of investing today. One practically needs to empty his or her mind of all the erroneous information that has been implanted there over the years and rediscover a correct orientation to building wealth through investing.

Millions of people all over the world seek the key to building wealth, yet it remains an ever-elusive achievement even to those that have more resources than the average Joe. In fact, it doesn't matter if you are black, white, Latino, Asian, Arab, Christian, Buddhist, Muslim, Brazilian, Japanese, Kuwaiti, British, German, Spanish, Italian, Cuban, Chilean, Argentinian, American, or Canadian, the key to building wealth is the same no matter your nationality, ethnicity, race, or religion. Yet so many people seek the wrong solutions such as changing investment firms from Merrill Lynch to Goldman Sachs to J.P. Morgan in seek of higher returns, or speculating in assets they don't understand. And the great majority of people that have been searching in this manner to build wealth are still searching today.

Why?

The answer is quite simple. All of these investors have a particular shared denominator of failure and another denominator highly predictive of success that is missing. Their common denominator of failure is their motivation to find the easiest method to build wealth. Remember Lesson #13 that we learned from Navy SEALs about investing? – The safest way is often not the easiest way. The placement of their money in someone else's hands to manage, the purchase of newsletters to provide their stock picks for them, and the greed driven behavior of gambling in speculative assets are just some of the many pursuits investors undertake in search of wealth. Their common missing ingredient and their reason for lack of success is their exhaustion of all possible methods to build wealth except for one - Seizing personal responsibility for learning how to manage their own money.

So the million dollar question is literally this: What is the fastest way to build wealth?

Ready for the answer? Take the time to learn a proper investing system, seize responsibility for your financial future, and manage your own money. Unfortunately there are truly no viable alternatives to this answer. There is a reason that the best method to accomplish something is almost never the easiest way. When it comes to investing, it is simply amazing that the vast hordes of investors believe that the easiest ways to invest are also the best ways to invest. We're here to show you why this is the furthest thing from the truth. So without further ado, here are the:

101 Reasons Why Managing Your Own Money is the Safest & Quickest Way to Build Wealth

(1) No one will ever care more about the performance of your money than you. Period. No financial consultant or investment firm will ever care more about the performance of your portfolio than you. Reasons #2 and #3 are quite lengthy because they help clarify reason #1.

(2) A financial consultant's job is to make his or her firm wealthy, NOT to make you wealthy. These two objectives are vastly different. This is perhaps the second most important reason why you must take responsibility for managing your own money. Most people do not realize that most financial consultants are nothing more than glorified salesmen and saleswomen, even if they do work for a prestigious investment firm. If you currently employ a financial consultant, the next time you visit the office, make a point to speak to the branch manager and ask him for the annual returns

of the top five best-paid financial consultants in his office over the last five years. Then ask him which financial consultants in the office have earned the best returns for their clients over the last five years and ask to see these returns.

Don't let the branch manager answer your questions by giving you the annual returns of the best five internal or external money managers that the investment firm utilizes. This response does not answer your question. First of all, it is highly unlikely that the top producers hire the top five best performing money managers year after year as any major global investment firm utilizes hundreds of money managers. By this, I mean that most financial consultants make zero decisions about what stocks are purchased with the money that you give them. They hire either internal or external money managers to do this for you. Thus, every branch manager, if they are truly concerned about the returns he or she earns for his or her clients, should be able to tell you not only the five consultants in the office that earn the highest portfolio returns based upon the mix of money managers they hire, but also the returns his top five producers earn for their clients.

If a branch manager refuses to divulge this information, you have to wonder why. If they tell you they do not know, and they only know the returns of the various money managers, their offices employ, this is even more incredulous. Why would the manager assign such little significance to the kinds of returns his top producers are earning for their clients that he or she doesn't even track this information? And if he or she can provide this information, ask if the returns he or she can give you are the exact figures that his or her top financial consultants have yielded on average for all their clients or if they are just estimates. Again, if a manager is just guessing, you have to wonder why they wouldn't know this seemingly critical information.

Finally, if they know, but won't tell you, why would they not release this information? Shouldn't the best paid financial consultants in any office be earning their clients the best returns year after year after year over all other financial consultants by a very wide margin. And if not, why are they being compensated so highly? The answers to these questions, if you receive honest answers, should reveal that great salesmen are compensated very handsomely by their firms while almost zero premium is put on the ability of a financial consultant to earn great returns for their clients.

(3) Building on point (2), many investors will then say, OK. I'll find myself the financial consultant, the one that falls in the top 0.5% of all consultants that really know what they are doing, and I'll hire him or her. Here is why they are wrong again. Because most people never take the time to properly learn how to invest themselves, they never can understand the investment strategies of those that truly know what they are doing. This lack of understanding, despite any efforts on behalf of the consultant to educate the client, inevitably leads to incessant questioning of the consultant's actions, strategies, etc. which can grow very tiresome very quickly.

I have dropped large accounts in the past because of such meddling, sophomoric behavior from clients that had a lot of money. Furthermore, I have refused to accept large accounts as well because I could tell, in speaking with a prospective client, that he or she firmly held so many misconceptions about investing that he or she would be a nightmare to deal with. Consultants that truly know what they are doing, despite their efforts, can not educate anyone fully in 3-4 hours time if that person has been conditioned for years to believe the nonsense that global investment firms have taught him or her. Furthermore, because great consultants realize that so many widely believed concepts about investing are nonsense, and have achieved their great performance by realizing this, they will constantly be fighting an uphill battle against clients that believe this nonsense. Therefore the chances that they would keep these clients in the long run are slim to none.

Even if one finds the rare consultant that truly knows what he or she is doing, and truly has outperformed the markets significantly year in and year out, because these types of consultants invest so differently than the status quo, any lack of exposure to such intelligent investment strategies will undoubtedly cause fear. It is human nature that ignorance leads to fear. In turn, fear causes incessant badgering and questioning, a behavior that 100% of the time will cause a great financial consultant to terminate a relationship with a client.

Because great consultants achieve their outperformance by making decisions that go against the grain of what 99% of other financial consultants do, a great level of understanding of how to invest properly is necessary for one to even to maintain a relationship with a great consultant. In the end, even if one doesn't wish to manage his or her own money AND even if one is able to find that rare 1 in 1,000 financial consultant that really knows what he or she is doing, one still needs to learn a comprehensive investment system just to maintain a healthy relationship with their knowledgeable consultant. Hiring a truly gifted financial consultant still may not be the answer, because chances are that a truly gifted financial consultant will not hire you. Ultimately, this is why you should learn to manage your own money!

(4) Global investment firms always tout a message of trust in their commercials. But where is the historical performance that merits that trust? 6% to 10% a year?

(5) If being a financial consultant required such specialized knowledge, why do investment firms hire financial consultants from a vast array of backgrounds and degrees? The investment industry is most likely the industry that possesses the greatest amount of diversity regarding the former professional careers of its frontline personnel. This is because there is no specific set of knowledge required to be a great financial consultant. Only great people skills and sales skills. You cannot find a single other industry that is so willing to hire people from all walks of life. If you want to become a lawyer, you need a law degree. Want to

become a marketing executive with a large firm? You better have at least eight years of marketing experience with a Fortune 500 company. However, if you want to become a top manager at a prestigious investment firm, your degree is irrelevant as long as you have an uncanny ability to sell.

(6) Think about what #(5) implies. Think your financial consultant has an MBA or business degree in finance? Think again. The typical financial consultant does not have an MBA. However, even if he or she did have an MBA, it may not even be of any utility in selecting great stocks. The common denominator that all successful financial consultants have is a great knack for being able to sell.

(7) Misinformation disseminated by investment firms in order to keep clients dependent upon them is voluminous. Commercial investment firms thrive on this co-dependent relationship. That alone is a reason why you should cut the umbilical cord to investment firms and learn to do it yourself. There is a reason why investing legends like Warren Buffet state that he only reads firms' analyst reports when he wants a good laugh. He realizes the level of misinformation that is necessary to build client-firm dependency. You should too.

(8) You'll never build wealth quickly with diversified portfolios (diversified by asset allocation, diversified by style, diversified with mutual funds). But this is all investment firms do. I once met a top financial consultant at a major firm that believed in buying nothing but index funds for his clients. If this is how your money is being managed, do you really need to pay someone to buy index funds for you? Figure out the equation: A. Diversification won't create wealth. B. Investment firms diversify portfolios. C. I give my money to an investment firm, thus my portfolio is diversified. What's your conclusion?

You will never build wealth at an investment firm. Preserve it? Maybe. Slow Growth? Probably. Build Wealth? Fat chance.

(9) 6% to 10% will never help you build wealth. You must learn to at least earn 15% to 25% or more every year. At 8% a year, it will take you 9 years to grow $250,000 to $500,000 and 18 years to grow $250,000 to $1,000,000 in a non-taxable account, not considering the erosion in purchasing power due to inflation. At 25% a year, it will take you less than 7 years to grow $250,000 into a $1,000,000 in a non-taxable account. That's the difference between building wealth and preserving wealth. 6% to 10% a year helps you preserve wealth, not build it.

(10) Major global firms will NEVER find the best stocks in the global market and hold them in your portfolio.

(11) Reason #10 is true because major firms coverage of small and micro cap stocks are appallingly light. Firms must provide extensive coverage of large cap stocks, the Genentechs, the IBMs, the McDonalds, the General Electrics of the world to appease their clients. However, the Microsofts of the future are small and micro cap stocks now. You can't build wealth buying and holding the IBMs of the global stock world. The Apples and Googles that increase 400% or more are very rare among large cap stocks. Yes, I know that the great Warren Buffet was a buy and hold man, but today's investment world is much different than it was 50 years ago, or even 20 years ago. The explosive growth of derivative instruments and many more investment vehicles have formed an interdependency among assets that has never existed before. Furthermore, the actions of some nation's banks have introduced a very tangible fragility into the global economy today.

    Nothing in this world is static. Certainly, the global climate is not the same today as it was 50 years ago. The temperatures of the world's oceans are not the same is they were even 20 years ago. And financial markets are not the same today. Buy and hold blue

chip stocks if you want. But you will never bu
today.

(12) Information technology and the flattening
world now makes it easier for you to be much
than any financial consultant employed by any ~~ ~~e major
investment firms.

(13) Financial consultants, because of the payout grid that dictates
their salaries, are often motivated by selling you the highest
commission based products, not necessarily what is in your best
interest.

(14) Investors that have actually built wealth through investing like
Warren Buffet, George Soros, even Mark Cuban, have all managed
their own money. Investors that have already amassed great wealth
employ money managers. That should tell you something about
what's necessary to build wealth.

(15) Even large global investment houses only have the resources to
track about 1,500 stocks. The estimates of all stocks that trade
globally numbers about 75,000. Investors want coverage of the
most popular stocks in their country. This means that the great
majority of stocks that firms' analysts cover are large cap domestic
stocks. When I worked for a large Wall Street investment house,
many times I couldn't find any analyst coverage of many stocks I
wanted to buy that were traded in China, Hong Kong, or Brazil.
You want to own the best stocks in the world, you have to manage
your own money, period. Give your money to someone else to
manage, and chances are very high that you will never own the best
stocks and opportunities in the world.

(16) When was the last time you heard a truly unique approach to
investing from a financial consultant anywhere? If you decided to
meet10 different consultants at 5 different firms, most likely their

would sound like broken records. Now think about this?
w can it be that in an arena as creative as investing, that different
financial consultants from different firms that live on different
continents all apply the same principles and strategies when
managing your money? The answer is that practically ALL
investment strategies employed by the commercial investment
industry are sales driven, not return driven.

(17) If you utilize a money manager to handle your money, the
great majority of financial consultants don't understand much more
than you do about investing. Most people don't realize this because
they don't know the proper questions to ask their financial
consultants. Take care to learn the proper questions and you will
reveal their weaknesses.

(18) The great majority of financial consultants can be summed up
in one word. Salesman. Enough said.

(19) Investment firms convince you to do so many things that are
not in your best interest. We'll list these things now.

(20) If you don't want to duped into buying into bear markets and
close to market tops, learn to manage your own money.

(21) If you don't want to be cashed out during times of market
volatility and pay fees on cash because your consultant doesn't
know how to make you money during poor markets, then manage
your own money.

(22) Perform a Google Search as follows: "SEC fines, Citigroup,
Merrill Lynch, UBS Paine Webber, Morgan Stanley, J.P. Morgan"
and read all the articles that are returned. The SEC stands for the
Securities Exchange Commission, and they impose fines on
investment houses when they engage in illegal or unethical

behavior. Do you still believe that these firms have your best interest at heart after performing this search?

(23) Henry Blodget, once Merrill Lynch's top internet securities analyst, wrote in private emails that the internet stocks Merrill Lynch analysts were touting were "crap" and "junk" and that the only thing special about them were the investment banking fees these companies were paying to Merrill. (Source: The Washington Post, April 24, 2002). Though many firms claim to have separated their investment banking business from their brokerage business today, do you really believe that a huge investment banking client that has already paid massive fees to an investment firm will not pressure top management to tone down negative ratings regarding their company or to amplify otherwise already positive ones? Remember, Warren Buffet says he reads analysts' reports only when he needs a good laugh. How do most stock pickers at firms choose stocks for you? By reading their firm's analysts reports.

(24) It doesn't really make a difference in 99 cases out of 100 if an absolutely green financial consultant straight out of college manages your money or a 20 year veteran with silver hair manages your money. You'll receive roughly the same results because they both use the same firm-developed internal systems that help consultants choose money managers and the same firm-developed asset allocation models. If this doesn't scream sales optimization strategies over portfolio return optimization strategies, then I don't know what does.

Individuals that say they have tried managing their own money but have failed have never implemented a realistic or proper system to do so.

(25) There are courses that teach a comprehensive investment system available at http://www.SmartKnowledgeU.com. Just ensure that any investment course that you seek out does not

emphasize the same tired, ineffective strategies promoted by the commercial investment industry. Find a course that emphasizes Blue Ocean investment strategies, and it will be infinitely more helpful to your ability to build wealth quickly.

(26) There is a global investment crisis aka the Peak Investment Crisis that is brewing and inevitable though the vast majority of investors are unaware of it (and this is NOT a reference to any global market correction that may have happened recently). If you learn how to invest your own money now (the end of 2007), which means learning a comprehensive investment system, you are highly unlikely to be caught unprepared when this crisis hits and destroys trillions of dollars in the global stock market.

We are not saying that this investment crisis will happen tomorrow. But there are many undeniable facts, not theories, about the global economy that presage an economic disaster that will most likely happen sometime within a compact time frame moving forward from the end of 2007. Learn a proper investment system that teaches you to understand the global economy to guide your investment decisions and you will profit tremendously from this crisis.

(27) Most people that try to do it themselves and fail have no system. They buy stocks that are plastered all over the financial media, which more times than not, means that the stock has already had a fantastic run. After all, stocks that are languishing will not attract much media attention. Most people that fail do the worst thing possible. They buy high and when the stock corrects, they sell out low.

(28) Individuals often say they can't manage their own money, and as proof, they state that they have lost money when trying to do so. However, the majority of individuals that say this never learned a proper investment system before commencing the management of

their own money. If you are among this subset of investors, below are many more reasons why anyone absolutely can learn to manage their own money.

(29) In the past, learning how to invest was all about number crunching. Dry and boring. Today, Blue Ocean investment strategies have introduced a lot of creativity into investment strategies and have actually made learning how to invest fun.

(30) You mistake past attempts at managing your money as serious attempts. For example, your neighbor, a financial consultant, told you he had a hot tip for a can't miss stock. You bought and you lost big. You vow to leave investing to the experts. Sorry, but this is hardly qualifies for an attempt to manage your own money. Foolishness, yes. Serious go at managing your own money? Hardly.

(31) Mistake #2. You mistake years of investing for years of investing experience. If you've been investing for 30 years but have never managed your own money, you have zero years of investment experience when it comes to being able to do it own your own. Most people don't realize this, think they've learned enough by speaking with their investment advisor over the years, embark on their own and lose money. Learn an investment system first and this won't happen.

(32) Mistake #3. You believe that all the cumulative knowledge you've gained from being a client of a well-respected brokerage house should be enough to allow you to manage your money successfully. None of this information will help you build wealth. If you've built wealth through them, you wouldn't be trying to learn how to do it yourself. Forget about all these strategies and principles and seek out an investment system that doesn't have closing a sale as its number one goal.

(33) Mistake #4. In this ever increasing age of immediate gratification, you've never given yourself the proper time to learn a real investment system. You may have tried something for three months, and after questionable or poor results, discarded it. Ever try learning anything worthwhile within 3 months with great success? Learning how to invest and how to build wealth is not difficult yet it demands a certain level of commitment and time. Too many people these days expect a lot for nothing. They want a secret formula that will give them explosive growth.

They jump from one foolish spam email that screams "I'm almost positive this stock will give you 1,580% returns in six months" to the next $10,000 software program that promises to have cracked the "secret patterns and codes" that predict every single upleg in the markets in chase of quick profits. This is not learning a system. This is foolishness. There are secrets to building wealth, but they all involve learning proper systems of investing that won't make you rich overnight but will make you rich only when you assume a proper commitment to learning.

(34) Mistake #5. You actually spend an adequate investment of time learning a system, but you spend time learning the wrong things. You invest with these strategies but never build any wealth and declare that you're better off letting the "pros" handle it. Modern portfolio theory of diversification is over half a century old. There is nothing modern about it. Learn about the Blue Ocean of investment strategies that have updated yesterday's outdated strategies and you will finally learn the secrets about building wealth.

(35) Mistake #6. You start an investment club with industry experts. Experts in nanotechnology, in biotechnology, in pharmaceuticals, in precious metals, but still your investment club fails to make you rich. Industry experts are a great place to start. In fact, they will be able to shed more light on companies than the average person. Still if no one in your investment club has learned a

proper system of investing, all that insight is useless. You must have the framework available to take advantage of all that insight. That framework is a solid system of investing, and all members of your investment club should possess this.

(36) Mistake #7. Most people misunderstand what a solid investment system is. This is not something that you gain from reading a $39.99 book and not something that you can learn from "dabbling" in investing. Just as you would not expect to be able to solve complex algebra algorithms or problems without a comprehensive structured course or to learn how to fly a plane from reading a book, you need a comprehensive structured course to truly learn a system. Find one and learn it.

(37) Most people don't utilize leverage when learning an investment system. If your strength is not independent learning, then find a tutor to aid you. Understanding your personal strengths and weaknesses are paramount to investing success. If you have learned a great investment system but don't have time to apply it properly, form an investment club and leverage the ideas of others to save time.

(38) A talking, or screaming, head on some financial news channel on TV told you about a can't miss stock. You bought and you lost again. See Reason #33. This is not a serious attempt to manage your money but mere foolishness.

(39) You paid lots of money for an investment newsletter subscription. You bought everything they recommended but didn't really earn much money beyond what you earned before you bought the subscription. To build wealth, it's not good enough to know just what to buy. You must know when to buy, how to buy, when to sell, and how to sell as well. This is a complete investment system. Furthermore, newsletters that provide coverage on 100 stocks will never provide any utility to you unless you have already

learned an investment system that allows you to filter down that list of 100 to only the best ones.

(40) You purchased books on value investing, how to invest like Warren Buffet, technical investing, and so on, but you still have not had huge successes with your investments. These are the wrong types of books to consult in learning an investment system and thus, the reason for failure. Traditional decades old strategies should not be applied today. Mimicking someone else's style does not work. I'm sure basketball players would like to elevate their game to the level of Michael Jordan's game, but mimicking his style won't make them play like Jordan.

(41) You've tried managing your own money and have had years of great success but also years of huge losses. You decide that a steady 8% a year, just like the investment firms have been telling you for so many years, is the way to go. Sounds like you've been speculating versus having learned a solid investment system. While you are going to have some years that are much more spectacular than others when investing you shouldn't have years where you gained 40% and years where you lost 50%. That can only happen because you've been speculating and still have not learned a proper investment system.

(42) You only buy stocks on tips from "experts" already in the investment industry. You figure this is the quick, painless way to find the best stocks in the world to invest in. However, it seems to be hit or miss with the stocks you have bought. Again, this is not learning an investment system. Remember that experts that tend to give away loads of free advice are merely salesmen. Believe it or not, I have encountered fools on the internet that react angrily to my polite refusals to give them the free advice and free stock picks that they seek. Experts will never give away their best advice for free. Only salespeople will.

(43) The reason all the instances above are NOT justifications for why you can't manage your own money is because none of the above examples included a systematic method of investing. Would you ever just take the recommendation of a friend that Island XYZ is the best island in the world and blindly fly there for your honeymoon without performing any research yourself? Would you ever just quite your job and start a construction business tomorrow because your neighbor is making a killing in the construction industry? These are the exact fly-by-the-seat-of-your-pants decisions that investors make ALL THE TIME when managing their own money, and then when struck with failure, conclude that they can't manage their money.

(44) Become a member of an elite group, the less than 3% of individual investors that actually learn how to invest for themselves. There is a reason that so few investors actually build great wealth through investing. I'm not talking about the investors that made $25 million from real estate and then grow that amount through investing in the stock markets. I'm talking about the investors that started with a very small investment in the stock market and amassed a fortune through investing. The reason that so few investors amass a fortune through investing is that so few are willing to truly learn an investment system that teaches them how to invest themselves.

(45) There is a reason why you consistently hear statistics like 3% of individuals own 95% of the wealth, no matter what country you visit. The reason is that these 3% of people took the time to learn how to manage their money themselves and thus have truly built wealth.

(46) Like attracts like. Of all the investors I've met in my life, less than 1% actually learned how to do it themselves. However, the best ideas outside of my own that I've encountered have come from discussions with these 1% of investors. If you have something to

offer to someone else, they will freely offer their views to you as well. There's something about human nature, unless you are a great philanthropist, that makes people dislike others that are not willing to put in the work themselves and instead only look for free handouts (advice) from the people that have put in the work.

You say you don't have time to manage your own money? Guess what? Your financial consultant has even less time.

(47) The only excuse that you have for not building wealth is not taking the time to learn an investment system. Given that this is potentially the most important pursuit regarding your financial security, there really is no excuse for not learning how to invest yourself.

(48) If you don't believe that your returns should be limited to the knowledge of your financial consultant, then manage your own money. For example, how many times have you asked your financial consultant, I'd like to invest in gold, or I'd like to invest in dollar declining funds, or I'd like to invest in Chinese markets, only to have your financial consultant stare at you blankly and say, "the safest way to invest is what I'm doing for you now."

I once heard this anecdotal story. A wealthy individual asked his financial consultant, one of the top producers at his firm, why he didn't own any stocks in the Chinese stock market. The consultant said just give me some time and I'll get you a list of stocks that we can buy. When he produced the list, the list contained the American-based Chinese restaurant chain P.F. Changs. If this is the kind of advice a top producer gives, you may think how can he be a top producer? Just read this entire list, and you'll realize how easy it is for these types of situations to exist at even a top investment firm.

You want to know how a top producer at a prestigious global firm can give such shoddy advice? It's because he's not paid to produce great returns for you. He's paid to close sales. You want to duplicate this experiment today? If you live outside of Canada, then go to your financial consultant and ask him what he thinks are a couple of the best Canadian junior gold mining stocks and why? Ask him or her to answer on the spot. Given that gold stocks in 2007 and into 2008 are one of the best assets to own, any competent financial consultant should be able to answer this question on the spot.

(49) If you believe that diversification is the pathway to mediocrity because even a 2000% gain isn't going to help you much if it constitutes 1.5% of your entire portfolio, then manage your own money.

(50) In my many years working for global investment firms, I once heard one of the top producers call a client and tell the client to urgently sell shares of a specific stock and then immediately call another client and tell this client to buy the shares of the same stock. There are plenty of people like this working for global investment firms that are rewarded by these firms for such actions (because these actions earn the firm money). Do you really want someone like this managing your money?

(51) The only excuse for not learning an investment system is laziness and a lack of commitment to building wealth, NOT A LACK OF TIME. Even if you work full time, it will take no longer that a few hours a week for one year to master an investment system with the proper course. That is one year of sacrifice of perhaps missing your favorite TV shows. That is not a lot of sacrifice for a lifetime of building wealth and security for your family. Again the only excuse is laziness or a lack of desire.

(52) So you don't care that your financial consultant knows nothing about stock picking. You only care that he utilizes expert money managers on your behalf. Wrong again. An estimated 98% of institutional money managers track the domestic indexes in their own country. You still won't own the best stocks in the world even

if your financial consultant employs money managers to manage your money.

(53) Financial consultants have hundreds of clients. How much personal attention do you think your account is receiving, especially if it is less than USD $5 million in size? If you have no time to manage your own money, that is still more time than your financial consultant spends managing your money.

(54) To save time, financial consultants often gain exposure in foreign markets for you by buying mutual funds. Mutual funds, because of all the fees associated with them, are horrible investment vehicles. Furthermore, mutual finds diversify away the performance of any great individual stocks they hold.

(55) Mutual funds were invented to allow investment firms to sell more product in less time. Selling a mutual fund requires a fraction of the time that would be required if financial consultants had to search and find the best companies in the world. It also allows financial consultants to invest you in asset classes, regional markets and so on, with zero knowledge of how to invest intelligently. When it comes to investing, knowledge equals power, and power builds wealth. You want knowledge, there is no alternative but to learn to invest yourself. If your financial consultant purchases mutual funds for you, it is because he/she has not time to find individual stocks for you.

(56) Mutual funds, due to their institutional nature, will often tank during global market corrections as massive amounts of money are redeemed. Yet so many firms push mutual funds. Furthermore, to be able to meet redemptions, mutual fund managers must hold a certain portion of their fund in cash in order to manage liquidity in the fund. Do you really want to pay a firm to hold cash for you because when you buy a mutual fund you pay for inefficiency. 100,000 times out of a 100,000 times, a great individual stock is better to own than a great mutual fund.

(57) Time is the one commodity that financial consultants do not have. Is this good if they are managing your money?

(58) Here is the typical breakdown of management directives for financial consultants. 70% of all time spent marketing and meeting new prospects. 30% of all time spent with accounts, including routine account maintenance. Is this the equation you want for the management of your money?

(59) If time is the commodity you say that you lack, and this is why you employ a financial consultant instead of managing your own money, this is also a poor excuse for the following reason. Most people work so hard to have a nest egg to invest and then spend no time whatsoever in protecting and growing that nest egg (In essence, handing your money to someone else to manage it IS spending NO TIME protecting and growing it).

(60) You should make two to three to eight times the returns from managing your own money than you do by handing it to someone else. If time is the commodity you lack to manage your own money, do you see how this is a circular argument? You lack time because you don't earn enough returns on your investments. But if you made much greater returns you would CREATE MUCH MORE FREE TIME for yourself, because you would not have to work so hard at your job or you would have the luxury of being able to turn down a promotion in exchange for having a better quality of life.

(61) Being wealthy is NOT just about having more money than your neighbor. It's also about having the leisure time you desire to enjoy life. By committing more time NOW to learn an investment system, you will free up much more time in your FUTURE. Everything has an initial period of sacrifice. Learning how to invest however, yields such monumental rewards down the road that it is very much worth the initial period of sacrifice.

(62) If you are RETIRED, then you absolutely have ZERO excuse for not learning how to manage your own money. Traditional education offers very little utility in building wealth in the real world. Because of this, you must seek investment courses outside of traditional education that will teach you how to truly build wealth.

(63) It's truly not difficult to manage your own money. The reason so many people don't know how to do it is that there are very few good courses that teach people how to do this. The scarcity of such classes is purposeful as the institutions that control stock markets in this world don't want people to know what they know. By this, I mean that they take a much different approach to managing their own institutional accounts than in managing private individual accounts. The information that they closely guard, the information that they shield from their clients, is exactly the information that would make their existence moot.

(64) Perhaps the most important class that could be taught in secondary education classes is one called "How to invest money". However, this class is not taught in traditional forums of education. Therefore it's up to you to learn how to do it yourself outside the realm of traditional educational.

(65) People that try and fail, fail not because they aren't capable. They fail because they seek the wrong type of information about investing. Forget about fundamental investing and learn the Blue Oceans of investment strategies.

(66) Saying you can't do something is a poor excuse for not even trying. Managing your money in the global stock market is no more complicated than an 8th grade level mathematics class. It just takes commitment and the patience to learn BEFORE entering the stock markets.

(67) Investment firms spread tons of misinformation about the complexity of investing in an attempt to force you to entrust them with your money. Anyone that tells you it is impossible to beat the "pros" should automatically not be trusted because they are feeding you a diet of investment crap. Of course they want you to believe this. If you didn't, they would be out of business. If you ever wondered why you have never made tons of money while your money was being managed by an investment firm, stop believing their myths.

(68) You must get over the immediate gratification aspect of managing your money. This is a lifetime pursuit. In the beginning it will require more time. Down the road, doing so will CREATE MORE LEISURE TIME as your returns flourish.

(69) Learning to manage your own money will create a legacy for your children. Since your children will never learn how to do so within the confines of traditional education, after you learn, you can teach your children and give them a head start in building wealth that will place them 10 steps ahead of all their peers.

(70) Seizing control of this significant part of your life will teach you how to seize control of other parts of your life as well.

(71) Learning how to manage your own money will give you a greater appreciation for the movie "The Wizard of Oz". Every time you watch it you'll realize that in the past you were the tin man or the lion or Dorothy and that investment firms were the man behind the curtain. If you don't seek out a proper investment system now, and you are beginning your investment life, you will inflict significant harm on the mindset required to build wealth by internalizing mainstream advice. Learning a proper investment system now allows you to filter out all the white noise of the investment world.

(72) Most money managers have a very nationalistic slant in the management of portfolios, tracking the major indexes in your country. Or if you do not live in a country that has one of the major developed markets in the world, then they tend to have a very regional bias. For example, if you live in Indonesia, if a manager does not invest you heavily in the Indonesian stock market, perhaps the manager is heavily invested in China. The problem with this strategy is that even great markets, especially fast growing ones, eventually become overbought and overheated, and a narrow regional or domestic focus exposes your portfolio to a lot of risk. If you want a global portfolio that will capitalize on the fastest growing countries in the world while capturing other assets in more developed markets for an element of stability, you simply must learn to do it yourself.

(73) Building on the above, managers that seek out foreign markets primarily do this by purchasing emerging or developing market mutual funds. In major foreign markets, you want to own the best individual stocks, not mutual funds.

(74) You'll be fed years of junk by establishing a relationship with a global investment firm. Not being fed years of junk that may take you years to "unlearn" is worth the price of learning how to do it yourself.

(75) Making money in stock markets is about picking the right stocks in the right markets at the right time. Learn to do this and you'll become wealthy.

(76) I have yet to encounter a single money manager at a commercial investment firms that currently utilizes the proper filters to find the best stocks in the world. You need to learn yourself if you ever want to apply the best investment systems in the world.

(77) Investment firms' goals are very different than yours. Their goal is to gather as many assets as possible and earn as many client fees as possible. This goal leads to strategies that do not maximize the returns on your portfolios.

(78) Even if you take shortcuts to managing your money, like paying for investment newsletter subscriptions, the only way you can build wealth is if you learn a proper investment system that allows you to leverage the information of top-tier investment newsletters. Notice again that we say top-tier investment newsletters, because just like financial consultants, perhaps less than 1% of investment newsletters are actually worth your money. However, for the information of the best investment newsletters in the world to be worth anything to you, you must learn an investment system that allows you to invest in their stock picks with efficiency and at low risk/high reward entry points.

(79) You just can't mimic what successful investors buy or buy what a newsletter tells you to buy if you want to build wealth. If this were the case, there would be a million other Warren Buffets out there who just inspect the Berkshire Hathaway annual reports every year and copy the Berkshire portfolio. Besides knowing what to buy, you also have to know how much to buy, when to buy, and when to sell among other things. Thus you must learn an investment system that you can trust.
(80) Learning how to invest yourself is a much more important determinant of wealth than mainstream pursuits such as obtaining a CFP, a CFA or other advanced degrees. Get a degree in learning how to invest instead.

(81) The stocks that will make you wealthy over time are the ones nobody knows about. Therefore you can't depend on Bloomberg, CNBC, Jim Cramer, or Reuters to tell you about them. You must learn a system that helps you identify them.

(82) Once you learn to invest, you can employ a domino effect to really quicken the pace of your wealth building. Once you convince some of your friends to learn how to invest, form an investment club. I guarantee you that if you have a group of five to ten or even 20 people that have truly learned an investment system, the ideas generated by this group will be 100 times better than a 100,000 financial consultants.

(83) Most people that believe that learning a system is not worthwhile have read stories similar to the following: We conducted an experiment to test the randomness of the stock market by having a monkey with painted feet dance around on a stock page. We built a portfolio out of those 20 stocks and it outperformed the 10 top money managers in our country. In 2006, five Playboy playmates outperformed a well-known U.S. mutual fund, the Legg Mason Value Fund, in a paper investing contest. People point to this as proof that investing in the stock markets is random and a crap shoot. Maybe it says more about the quality of people in the investment profession, but read below for a better explanation.

(84) Several things make the above argument highly flawed. Number one, playing make-believe with an imaginary portfolio can not mimic reality. Tell the Playboy playmates or the person managing a portfolio with monkey selected stocks to actually invest large sums of their own money in these picks and see if the results are the same at the end of the year. For example, the Playboy playmates were asked to choose a portfolio consisting of only five stocks.

At a million dollars, every position would have $200,000 to start. However, own $200,000 in a stock that all of a sudden loses $50,000 and see if they would really hold on to it to see the 30% gain at the end of the year. Or see if they have a system two years out where they protected their profits at the end of year one or lost them all. Imaginary contests do not and can not mimic results in the real world.

(85) If you are a baby boomer just starting a family in 2007, with skyrocketing education costs that now may even outpace inflation, it is estimated that tuition at the top schools could cost half a million to a million dollars by the time your children are ready to enter college. If you don't want the cost of your children's education to bankrupt you, you better learn how to build real wealth now.

(86) By building a legacy for your children as well as teaching them something they will never learn in school, you will ensure that they won't still be draining your resources and living at home when they are 25 years old.

(87) You'll never have to utter these 3 questions again, "What stock(s) should I buy?", "What stock(s) should I sell?"; and "What markets should I invest in?"

(88) You'll never have to utter this question again, "Where is the best place to invest my money?"

(89) You'll never have to utter this question again, "How do I handle the global market corrections?"

(90) You'll never have to utter this phrase again, "Your fees seem really high for the returns you've been earning me lately."

Learning a proper investment system will drastically decrease the mistakes you make in investing your money, the inefficiencies that currently plague your returns, and the amount of fees you pay over your lifetime while dramatically increasing your returns and your leisure time. That is a payoff

that is well worth many times the initial investment of time and money.

(91) Your returns will never be plagued again by consultants that keep you fully invested in traditional stocks through global market corrections and having to hear "your best off staying fully invested through this time."

(92) Markets are not efficient. Just think of how many major news stories have recently been scooped by blogs instead of the major media outlets. Financial information is the same. Learn how, why, when, where, and what to look for and your investment system will yield stock picks with low-risk, high-return set ups.

(93) A certain amount of volatility in your portfolio is necessary to build wealth quickly. However, volatility does not equate to risk though investment firms lead you to believe this. Do you think Warren Buffet and George Soros built their fortunes without investing in a proportion of assets that were volatile? However, intelligently investing in volatile assets requires that one learns a solid investment system.

The overwhelming number of financial consultants never learn an investment system. They learn investment theories and strategies, and most of all, sales strategies, but NOT an investment system. Diversification is NOT an investment system. Asset allocation is NOT an investment system. Learning a solid investment system requires more time. Therefore it is up to you to learn a wise investment system.

(94) The overwhelming curriculum of global investment firms' financial consultant training courses are spent on sales strategies. Ask a graduate of a big time firm's financial training course to pick the best gold and uranium stocks for you and the overwhelming majority of them will be clueless. But he or she will be adept at

convincing you to entrust them with the management of your money. This should tell you something.

(95) Financial and fundamental analysis are dinosaur investment strategies when it comes to utilizing the best predictive information for stock appreciation. Modern Portfolio Theory was invented in the early 1950's. Does that sound "modern" to you? Do you want to be a dinosaur or move into the modern world of investment strategies?

(96) A one time $10,000 investment in learning an intelligent investment system primed to take advantage of the explosive growth in top-tier investment information is worth 1,000 times more than $20,000+ annual fees paid every year to an investment firm on a million dollar account.

(97) Learning how to invest yourself, even if you have a large account domiciled at a global investment firm already, will save you loads of money over time. Say you have a $5,000,000 account and pay 1.5% annual management fees, then your annual fees amount to $75,000 (the truth is if you have been sold hedge funds, your fees are probably much higher than this because hedge funds typically charge you 20% of your profits AND 2% management fees).

In ten years, you have paid a firm more than $750,000 in management fees (presuming you account is growing). For a tiny fraction of that money, you can learn a comprehensive investment system, manage your own accounts, and never have to pay management fees again.

(98) How many times in your life when it was absolutely 100% necessary for something to be done right, did you decide to do it yourself? Isn't your financial future something that is worthy of being placed in this category?

(99) How many times a year do you sit down with your financial consultant face to face to have a serious discussion about your stock portfolio? How many times a year do you take your car in for routine maintenance, including oil changes and car washes? Which is more important to maintain, your car or your financial livelihood? Some may say their car, but you get my point.

(100) Learning a comprehensive investment system and how to invest your own money will lead you to learn about many non-traditional asset classes, i.e., the asset classes that the institutional divisions of global investment houses invest in but rarely purchase for high net worth individuals. These non-traditional asset classes may very well provide some of the best returns in the markets over the next five years.

And finally, REASON 101!

(101) We're not saying that all financial consultants stink. Just the great majority of them. There are great ones out there. Most of them are probably independent. And I do recall one financial consultant that told me he avoided the firm's top ten stock picks like the plague. So they do exist. It's just that the energy expended to find one would probably be better spent investing in yourself and learning how to invest yourself.

APPENDIX III

SmartKnowledgeU™ Services Available at Our Online Website

For more information and current service prices, please visit us at
http://www.SmartKnowledgeU.com

THE PLATINUM LEVEL MEMBERSHIP

33 Learning Modules, 500+ Pages of Content, 24 Practice
Exercises, 139 Lessons, 166 Exam Questions, More than 109 Hours
of e-learning, and 6-months of supplemental learning. Our online
investment education course teaches you our proprietary Blue
Ocean investment strategies and a comprehensive investment
system that will grant you a legitimate shot of earning 25%+ returns
for the rest of your life. Learn strategies that enable you to uncover

stocks that are virtually guaranteed to return you a minimum of 40% returns in a couple of years or less.

More importantly, our Platinum Level membership teaches you how to make a fortune from the ongoing monetary crisis that is affecting all investors worldwide today. It includes 4 very Special Reports specifically dedicated to guiding you through this crisis:

(1) The Best Investment for the Next 5 Years,
(2) The Crisis Investing Report,
(3) The Coming Global Crisis, Part I; &
(4) The Coming Global Crisis, Part II.

These reports contain more than 100 pages of the most detailed information available anywhere in the world regarding various Central Banks' management of their paper currency and gold reserves and why their actions spell out a disastrous and volatile future for many global financial markets. These reports contain proprietary information, graphs, and charts unavailable anywhere else that enable you to confidently invest and make a fortune in the ongoing gold bull market.

Each year, to keep our Platinum Members up-to-date we issue new modules and timely special bulletins. In 2008, we added 9 new Learning Modules that provided ongoing guidance to all Platinum Members to ensure that they don't stray off track in earning a fortune from this burgeoning global economic crisis:

Module 25 - Precious Metal Stocks Options Trading – Is it For You?;
Module 26 - Can a Financial Meltdown Be Avoided?; and
Module 27 - Venturing Deep Inside the Investment Matrix
Module 28 - A History of the Gold Standard
Module 29 - How to Avert the Greatest Financial Disaster of Our Lifetime
Module 30 - How to Predict Corrections in Gold/Silver Prices
Module 31 - The Crisis is Upon Us

Module 32 - Patience is the Name of the Game
Module 33 - The Fed's Attempt to Revive a Flatlining Dollar

In addition to the 9 new modules, each of which may is normally 20-30 pages long, we issued 16 Special Alerts in 2008, short summaries of the fast changing situations in the macroeconomic and investment environment. Finally, our Platinum Level membership **provides information about asset classes OTHER THAN GOLD that are also poised to boom from this crisis, with one asset class that may even outperform gold. We further provide specific lessons on how to identify the best gold stocks in the world, the best non-stock assets to hold during this crisis, and how to use the volatility inherent in precious metals to your benefit to earn greater profits.**

If you truly must know everything you possibly can and gain every possible advantage in building a fortune from this coming crisis, then the Platinum Level Membership is for you.

THE CRISIS INVESTMENT OPPORTUNITIES NEWSLETTER

Learn what makes the SmartKnowledgeU™ proprietary investment system so unique. Although we reserve the details of how we select the stocks that comprise our Crisis Investment Opportunities model portfolio for our Platinum Level members only, the Crisis Investment Opportunities newsletter will definitely enable you to profit from ongoing volatility in global stock markets while many people lose great sums of money. Undoubtedly, our portfolio took a hit in late 2008 when the US Treasury and US Federal Reserve allegedly engineered a massive correction in gold and silver, but the important thing to understand is that we firmly believe we are positioned correctly to benefit from this monetary crisis as it deepens in 2009. Still, since we launched the Crisis

Investment Opportunities newsletter in June 15, 2007, as of January 29, 2009, we have outperformed almost all major global market indexes by 30% to 50% as of the start of 2009.

Some of the positions we have already closed out include weighted gains of 76.06%, 99.73%, 24.71%, 72.04%, 31.23%, 20.39% and 48.46%. Our strategy for the Crisis Investment Opportunities model portfolio is to only add stocks or non-stock assets to the portfolio when they present a low-risk, high-reward entry point. As I stated in the previous sentence, we not only hold stocks in this portfolio but we also hold other non-paper investments as well that we believe will strongly perform as this monetary crisis deepens.

Visit http://www.smartknowledgeu.com and download our fact sheet to view up-to-date, current returns of our Crisis Investment Opportunities model portfolio.

PRIVATE ONE-ON-ONE CONSULTATIONS

During my Private Consultation sessions, I provide very detailed and specific information that will grant you unquestionable confidence to take actionable steps to not only protect your net worth but also to greatly expand it as this crisis unfolds. During a Private Consultation session,

I will review:

√ Specific compelling information unavailable in our public workshops regarding the severity of the dollar crisis as well as detailed explanations of my suggested portfolio allocation guidelines for both stock and non-stock assets.

√ Specific reallocation guidelines by asset class for your portfolio tiered by medium and aggressive risk tolerance levels and insight into which allocation guideline is our favorite.

I will provide:

√ Consultation on two other largely ignored asset classes besides gold that are poised to enormously benefit from this impending crisis.

√ Consultation on which global markets you should avoid and which global markets are likely to be insulated from this impending crisis.

√ A list of our favorite stocks in each of our favored asset classes to guide your future portfolio reallocation and specific stock selection.

Plus I will provide these additional BONUSES FOR FREE:

√ Consultation on what non-stock asset class has one of the greatest upsides to this imminent crisis, the safest low-risk, high-reward asset among this asset class to purchase, and personal instruction on how to buy this valuable asset without fear that you are overpaying.

√ Consultation on how to protect the purchasing power parity of your paper currency (specifically against a falling U.S. dollar) as this crisis deepens and why procrastinating can really hurt your financial future. What I have to say about the Euro and Pound Sterling may surprise you.

For more information, please contact us at
info@smartknowledgeu.com or visit us at
http://www.SmartKnowledgeU.com

Visit us at our blog, http://www.theUndergroundInvestor.com and
join our group, "Crisis Investing", at http://www.facebook.com.

GOOD INVESTING!

FOOTNOTES

[1] Ellyn Spragins, "$15k to get into Harvard - 5 ways to stop the madness," 20 Nov 2006, http://money.cnn.com/2006/11/18/pf/college/harvard_or_bust.moneymag/index.htm

[2] BBC News, "Top bosses earn $11m a year," 22 Jun 2006. http://news.bbc.co.uk/2/hi/business/5107550.stm

[3] Ibid.

[4] PR Newswire, "Optimistic Teens May Need Financial Reality Check, Schwab Survey Shows," 27 March 2006, http://sev.prnewswire.com/banking-financial-services/20070327/SFTU08327032007-1.html

[5] Ibid.

[6] Ibid.

[4] Bill Bonner, "The life of Brian: how the Amaranth trader lost $6bn," Sept. 29, 2006, http://www.moneyweek.com/file/19182/the-life-of-brian-how-the-amaranth-trader-lost-6bn.html

[7] Sebastian Boyd, "Citigroup pays price years after Dr. Evil," 25 July, 2006, http://www.iht.com/articles/2006/07/24/bloomberg/bxciti.php

[8] BBC News, "Japan closes Citigroup branches," 17 September, 2004, http://news.bbc.co.uk/2/hi/business/3666828.stm

[9] Ben White, "WorldCom Ex-Leaders Reach Deal in Lawsuit," 19 March, 2005, http://www.washingtonpost.com/wp-dyn/articles/A48610-2005Mar18.html

[10] PBS Frontline, "The Global Settlement: An Overview," 28 April, 2003, http://www.pbs.org/wgbh/pages/frontline/shows/wallstreet/fixing/settlement.html

[11] John Holusha, "Huge Profits at Goldman Bring Big Bonuses," 12 December 2006, http://www.nytimes.com/2006/12/12/business/12cnd-earn.html?ex=1178942400&en=efc89e23b6eb3e04&ei=5070

[12] CNN.com, "Financial Advisor Fired Over Enron Advice," 26 March 2002, http://archives.cnn.com/2002/US/03/26/enron.adviser/index.htm

[13] Roddy Boyd, "AG, SEC Looking into Analyst's Firing," 4 October 2006, https://www.nypost.com/seven/10042006/business/ag__sec_looking_into_analysts_firing_business_roddy_boyd.htm

[14] Netty Ismael, "Morgan Stanley's Xie Quit After Singapore E-Mail," 5 October 2006, http://72.14.235.104/search?q=cache:oGqsd32awLEJ:www.bloomberg.com/apps/news%3Fpid%3D20601087%26sid%3DaK7UIXigIxjM%26refer%3Dhome+blomberg,+andy+xie,+money+laundering+center+for+corrupt+Indonesian+businessmen&hl=en&ct=clnk&cd=1

[15] David Teather, "Insurers accuse Morgan Chase of fraud", 6 March 2002, http://www.guardian.co.uk/enron/story/0,11337,662706,00.html

[16] Matt Krantz, "CNBC's Cramer Boasts of Manipulating Markets," 23 Mar 2007, http://www.usatoday.com/money/markets/2007-03-23-cramer-usat_N.htm
[17] Ibid.
[18] Ibid.
[19]Eric Schlosser, Fast Food Nation, (London: Penguin Books, 2002), p. 143.
[20]Roger Edleson, "Poor Returns," The Financial Times, 2001 June 18.
[21]Kay Johnson, "Vietnam's Stock Market Madness", 22 Feb 2007, http://209.85.175.104/search?q=cache:Gah-IwNzJOwJ:www.time.com/time/magazine/article/0,9171,1592579,00.html+norit aka+akamatsu,+vietnam,+economist&hl=en&ct=clnk&cd=7&gl=th
[22] Ibid.
[23] Ibid.
[24] Ibid.
[25] Howard Zinn, A People's History of the United States, (New York:HarperPerenniel, 1995), p.251.
[26] Mongabay.com, "Global food prices rise 40% in 2007 to new record," 27 Dec 2007, http://news.mongabay.com/2007/1227-fao.html
[26] Reuters.com, "Goldman Sachs says sell gold in 2008," 29 Nov 2007, http://www.reuters.com/article/rbssIndustryMaterialsUtilitiesNews/idUSL298967 7420071129
[27] Gabriel Madway, "Paulson: Subprime mortgage fallout 'largely contained'", 13 March 2007, http://www.marketwatch.com/news/story/paulson-subprime-mortgage-fallout-largely/story.aspx?guid=%7B5F1FC5A7-B457-4875-BEEE-D7F73282ED9F%7D
[28] Forbes.com,"A Smarter Way to Build a Global Portfolio," 2006, http://www.newsletters.forbes.com/servlet/ControllerServlet;jsessionid=af906768 104f4f8f8abea3b868f9e385?Action=DisplayPage&Locale=en_US&SiteID=es_7 64&id=ProductDetailsPage&productID=36420700
[29] Art Lutschaunig,"Overrelying on the Long Term," 1 August 2007, http://209.85.175.104/search?q=cache:0UaOQcwZSygJ:www.onwallstreet.com/a rticle.cfm%3Farticleid%3D3704+Ibbotson+Associates,+12.6%25,+small+cap&h l=en&ct=clnk&cd=2&gl=th
[30] PBS Frontline."The Global Settlement: An Overview," 28 April, 2003, http://www.pbs.org/wgbh/pages/frontline/shows/wallstreet/fixing/settlement.html
[31] Dan Ackman,"The Trial of Henry Blodget", January 6, 2003, http://www.forbes.com/2003/01/06/cx_da_0106topnews.html
[32] Gretchen Morgensen. "The Final Frontier for Wayward Wall Street?", 21 Dec 2002, http://query.nytimes.com/gst/fullpage.html?res=9A05E0D61F3DF932A15751C1 A9649C8B63; and the Securities and Exchange Commission.

[33] Brooke A. Masters and Carrie Johnson, "SEC May Alter Mutual Fund Governance," 23 June 2004, http://www.washingtonpost.com/wp-dyn/articles/A61925-2004Jun22.html

[37] Alan J. Ziobrowski, Ping Cheng, James W. Boyd, and Brigitte J. Ziobrowski, "Abnormal Returns from the Common Stock Investments of the U.S. Senate," Journal of Financial and Quantitative Analysis Vol. 39, No. 4 (December 2004).

[38] J.S. Kim, the Underground Investor blog, 25 Sept. 2006, http://www.theundergroundinvestor.com/2006/09/25/a-i%E2%80%99m-not-looking-so-smart/

[34] Liz Peek, "Dark Pools Threaten Wall Street," 16 October, 2007, http://www.nysun.com/article/64598.

[35] Edgar Ortega and Yalman Onaran,"Bourses lose business to the 'dark pool'," 5 Dec 2006, http://www.iht.com/articles/2006/12/04/bloomberg/bxexchange.php

[36] Anuj Gangahar,"Banks begin to dip into 'dark pools'," 18 Oct 2006, http://www.ft.com/cms/s/511e0a94-5ede-11db-afac-0000779e2340.html

[39] Investopedia Staff, "Dissecting The Bear Stearns Hedge Fund Collapse," 2008, http://www.investopedia.com/articles/07/bear-stearns-collapse.asp

[40] United Press International, "Bear Stearns freezes hedge fund's assets," 1 Aug. 2007, http://www.newsdaily.com/Business/UPI-1-20070801-12453600-bc-us-bearstearns-freeze.xml

[41] George Goodman, "Paper Money", 1981, http://www.pbs.org/wgbh/commandingheights/shared/minitext/ess_germanhyperinflation.html